MY LIFE AND TIMES

BY

JEROME K. JEROME

British Library Cataloguing-in-Publication Data
A catalogue record for this book is available from the
British Library

JEROME K. JEROME FROM A RECENT
PORTRAIT

Jerome K. Jerome

Jerome Klapka Jerome was born in Walsall, England in 1859. Both his parents died while he was in his early teens, and he was forced to quit school to support himself. Jerome worked for a number of years collecting coal along railway tracks, before trying his hand at acting, journalism, teaching and soliciting. At long last, in 1885, he had some success with *On the Stage – and Off,* a comic memoir of his experiences with an acting troupe. Jerome produced a number of essays over the following years, and married in 1888, spending the honeymoon in "a little boat" on the Thames.

In 1889, Jerome published his most successful and best-remembered work, *Three Men in a Boat.* Featuring himself and two of his friends encountering humorous situations while floating down the Thames in a small boat, the book was an instant success, and has never been out of print. In fact, its popularity was such that the number of registered Thames boats went up fifty percent in the year following its publication. With the financial security provided by *Three Men in a Boat,* Jerome was able to dedicate himself fully to writing, producing eleven more novels and a number of anthologies of short fiction.

In 1926, Jerome published his autobiography, *My Life and Times.* He died a year later, aged 68.

CONTENTS

MY LIFE AND TIMES

INTRODUCTION

I remember a night in Philip Bourke Marston's rooms. He was blind and wrote poetry, and lived with his old father, Dr. Westland Marston, the dramatist, in the Euston Road. They had turned us out of Pagani's; it must have been about twelve o'clock.

Pagani's was then a small Italian restaurant in Great Portland Street, frequented chiefly by foreigners. We were an odd collection of about a dozen. For a time— until J. M. Barrie and Coulson Kernahan came into it—I was the youngest. We dined together once a fortnight in Pagani's first-floor front at the fixed price of two shillings a head, and most of us drank Chianti at one and fourpence the half flask. A remnant of us, later on, after Philip Marston's death, founded the Vagabonds' club. We grew and prospered, dining Cabinet Ministers, Field Marshals—that sort of people—in marble halls. But the spirit of the thing had gone out of it with poor Philip.

At Pagani's, the conversation had been a good deal about God. I think it was Swinburne who had started the topic; and there had been a heated argument, some taking Swinburne's part and others siding with God. And then there had been a row between Rudolph Blind, son of Karl Blind, the Socialist, and a member whose name I forget, about a perambulator. Blind and the other man, whom I will call Mr. X, had bought a perambulator between them, Mrs. Blind's baby and the other lady's baby being expected to arrive the same week. All would have gone well but that Mr. X's lady had presented him with twins. Blind's idea was that the extra baby should occupy the floor of the perambulator. This solution of the problem had been put before Mrs. X, and had been rejected; she was not going to have her child made into a footstool. Mr. X's suggestion was that he should buy Blind out. Blind's retort was that he wanted only half a perambulator and had got it. If bought out, it must be at a price that would enable him to purchase an entire perambulator. Blind and X were still disputing, when all at once the gas went out. It was old Pagani's customary method of hinting that he wanted to go to bed.

Philip, to whom all hours were dark, guided us downstairs; and invited us to come round to his rooms and finish up the evening. He wanted to introduce me to his old father, who was an invalid and did not, as a rule, come to these gatherings. Accordingly, some half-a-dozen of us walked round with him, including Dr. Aveling (who wrote under the name of Alec Nelson and who had married a daughter of Karl Marx) and F. W. Robinson, the novelist, who was then running a monthly magazine called *Home Chimes*. Barrie was writing articles for it, and I was doing a monthly "Causerie" titled "Gossips' Corner" and headed with the picture of a solemn little donkey looking over a hedge. At first, I had objected to the presence of this donkey, but Barrie took a fancy to him, and pleaded for him; and so I let him stay. Most of the writers since famous were among its contributors.

In Fitzroy Square we stopped to discuss the advisability, or otherwise, of knocking up Bernard Shaw and taking him along with us. Shaw for some time had been known to the police as one of the most notorious speakers in Hyde Park; and his name was now becoming familiar to the general public as the result of scurrilous attacks, disguised as interviews, that were being made upon him by a section of the evening press. The interviewer would force his way into Shaw's modest apartment, apparently for no other purpose than to bully and insult him. Many maintained that Shaw must be an imaginary personage. Why did he stand it? Why didn't he kick the interviewer downstairs? Failing that, why didn't he call in the police? It seemed difficult to believe in the existence of a human being so amazingly Christian-like as this poor persecuted Shaw appeared to be. As a matter of fact, the interviews were written by Shaw himself. They certainly got him talked about. Three reasons decided us against waking him up on the present occasion. Firstly, no one was quite sure of the number of the house. Secondly, we knew his room was up six flights of stairs; and none of us seemed eager for the exercise. Thirdly and lastly, the chances were a hundred to one that, even if we ever got there, Shaw wouldn't come down, but would throw his boot at the first man who opened the door.

The Euston Road had not a good reputation in those days. I expect it was the cheapness of the locality that kept the Marstons there. Philip made very little by his writings; and his father's savings could not have been of any importance. In those days, if a dramatist made five hundred pounds out of a play, he was lucky. The old gentleman was in bed when we reached the second floor, but got up and joined us in a dressing gown that had seen better days. Philip, a while before, had been sent a present of really good cigars by an admirer; and sound whisky was then to be had at three-and-six a bottle; so everything went merry as a marriage bell. Philip's old father was in a talkative mood, and told us stories about Phelps and Macready and the Terrys. And this put Robinson on his mettle, and he launched out into reminiscences of Dickens, and Thackeray whom he had helped on the *Cornhill Magazine*, and Lewis and George Eliot. I remember proclaiming my intention of writing my autobiography, when the proper time arrived: it seemed to me then a long way off. I held—I hold it still—that a really great book could be written by a man with sufficient courage to put down truthfully and without reserve all that he really thought and felt and had done. That was the book I was going to write, so I explained. I would call it "Confessions of a Fool."

I remember the curious silence that followed, for up till then we had been somewhat noisy. Aveling was the first to speak. He agreed that the book would be interesting and useful. The title also was admirable. Alas, it had already been secured by a greater than myself, one

August Strindberg, a young Swedish author. Aveling had
met Strindberg, and predicted great things of him. A
German translation of the book had just been published.
It dealt with only one phase of human folly, but that a
fairly varied and important one. The lady of the book I
met myself years later in America. She was still a
wonderfully pretty woman, though inclined then to
plumpness. But I could not get her to talk about
Strindberg. She would always reply by a little gesture, as
of putting things behind her, accompanied by a
whimsical smile. It would have been interesting to have
had her point of view.

The majority were of the opinion that such a book
never had and never would be written. Cellini's book, if
true, was mere melodrama. Pepys had jotted down a
mountain of trivialities. Rousseau, having confessed
himself the victim of an imbecility tolerably harmless,
and more common than he thought, got frightened and,
for the rest of the book, had sought to explain away his
vices, and to make the most of his virtues. No man will
ever write the true story of himself; and if he did Mudie's
subscribers would raise shocked eyes to heaven, and ask
each other if such incomprehensible creatures could
possibly exist. Froude ventured to mention the fact that
the married life of Mr. and Mrs. Carlyle had not been
one long-drawn-out celestial harmony. The entire
middle-class of England and America could hardly
believe its ears. It went down on its knees and thanked
God that such goings-on happened only in literary and
artistic circles. George Eliot has pointed out how we dare

not reveal ourselves for fear of wounding our dear ones. That the beloved husband and father, the cherished wife, the sainted mother, could really have thought this, felt that, very nearly done the other! It would be too painful. Society is built upon the assumption that we are all of us just as good as we should be. To confess that we are imperfect, is to proclaim ourselves unhuman.

So every volume of "My Memoirs," every "Book of my Life" conforms to the strict convention. If, for the sake of a moment's variety, we hint at the possession of a vice, it resembles those of the Vicar of Wakefield, and "leans to virtue's side."

The American publisher, whom we had playfully dubbed "Barabbas," told us that Mark Twain had told him that he, Mark Twain, was writing a book of reminiscences, speaking quite frankly about everybody he had met. To avoid trouble all round, Twain was instructing his executors not to publish the book until twenty years after his death. Some time later, when I came to know Mark Twain, I asked him if it were true. "Quite true," he answered; "I am going to speak of everybody I have met, exactly as I have found them, nothing extenuating." He also added that he might, before he left London, be asking of me a loan, and hoped that, if he did, I should not turn out to be a mean-spirited skinflint. I still think the book was a myth, put about by Mark Twain for the purpose of keeping his friends nervous, and up to the mark. A sort of a book of the kind has, it is true, been published, since I wrote this chapter; but it isn't a bit the book he threatened. Anyhow, he never turned up for that loan.

The others drifted away, one by one. The old gentleman had retired to bed. Philip asked me to stop on awhile. I was living close by, in Tavistock Place. The site of the house is now occupied by the Passmore Edwards Institute. Passmore Edwards, who was then the proprietor and editor of *The Echo*, the first newspaper in London published at a halfpenny, had been a great friend of my father, back in the days when they were both young men. My father always claimed that it was he and Passmore Edwards who had introduced golf into the South of England. I do not press the point, not being sure of the view that may be taken of the matter on the Day of Judgment. Perhaps he was only boasting. They used to play it on the sands at Westward Ho. My father, at the time, was farming land the other side of the river, above Instow. Westward Ho was then a wild stretch of desolate sealand bounded on the north by the great pebble ridge. They used it as a bunker at low tide. It must have taken some getting over. I shared the ground floor of number nineteen Tavistock Place with a chum, George Wingrave by name. The rooms above us were occupied by two sisters. The elder was the mistress of a gentleman who is now a well-known member of Parliament, in addition to being a magistrate, inclined to deal severely with human faults and frailties. She committed suicide a day or two after he was married. I remember our quaint little old landlady, Mrs. Peedles— "Mrs. P." George and I always called her for short—

bursting in upon me with a white, scared face while I was writing. We found her unconscious, her sister kneeling by the sofa holding her in her arms; but she died before we could get help. Fortunately for our present well-known legislator, his father was a man of means and influence. "An overdose of morphia" was, I think, the verdict. It came out that she had been suffering from sleeplessness. She had been a quiet, reserved girl. The younger sister was religious.

So soon as we were alone, Philip re-introduced the subject of reminiscences. Asking me not to talk about it, he told me he had done the very thing we had decided to be impossible—had kept a diary, writing down the thoughts that came to him, his dreams and desires. Or, to speak more strictly, typing them. Since his blindness, he had become marvellously proficient on the typewriter. It was a curious mixture, this diary, according to his own account. One Philip was an evil thing, full of lusts and horrors, lower than any beast that crawled the earth. And another Philip was quite beautiful, and Christ would have loved him. And, in addition to these two, was yet a third Philip, who stood apart from both. Philip could not make out who this third one was. He seemed to be always just behind the other two, watching them both with passionless eyes. "There are times," so Philip explained to me, "when he looks into my very soul and I shrivel up with shame; and there are rare moments when I feel as if he had entered into me and we were one."

From another, I might have deemed this idle talk; but Philip was a curious fellow. Much tragedy had entered his life that must have gone to the making of him; and in him the animal and spiritual were both strongly developed. Behind that veil of darkness, there must have been many a grim struggle between them. Myself I always believed in the existence of that book about which we talked that night. I was abroad when he died. On my return I spoke about it to his father and he promised to make search for it.

But we never found it.

Chapter I

BIRTH AND PARENTAGE

I was born at Walsall in Staffordshire on the 2nd of May, 1859. My father, at the time, was the owner of coal mines on Cannock Chase. They were among the first pits sunk on Cannock Chase; and are still referred to locally as the Jerome pits. My mother, whose name was Marguerite, was Welsh. She was the elder daughter of a Mr. Jones, a solicitor of Swansea; and in those days of modest fortunes had been regarded as an heiress. It was chiefly with her money that the coal-pits had been started. My mother's family were Nonconformists, and my father came of Puritan stock. I have heard my mother tell how she and her sister, when they were girls, would often have to make their way to chapel of a Sunday morning through showers of stones and mud. It was not until the middle of the century that the persecution of the Nonconformists throughout the country districts may be said to have entirely ceased. My father was educated at Merchant Taylors School, and afterwards studied for an architect; but had always felt a "call," as the saying is, to the ministry. Before his marriage, he had occupied his time chiefly in building chapels, and had preached in at least two of them. I think his first pulpit must have been at Marlborough. A silver salver in my possession bears the inscription: "Presented to the Reverend Clapp Jerome by the congregation of the Independent Chapel, Marlborough, June 1828." And at that time he could not have been much over one and twenty. From Marlborough he went to Cirencester. There he built the Independent Chapel, and I see from a mighty Bible, presented to him by the "Ladies of the Congregation," that it was opened under his ministry on June 6th, 1833. Altered out of all recognition, it is now the Cirencester Memorial Hospital on the road to the station. I have a picture of it as it appeared in my father's time. From an artistic point of view the world cannot be said to progress forwards.

On his marriage, my father settled down in Devonshire, where he farmed land at Appledore above Bideford; and also started a stone quarry. But the passion to be preaching never left him. In Devonshire, he preached whenever he got the chance, travelling about the country; but had no place of his own. When he gave up farming to go to Walsall, it was partly with the idea of making his fortune out of coal, and partly because a permanent pulpit had been offered him.

Sir Edward Holden of Walsall, a still vigorous old gentleman of over ninety, with whom I dined not long ago, tells me my father was quite a wonderful preacher, and drew large congregations to Walsall from all round the district. He preached at first in the small Independent Chapel that he found there. Later, the leading Nonconformists in the town got together, and the Congregational church in Bradford Street, which is still one of the features of the town, was built for him, my father giving his services as architect. It stands on the top of the hill, and in those days looked out over fields to

Cannock Chase. It would be easy, as things turned out, for a wise man to point the obvious moral that if my father had followed sound Biblical advice—had stuck to his preaching, for which God had given him the gift, and had left worldly enterprise to those apter in the ways of Mammon, it would, from every point of view, have been the better for him. But if success instead of failure had resulted, then he would no doubt have been praised as the ideal parent, labouring for the future welfare of his children. It was the beginning of the coal boom in Staffordshire, and fortunes were being made all round him, even by quite good men. In my father's case, it was the old story of the man who had the money calling in to his aid the man who had the experience. By the time my father had sunk his last penny, he knew all that was worth knowing about coal mining; but then it was too late. The final catastrophe seems to have been hastened by an inundation; and to cut a long story short, my father, returning home late one evening after the rest of the household were asleep, sat himself down on the edge of my mother's bed and broke to her, as gently as possible, the not unexpected news that he was a ruined man. I see from my mother's diary that the date coincides with the first anniversary of my birthday.

A few hundreds, all told, were perhaps saved out of the wreck. We moved into a small house in Stourbridge, near by; and, having settled us there, my father, ever hopeful to the end, went off by himself to London, with the idea of retrieving our fortunes through the medium of the wholesale ironmongery business. He seems to have taken premises with a wharf in Narrow Street, Limehouse, and at the same time to have secured by way of residence the lease of a small house in Sussex Street, Poplar. He describes it, in his letters, as a corner house with a garden; and my mother seems to have pictured it as something rural. Poor Lady! It must have been a shock to her when she saw it. Sometimes, when in the neighbourhood of the City, I jump upon an East Ham 'bus and, getting off at Stainsby Road, creep to the corner and peep round at it. I can understand my father finding one excuse after another for not sending for us. Of course he was limited by his means and the wish to be near his place of business in Narrow Street. Also, no doubt, he argued to himself that it would only be for a little while—until he could afford one of the fine Georgian houses in the East India Dock Road, where then lived well-to-do ship-owners and merchants. There, till we joined him, two years later, my father lived by himself, limiting his household expenses to five shillings a week. For the ironmongery business was not prospering; and at Stourbridge there were seven of us, in all, to be kept. My mother did not know at the time— not till a friend betrayed him to her and then she took matters into her own hands, and began her packing.

But before that, a deeper trouble than any loss of money had all but overwhelmed her. My little brother Milton had died after a short illness when six years old. A dear quaint little fellow he seems to have been: though maybe my mother's love exaggerated his piety and childish wisdom. On each anniversary of his death, she confides to her diary that she is a year nearer finding him again. The last entry, sixteen years afterwards and just ten days before she died herself, runs: "Dear Milton's birthday. It can be now but a little while longer. I wonder if he will have changed."

My brother's death left a gap in the family. My younger sister, Blandina, was eleven years older than myself; and Paulina, the elder, was a grown-up young woman with a Sunday School class and a sweetheart when I was still in frocks. The sweetheart was one Harry Beckett, an engineer. My mother at first entertained hopes of his conversion; but later seems to have abandoned them on learning that he had won in open competition the middleweight championship of Staffordshire. She writes him down sorrowfully as "evidently little better than a mere prize fighter," and I gather there were other reasons, rendering him undesirable from my parents' point of view. The end, I know, was tears; and Harry departed for Canada. He turned up again in the eighteen eighties and dropped in unexpectedly upon my sister. I happened to be staying with her at the time. She was then the mother of seven hefty boys and girls. A big handsome fellow he was still, with laughing eyes and kindly ways, I had taken to the writing of stories and was interested in the situation. He was doing well in the world; but he had never married. Perhaps he did mix his whisky and water with less water than there should have been as we sat together in the evening, we three—my brother-in-law was away up north on business—but as I watched them, I could not help philosophising that life will always remain a gamble, with prizes sometimes for the imprudent, and blanks so often to the wise.

It is with our journey up to London, when I was four years old, that my memory takes shape. I remember the train and the fields and houses that ran away from me; and the great echoing cave at the end of it all—Paddington station, I suppose. My mother writes that the house was empty when we reached it, the furniture not turning up till four days later. "Papa and I and Baby slept in the house." There must, of course, have been a little furniture, for my father had been living there. I remember their making me up a bed on the floor. And my father's and mother's talk, as they sat one each side of the fire, mingled with my dreams. "Mrs. Richard put up the two girls, and Fan and Eliza slept at the Lashfords'." Eliza, I take it, must have been a servant. Aunt Fan was my mother's sister who lived with us: an odd little old lady with corkscrew curls and a pink-and-white complexion. The pictures of Queen Victoria as a girl always remind me of her.

My recollections are confused and crowded of those early days in Poplar. As I grew older I was allowed to wander about the streets a good deal by myself. My mother was against it, but my father argued that it was better for me. I had got to learn to take care of myself.

I have come to know my London well. Grim poverty lurks close to its fine thoroughfares, and there are sad, sordid streets within its wealthiest quarters. But about the East End of London there is a menace, a haunting terror that is to be found nowhere else. The awful silence of its weary streets. The ashen faces, with their lifeless eyes that rise out of the shadows and are lost. It was these surroundings in which I passed my childhood that gave to me, I suppose, my melancholy, brooding disposition. I can see the humorous side of things and enjoy the fun when it comes; but look where I will, there seems to me always more sadness than joy in life. Of all this, at the time, I was of course, unconscious. The only trouble of which I was aware was that of being persecuted by the street boys. There would go up a savage shout if, by ill luck, I happened to be sighted. It was not so much the blows as the jeers and taunts that I fled from, spurred by mad terror. My mother explained to me that it was because I was a gentleman. Partly that reconciled me to it; and with experience I learned ways of doubling round corners and outstripping my pursuers; and when they were not actually in sight I could forget them. It was a life much like a hare must lead. But somehow he gets used to it, and there must be fine moments for him when he has outwitted all his enemies, and sits looking round him from his hillock, panting but proud.

My father had two nephews, both doctors, one living at Bow; and the other at Plaistow, which was then a country village. Bow was a residential suburb. One reached it by the Burdett Road. It was being built on then, but there were stretches where it still ran through scrubby fields and pastures. And beyond was Victoria

Park, and the pleasant, old-world town of Hackney. Further north still, one reached Stoke Newington, where dwelt grand folks that kept their carriage. I remember frequent visits to one such with my young sister, Blandina. I see from my mother's diary that a mighty project was on foot; nothing less than the building of a new railway: from where to where, I cannot say. In the diary it is simply referred to as "Papa's Railway." For us it led from Poverty to the land of "Heart's Desire." I gather that the visits to Stoke Newington were in connection with this railway. Generally we were met at the iron gates by a very old gentleman—or so he appeared to me—with a bald, shiny head and fat fingers. My sister was always the bearer of papers tied up with red tape, and these would be opened and spread out, and there would be talking and writing, followed by a sumptuous tea. Afterwards, taking my sister's hand in his fat fingers, he would tuck her arm through his and lead her out into the garden, leaving me supplied with picture-books and sweets. My sister would come back laden with grapes and peaches, a present for Mamma. And whenever the weather was doubtful we were sent home in the deep-cushioned carriage with its prancing horses. Not to over-excite our neighbours of Sussex Street, it would stop at the end of the Burdett Road, and my sister and I would walk the rest of the way.

Our visits grew more and more frequent, and my mother's hopes for "Papa's Railway" mounted higher and higher. Until one afternoon my sister came back out of the garden empty-handed, and with a frightened look in her eyes. She would not ride home in the carnage. Instead we walked very fast to Dalston Junction, from where we took the train; and I could see that she was crying under her veil. It must have been an afternoon early in November. I remember his having asked my sister if she would like to see the Lord Mayor's show. My mother writes in her diary under date November 16th, "Papa's railway is not to be proceeded with. We are overwhelmed with sorrow. Every effort my dear husband makes proves unsuccessful. We seem shut out from the blessing of God."

Even my father seems to have lost hope for a while. A page or two later I read, "Dear Jerome has accepted a situation at Mr. Rumbles'. A hundred a year from nine till eight. Feeling very low and sad."

On November 13th, my mother tells Eliza that she can no longer afford to keep her. "She wept and was very sorry to leave."

"December 2nd. Jerome had his watch stolen. An elegant gold lever with his crest engraved that I gave him on our wedding day. Oh, how mysterious are God's dealings with us!"

On December 4th, the sun seems to have peeped out. "Dear Blandina's birthday. Gave her my gold watch and a locket. She was very much delighted. Dear Pauline came home. A very pleasant, cheerful day, notwithstanding our heavy trials." But early the following year it is dark again.

"January 12th. A very severe frost set in this week. Skating by torchlight in Victoria Park. Coals have risen eight shillings a ton. It is a fearful prospect. I have asked the Lord to remove it.

"January 18th. To-day *suddenly*, to the surprise of all, a thaw began. The skating by torchlight all knocked on the head. Coals have gone down again just as we were at the last. 'How much better are ye than many sparrows.'"

My sisters seem to have taken situations from time to time. As governesses, I expect: the only calling then open to a gentlewoman. I read: "Pauline to Ramsgate. Oh, how intensely do I wish we could all continue to live together!" And lower down on the same page: "Blanche to Mrs. Turner's. Am feeling so lonely. The briars are too many for my feet to pass through; and the road is rough and dark."

And then a week or two later, I likewise take my departure, but fortunately only on a brief visit to friends in the north of London. I am seen off at the station. My mother returns to the empty house and writes, "Dear Luther went off delighted. Gracious Father, guard and protect my little lamb until he returns."

Writing the word "Luther" reminds me of an odd incident. I was called Luther as a boy, not because it was my name, but to distinguish me from my father, whose Christian name was also Jerome. A year or two ago, on Paddington platform, a lady stopped me and asked me if I were Luther Jerome. I had not heard the name for nearly half a century; and suddenly, as if I had been riding Mr. Wells' Time Machine backwards, Paddington station vanished with a roar (it may have been the pilot-engine, bringing in the 6.15) and all the dead were living.

It turned out we had been playmates together in the old days at Poplar. We had not seen each other since we were children. She admitted, looking closer at me, that there had come changes. But there was still "something about the eyes," she explained. It was certainly curious.

For some reason, about this time, there seems to have crept into my mother's heart the hope that we might get back possession of the farm in Devonshire to which my father had brought her home after their honeymoon, and that she might end her days there. It lies on the north side of the river above Bideford, and is marked by a ruined tower, near to which, years ago, relics were discovered proving beyond all doubt that the Founder of our House was one "Clapa," a Dane, who had obtained property in the neighbourhood about the year Anno Domini one thousand. It was Clapa, I take it, who suggested our family crest, upraised arm grasping a battle-axe, with round about it the legend "Deo omnia data." But as to how much Clapa owed to God and how much to his battle-axe, found rusted beside his bones, history is silent. Be all this as it may, my mother never seems to have got over the idea that by some inalienable right the farm still belonged to us. Always she speaks of it as "our farm." Through the pages of her diary one feels her ever looking out towards it, seeing it as in a vision beyond the mean streets that closed her in, and among which in the end she died. One day she writes: "Dear Jerome has told me about Norton and our farm. Why should it not be? With God all things are possible." Later on, a large hamper arrives from Betsey, the farmer's wife. Betsey in my mother's time had been the dairymaid; and had married the carter. With the hamper, Betsey sends a letter containing further news concerning Norton— whoever or whatever "Norton" may be. My mother writes: "Well, God can restore even that to us. Oh, that I had more faith in God!"

Among all their troubles, one good thing seems to have been left to my father and mother: their love for one another. It runs through all the pages. There was a sad day when my sister Pauline lay dangerously ill. My mother returns from a visit to her.

"Gracious Father, sustain me that I may never distrust Thee, though wave follow wave in overwhelming succession. Came home with Papa, whose love is so constant and true. Mrs. Cartwright sent some apples and a can of cream, and Mrs. E. a pair of boots for Luther. 'His mercy endureth for ever.'"

"May 2nd, 1865. Dear little Luther's birthday. Six years old. Gave him a dove. Papa gave him 'Robinson Crusoe.'"

About this time, and greatly to my mother's joy, I "got religion," as the saying is. I gave up taking sugar in my tea, and gave the twopence a week to the Ragged School in Threecolt Street. On Sundays, I used to pore over a great illustrated Bible and Fox's "Book of Martyrs." This used to be a popular book in religious houses, and children were encouraged to wallow in its pictures of hideous tortures. Old Fox may have meant Well, but his book makes for cruelty and lasciviousness. Also I worried myself a good deal about Hell. I would suggest to our ecclesiastical authorities that they should make up their mind about Hell and announce the result. When I was a boy, a material Hell was still by most pious folks accepted as fact. The suffering caused to an imaginative child can hardly be exaggerated. It caused me to hate God, and later on, when my growing intelligence rejected the conception as an absurdity, to despise the religion that had taught it. It appeared one could avoid Hell by the simple process of "believing." But how was I to be sure that I did believe, sufficiently? There was a mountain of rubbish on some waste land beside the Limehouse canal: it was always spoken of locally as the "mountain." By way of experiment, I prayed that this mountain might be removed. It would certainly have been of advantage to the neighbourhood; and as, by comparison with pictures I had seen, it was evidently but a very little mountain, I thought my faith might be sufficient. But there it remained morning after morning, in spite of my long kneelings by my bedside. I felt the fault was mine and despaired.

Another fear that haunted me was the Unforgivable Sin. If only one knew what it was one might avoid it. I lived in terror of blundering into it. One day—I forget what led to it—I called my Aunt Fan a bloody fool. She was deaf and didn't hear it. But all that night I lay tossing on my bed. It had come to me that this was the Unforgivable Sin, though even at the time, and small though I was, I could not help reflecting that if this were really so, there must in the Parish of Poplar be many unforgivable sinners. My mother, in the morning, relieved my mind as to its being the particular Unforgivable Sin, but took it gravely enough notwithstanding, and kneeling side by side in the grey dawn, we prayed for forgiveness.

I return to my mother's diary.

"Jan. 1st, 1866. So time rolls on with its sorrows, conflicts, its unrealized hopes. But these will pass away and be followed by the full, unmeasured bliss of Eternity. Doctor Cumming prophesies this year to be our last. He seems to overlook the second coming of Christ, with the glorious ingathering of Jew and Gentile. Spent the evening with our friends in Bedford Square. Enjoyed our visit very much.

"Jan. 31st. Old Wood made another proposal of marriage (to my sister Blanche, I take it. Wood, no doubt, was the name of the bald-headed old gentleman of Stoke Newington). But God graciously preserved her from being influenced by his wealth. Yet our path is very cloudy and full of sorrow.

"May 22nd. Peace meeting at Cannon Street Hotel. Papa made a beautiful speech. Caught cold coming home.

"June 7th, 1867. Our wedding day. Twenty-five years have passed since together we have borne the joys and sorrows, the mercies and trials of this weary way. But we can still say, 'Hitherto hath the Lord helped us and preserved us.' But oh, when will it be eventide with us? 'And at eventide it shall be light.'

"June 30th. 3.45 a.m., heard a queer noise. Came downstairs to ascertain the cause. A black-and-white cat sprang from the room. Dear little Fairy's cage was open, his feathers scattered all about. A thrill of anguish passed through me, and I called aloud in my sorrow. All came downstairs to mourn our loss. It was no use. We were all retiring, when a call from Luther made me rush downstairs again. In the drawing-room there I beheld the little panting innocent clinging to the muslin curtains, and so delighted to pop once more into his cage. We were all now overjoyed and overwhelmed with astonishment at the bird's safety. How he escaped is a mystery. The Lord must have known how it would have grieved us all.

"July 18th. This morning we started to pay our long-talked-of visit to Appledore, and although we anticipated much pleasure, I had no idea of realizing half the kind attention and reception I and the dear children received. Everybody seemed to remember all my acts of kindness which I had long ago forgotten, and quite overwhelmed me with their love and affection. We enjoyed ourselves excessively. My visit has been to me like the refreshing rain after a long and dreary drought."

To me, too, that visit was as a glimpse into another world. At Stourbridge, as a little chap, I must have seen something of the country. But I had forgotten it. Through the long journey, I sat with my face glued to the window. We reached Instow in the evening. The old ferryman came forward with a grin, and my mother shook hands with him, and all the way across they talked of strange names and places, and sometimes my mother laughed, and sometimes sighed. It was the first time I had been in a boat, and I was afraid, but tried to hide it. I stumbled over something soft, and it rose up and up until it was almost as tall as myself and looked at me. There must have been dogs in Poplar, but the few had never come my way, and anyhow nothing like this. I thought he was going to kill me and shut my eyes tight; but he only gave me a lick all over my face, that knocked off my cap. The old ferryman swore at him, and he disappeared with a splash into the water. I thought he would be drowned and called out. But everybody laughed, and after all he wasn't, for I met him again the next day. A group of children was gathered on the shore, but instead of shouting or making faces at me they only looked at me with curious shy eyes, and my mother and sisters kissed them, and by this time quite a number of grown-ups had gathered round us. It was quite a time before we got away from them. I remember the walk up the steep hill. There were no lamps that I could see, but a strange light was all about us, as if we were in fairyland. It was the first time that I had ever climbed a hill. You had to raise your feet and bend your body. It was just as if someone were trying to pull you backwards. It all seemed very queer.

The days run into one another. I cannot separate them. I remember the line of reapers, bending above the yellow corn, and feeling sorry for it as it went down before their sickles. It was one evening when I had stolen away by myself that I found the moon. I saw a light among the tree-tops and thought at first to run home in fear, but something held me. It rose above the tree-tops higher and higher, till I saw it plainly. Without knowing why, I went down upon my knees and stretched out my arms to it. There always comes back to me that evening when I hear the jesting phrase "wanting the moon." I remember the sun that went down each night into the sea the other side of Lundy Island, and turned the farmhouse windows into blood. Of course he came to Poplar. One looked up sometimes and saw him there, but then he was sad and sick, and went away early in the afternoon. I had never seen him before looking bold and jolly. There were picnics on the topmost platform of the old, grey, ruined tower, that still looks down upon the sea. And high teas in great farmhouses, and with old friends in Bideford, where one spread first apply jelly and then Devonshire cream upon one's bread, and lived upon squab pies and junkets, and quaffed sweet cider out of goblets, just like gods.

I got left behind on the way home—at Taunton, I think. We had got out of the train for light refreshment. My mother had thought my sisters were looking after me, and they had thought I was with her. It seemed to me unlikely we should ever meet again in spite of the assurances of a stout gentleman in gold buttons and a braided cap. But I remember consolation coming to me with the reflection that here at least was interesting adventure, worthy of being recorded in my diary. For, unknown to all but my Aunt Fan, I was getting together material for a story of which I myself would be the hero. This notion of writing must have been my own entirely, for though my father could claim relationship with Leigh Hunt, I cannot remember hearing as a child any talk about literature. The stout gentleman with the gold buttons came back to me later, bringing a lady with him. She sat down beside me and guaranteed to take me back to my Mamma. There must have been something about her inviting confidence. I told her about the book, and how I was going to use for it this strange and moving incident. She greatly approved and was sure that I should succeed because I had the right idea. "There is only one person you will ever know," she told me. "Always write about him. You can call him, of course, different names."

By some magic, as it seemed to me, the kind lady and myself reached Paddington before my mother got there, so that, much to her relief, I was the first thing that she saw as she stepped out of the train. My mother hoped I had not been a trouble. But the kind lady assured her I had been most entertaining. "I always find people interesting when they are talking about themselves," the kind lady explained. And then she laughed and was gone.

Returning to our life in Poplar, things, I fancy, must have lightened a little, for a servant seems to have been engaged again. They come and go through the remainder of my mother's diary.

"Nov. 11th. Jane very rude, felt she was going to give me notice, so I gave her notice first. How different servants are to what they were!

"Dec. 2nd. Jane left. Sarah came. Anyhow it can't be a change for the worse."

It appears from an entry on December 16th, 1868, that chiefly through the help of a Mr. Halford I obtained a presentation to the Marylebone Grammar School, then called the Philological School, at the corner of Lisson Grove. I read: "It has been an anxious time, but God has blessed dear Papa's efforts. The committee examined

Luther this day, and the little lad passed through with
flying colours. He will begin his school life in January. I
must give up calling him Baby."

So ends my childhood. It remains in my memory as
quite a happy time. Not till years later did I learn how
poor we were—of the long and bitter fight that my
father and mother were waging against fate. To me it
seemed we must be rather fortunate folk. We lived in the
biggest house in Sussex Street. It had a garden round
three sides of it with mignonette and nasturtiums that
my mother watered of an evening. It was furnished more
beautifully, I thought, than any house I had ever seen,
with china and fine pictures and a semi-grand piano by
Collard and Collard in the drawing-room, and damask
curtains to the windows. In the dining-room were
portraits of my father and mother by Muirhead, and
when visitors came my mother would bring out the silver
teapot and the old Swansea ware that she would never let
anyone wash but herself. We slept on mahogany
bedsteads, and in my father's room stood the Great
Chest. The topmost drawer was always locked; but one
day, when the proper time arrived, my father would open
it, and then we should see what we would see. Even my
mother confessed she did not know—for certain—what
was hidden there. My father had been a great man and
was going to be again. He wore a silk hat and carried a
walking-stick with a gold head. My mother was very
beautiful, and sometimes, when she was not working,
wore silks and real lace; and had an Indian shawl that
would go through a wedding-ring. My sisters could sing

and play and always wore gloves when they went out. I had a best suit for Sundays and visitings; and always enough to eat. I see from my mother's diary that one of her crosses was that for a growing boy I was not getting proper nourishing food, but of this I had no inkling. There was a dish called "bread and sop" which was sweet and warm and of which I was fond. For tea there would sometimes be golden syrup, and for supper bread with dripping spread quite thick. And on Sundays we had meat and pudding for dinner. If all things are as my mother so firmly believed, she has long known that her fears were idle—that notwithstanding I grew up to be an exceptionally strong and healthy man. But I would that the foreknowledge could have come to her when she was living, and so have removed one, at least, of her many sorrows.

Chapter II

I BECOME A POOR SCHOLAR

One of the advantages of being poor is that it necessitates the cultivation of the virtues. I learnt to get up early in the morning—the beginning of all things that are of good repute. From Sussex Street to Poplar station on the North London Railway I found to be a quarter of an hour's sharp walking. So I breakfasted at half-past six, and caught the seven-fifteen. The seven-thirty would have done it. But my father's argument was: "Better catch the seven-fifteen. Then, if you miss it, the seven-thirty will still get you there in time. But if you catch the seven-thirty, then if you don't, you're done." The train wound round Bow and Homerton, then a leafy neighbourhood of market gardens and old wooden houses. At Homerton still stood Dick Turpin's house, a substantial, comfortable-looking dwelling, behind a pleasant, walled-in garden, celebrated even then for its wonderful godetias, said to have been Dick Turpin's favourite flower. At Dalston Junction one changed, and went on through Highbury and old Canonbury to Chalk Farm. From there my way lay by Primrose Hill and across Regent's Park. Primrose Hill then was on the outskirts of London, and behind it lay cottages and fields. I remember a sign-post pointing out a footpath to Child's Hill and the village of Finchley. Sometimes of a morning I was lucky enough to strike a carriage going round the outer circle of the park, and would run after it and jump on to the axle-bar. But clinging on was ticklish work, especially when handicapped by a satchel and an umbrella; added to which there was always the danger of some mean little cuss pointing from the pavement and screaming "Whip behind," when one had to spring off quickly, taking one's chance of arriving upon one's feet or on one's sitting apparatus. School hours were from nine till three; and with luck I would catch the quarter to four from Chalk Farm and get back home at five. Then there would be tea, which was my chief meal of the day; and after that I would shut myself up in my small bedroom—in the winter with a blanket wrapped round me—and get to work on my home lessons. Often they would take me until ten or eleven o'clock, and difficulty enough I had to keep myself awake.

It was a silly system; and in most schools it still continues. But I do not propose to dwell upon my school life. It makes me too angry, thinking about it. Education is the most important thing in the world, and the most mismanaged: which accounts for the continued low intelligence of the human race. Carlyle's definition of school is a place of torment where youth is confined behind windowless walls and has books flung at it. If only they would fling the right books, it would be something. What a boy learns in six years at school, he could, With the aid of an intelligent bookseller, learn at home in six months. Whatever knowledge I possess I picked up for myself in later years. To the British Museum reading-room, with its courteous officials, I remain grateful; though, on the principle of making the punishment fit the crime, the party responsible for its heating arrangements ought to be suffocated. To the Young Men's Christian Association—not yet then affiliated to the Standard Oil Trust—I return thanks. But still more am I indebted to shabby, care-worn ladies and gentlemen, their names forgotten, who, for a sadly inadequate fee of sixpence to ninepence an hour, put their fine learning at my disposal.

I am not blaming my own particular school. A French proverb has it that in all things a man's choice lies, not between the good and the bad, but between the bad and the worse. Looking back, I am inclined to regard my dear father's selection—whether of chance or necessity—as one of the least worse. In one respect it might be cited as a model. Corporal punishment was never employed. Without it, excellent discipline was maintained among three hundred chance assorted youngsters, Tradition was relied upon. Philological boys did not have to be beaten before they would behave themselves. If a boy proved to be outside the method, he was expelled. During the five years that I was there, only three boys had to be shown out.

Man is born sinful. One does not have to accept literal interpretation of the Book of Genesis to be convinced of it. The Manicheans maintain that the world, including man, was Devil created; and evidence can be adduced in support of their theory. There are times when even one's better feelings incline one to the argument of the blow. There is no fiercer opponent of the stick than Bernard Shaw. He and Zangwill were taking a walk. They noticed a group of boys in a field with their heads close together. When two or three country boys are gathered together, and seem to be interested, one is justified in thinking evil. Observation confirmed suspicion. An animal's shrill cry of pain came from the centre of the group. Shaw, gripping his walking-stick, vaulted the gate. The boys let go their victim and fled: Shaw in full chase. "The young imps of Satan"—to adopt the language of a passing labourer— had the start and proved fleet of foot. Shaw returned panting; explaining in heated language what he had intended to do, if only he had overtaken them.

"But I thought," said Zangwill, "that you were opposed to all physical punishment."

"So I am," growled Shaw. "But I have never claimed to be consistent."

Justice may occasionally condone the whip; but the long martyrdom inflicted upon youth in the name of Education shows human nature in an ugly light. All cruelty has its roots in lust. The boy has been beaten, one fears, not for his own good, but for the pleasure of the Domini. When magisterial gentlemen pass eulogisms on the rod, and old club fogies write to the papers fond recollections of the birch, I have my doubts. They like to think about it.

It was one Dan of the lower third who first disturbed my religious beliefs. He came from the neighbourhood of Camden Town, and generally we would meet in the outer circle, and walk together across the park. It was nearing the end of the summer term, and examinations were in progress. I confided to him my reason for being sure that I was going to win the arithmetic prize. Every night and morning on my knees I was praying for it. My mother had explained to me the mountain failure. I had not understood the verse properly. God only grants blessings that are good for us. Now here was something that was good for me. God Himself must be able to see that. My father was keen about my winning the arithmetic prize: he had said so. And this time I really did believe. I hadn't really expected the dust-heap to disappear, but the arithmetic prize I regarded as already mine. Dan argued that I wasn't playing the game. If the arithmetic prize was to be decided by prayer, then what was the use of working? The boy who had swotted hard all the term could be out-distanced, in the end, by any lazy beggar putting in ten minutes on his knees just before the examination. And suppose two boys prayed for it, both believing. What would God do then?

"Don't see the good of working at anything, if you can get everything you want by praying," concluded Dan.

It was a new light on the subject. Something was wrong somewhere. I thought at first of putting the problem before my mother, but felt instinctively that she would not be able to answer it: not to my help. I had got to fight this thing out for myself. And I didn't win the prize. I didn't try: I didn't seem to want it, after that.

William Willett was one of my schoolmates. I take it William Willett did more to give pure enjoyment—both mental and physical—to the people, than all the forces of Parliament, Press and Pulpit put together during the last hundred years. But already evil hands are trying to undo his work. The Devil will never rest till he has killed the Daylight Saving Bill.

In holiday time, I took up again my wanderings, my season ticket enabling me to extend my radius. They hunted the deer round Highgate in those days. I remember sitting on a stile near the Archway and seeing the van drive up and the stag unloosed. Hampstead was a pleasant country town, connected with London by a three-horse 'bus. A footpath led from Swiss Cottage, through corn fields, to Church Row; and a pleasant country road, following a winding stream, led to the little town of Hendon. I was always a good walker. It was lonely country between Wood Green and Enfield. Once I fell into a snowdrift, just beyond Winchmore Hill. Fortunately some farm labourers heard my call, and came to my rescue. Walthamstow lay far off, surrounded by marshes, where cattle grazed. There was a fine old manor not far from Edmonton. I trespassed there one day. Old houses have always had a lure for me. The owner himself caught me; but instead of driving me off, took me into the house and showed me all over it. He told me how he had often passed it on his way to work, when he was a

boy, apprenticed to a carpenter: and how he had dreamt
dreams. I came to be a visitor there, right till the end. He
had worked his way up by saving and hard work; had
never smoked, had never drunk, had rarely played. At
sixty—two years before—he had tasted his first glass of
champagne; and at sixty-five he died, having drunk
himself to death. A kindly old fellow, with a touch of
poetry in him. He was passionately fond of music, and
had built himself an organ room. He left a young wife
and two children. The place is a boarding-house now.
Hackney was a genteel suburb. At the Claptons, quite
good class people dwelt. Of afternoons, they took the air
in roomy carriages they called barouches, drawn by great
glossy horses that pranced and tossed their heads. At
Highbury there used to be a fair with open-air
dancing—and cock fighting, it was said.

There was a strange house I came upon one
afternoon, down by the river. It was quite countrified;
but how I got there I could never recollect. There was an
old inn covered with wisteria. A two-horse 'bus, painted
yellow, was drawn up outside. The horses were feeding
out of a trough, and the driver and conductor were
drinking tea—of all things in the world—on a bench
with a long table in front of it. It was the quaintest old
house. A card was in the fanlight, over the front door,
announcing "Apartments to let." I was so interested that
I concocted a story about having been sent by my
mother; and asked to see the rooms. Two little old ladies
answered me. All the time they kept close side by side,
and both talked together. We went downstairs to a long

low room that was below the ground on the side of the road, but had three windows on the other, almost level with the river. A very old gentleman with a wooden leg and a face the colour of mahogany rose up and shook me warmly by the hand. The old ladies called him Captain. I remember the furniture. I did not know much about such things then, but every room was beautiful. They showed me the two they had to let. In the bedroom was a girl on her knees, sweeping the carpet. I was only about ten at the time, so I don't think sex could have entered into it. She seemed to me the loveliest thing I had ever seen. One of the old ladies—they were wonderfully alike—bent down and kissed her; and the other one shook her head and whispered something. The girl bent down lower over her sweeping, so that her curls fell and hid her face. I thanked them, and told them I would tell my mother, and let them know.

I was so busy wondering that I never noticed where I walked. It may have been for a few minutes, or it may have been for half an hour, till at last I came to the East India Dock gates. I never found the place again, though I often tried. But the curious thing is, that all my life I have dreamed about it: the quiet green with its great chestnut tree; the yellow 'bus, waiting for its passengers; the two little old ladies who both opened the door to me; and the kneeling girl, her falling curls hiding her face.

I still believe that one evening, in Victoria Park, I met and talked with Charles Dickens. I have recorded the incident fairly truthfully in "Paul Kelver." He was certainly most marvellously like the photographs; and he did say "Oh, damn Mr. Pickwick!" Around Poplar, town and country were struggling for supremacy. There were little dismal farms scattered about the marshes. An old man in a yellow smock, driving before him three or four cows with bells round their necks, used to pass our house every morning and evening. He had his regular customers who would come out with their jugs: and he would milk the cows in the street. One summer, a boy and a girl came with a herd of goats. But they were not so successful. The goats would not stand still to be milked, and were always straggling. There was trouble in the world even before Lloyd George's Limehouse speech. I remember the long processions of the unemployed. They didn't run to a band, but sang a dreary dirge:

"We've got no work to do—oo—oo, We've got no work to do—oo—oo, We're all of us poor starving men, We've got no work to do."

My mother's diary is still sad reading during all these years. My father fell ill. The long walk to and from the city each day was too much for him. Often I would go to meet him; and he would be glad of my arm.

Outside "The George" in the Commercial Road there used to sit a little clean old lady who sold pig's trotters, cooked, at three halfpence apiece. Sometimes we would take three home with us. My mother would warm them, and I would be sent out to where a baked potato man stood at the corner of Pigott Street, calling to the passers-by: "'Ere you are, 'Ere you are. Warm your 'ands and fill your belly for one 'alfpenny." And so we would feast and make merry. One reduces one's denominator. The result is much the same.

There seems to have been a "property" at Notting Hill. On February 2nd, 1870, my mother writes:

"We are enduring a fearful struggle to try and save our property at Notting Hill, the hard-earned savings and privations of years."

"March 10th. My birthday. How dark! Luther gave me a pencil case, and Blandina a handkerchief. Papa gave me all he had, his love. He has had to give up his situation.

"March 12th. Saw the Directors. They will take £670 for the Notting Hill property. May God direct me how to raise it. Mr. Griffiths sent a pork pie for Papa. How kind!

"March 21st. To the city and saw Mr. D. Very weary and sad at heart. Dined with Mr. G. at Wilkinson's à la mode Beef rooms. Very good.

"April 5th. Mr. N. thinks the mortgage may be effected. Saw Mr. Hobson and the Pelican. Mr. C. would not make an offer. Came home with a sick headache.

"April 25th. To city. Waited at Mr. M.'s office till quite weary. He never came. Saw Mr. H. He advises me to give it up."

And then on June 4th my mother writes:

"I will magnify Thee, O Lord, for Thou hast set me up, and not made my foes to triumph over me."

From which I gather my mother came home that afternoon with a lighter step than for many a long day, giving herself all the airs of a smart business woman, the owner of "property" at Notting Hill.

The Franco-Prussian War broke out that year. All we boys were for Prussia, and "Pro-French" was everywhere a term of opprobrium. The idea that England would, forty and odd years later, be fighting side by side with France against Germany, would then have seemed as impossible, as to some of us nowadays would be the suggestion that fifty years hence, or maybe sooner, Germany may be our ally against France, as she was at Waterloo.

My sister Paulina had married one Robert Shorland, known later on in sporting circles as the father of Frank Shorland, the long-distance bicycle champion; and that autumn we left Poplar and went to live near to her in New Southgate: Colney Hatch as it was then called. It was little more than a country village in those days, with round about it fields and woods. London was four miles off, by way of Wood Green and Hornsey, with its one quaint street and ivy-covered church: and so on till you came to the deer park at Holloway.

I remember a little dog, belonging to my wife. She had had him from a puppy, and all his life he had lived in London. He was friendly with the neighbouring cats, and used to play with a white rabbit, belonging to the children next door. When he was nine years old, we took him with us into the country, and in less than six months he was the worst dog in the village. When he wasn't poaching, or chivying cats up trees, or killing chickens, he was fighting. He died fighting. A red-haired female was at the bottom of it. In London he had never looked at them.

In Poplar, I had been a model boy. There must be the Devil in the country for dogs and boys. I got into a bad set. It included the Wesleyan minister's two sons, and also the only child of the church organist. Religion, as Gibbon observes, would seem to be powerless to control the evil instincts of the human race. We robbed orchards. We snared rabbits in Walker's wood. It stretched from Colney Hatch to Old Southgate. The family consisted of eleven brothers, all enthusiastic cricketers. They formed themselves into a club and became famous. A stream ran through a park on the way to Palmer's Green; and I learnt to tickle trout. We acquired King David's knack of casting stones from a sling. We aimed at birds and cats. Fortunately, we rarely hit them; but were more successful with windows.

There were squatters in those days. One had built himself a shanty where now is Holly Park, a region of respectability; and about it had pegged out some couple of acres. There he had remained undisturbed for years: until a new owner appeared, and the question arose how to get him out. It all depended on a right of way. If he had not that, he could be built round and imprisoned. Then he would be compelled to go. In the middle of the argument, the old man died; and the contest took a new turn. It seemed that where a corpse once passed was ever after a free way to living men: or so it was said. Three stout lads the old man had left behind him, together with two well-grown wenches who could also be useful with their hands, and events promised to be exciting. The landlord had his men waiting day and night to prevent the corpse from passing: while the family within the hut girded their loins, and kept the day and hour of the funeral to themselves. I had it, late one evening, from the son of the butcher, that the attempt was to be made at dawn the next morning; and was up before the sun, making my exit by the window and down the water spout. I was just in time to see the little band of mourners emerge from the cottage. The coffin was borne by the two eldest sons, assisted by a couple of friends. It was only a few hundred yards to the road. But the landlord's men had been forewarned. It was an unholy *mêlée*. The bearers left the footpath when the landlord's men came towards them, and tried to race to the road through a gap in the hedge a little lower down. But before they could reach it, one of them slipped and fell. The coffin came hurtling down, and around it and over it and all about it a battle royal took place. And while it was still raging, another coffin, carried by the two girls and their two sweethearts, had sprinted down the footpath and gained the road. The first coffin had broken open and was found to be full of stones. How it all ended I don't know. I think there was a compromise. But the party I was sorry for, was the corpse. It was he who had taught me how to tickle trout. He would have loved to be in that last fight.

My father died the following year; on June 3rd, so I learnt from my mother's diary.

"Dear Papa never wore his dressing-gown, for the Lord called him home this morning at half-past nine o'clock. A momentary summons, and he has gone to receive the reward of his labourings and sufferings of so many years."

He had contracted heart disease and had died stepping out of bed. I have never been able to agree with the Prayer Book. I should always pray myself for sudden death.

My father had never looked old to me. But that may have been because of his jet-black waving hair. It was not till after he was dead that I learnt it was a wig; for in bed, according to the fashion of that period, he always wore a night-cap. One never saw a bald-headed man in those days: men were more particular about their appearance.

I like to think that to my mother, during the last few years of her life, came peace. With the dying of hopes, perhaps went the passing of fears, also. It was a revelation to me, reading her diary. It did not come into my hands until some twenty years later. I had always thought of her as rather a happy lady. I used to hear her singing about her work, even in the grim house at Poplar; and I can remember our rare excursions to the town, to buy me a new suit of clothes or to pay a visit: how we would laugh and joke, and linger before the shop windows, choosing the fine things we would buy when "our ship came home"!

From among her last entries, I quote the following:

"Sept. 17th. My cousin Henry Tucker came to see me. He has grown quite an old man. Blandina came home for the afternoon. A very happy day.

"July 19th. To Croydon with Blanche. Mr. & Mrs. Clouter very kind. Enjoyed myself.

"December 4th. Dear Blanche's birthday. Dear Paulina and all the little ones came round and we were all very happy.

"Christmas Day. Blanche and Luther to Mrs. Marris. Fan & I to Paulina's. Had a pleasant quiet day. The Lord bless my loved ones."

After my father's death we moved to Finchley. There was a path through the fields to Totteridge, past a thatched cottage where lived a rosy-cheeked little old lady who sold fruit and eggs. She had been a farmer's wife in Devonshire. She and my mother became great chums, and would gossip together on a bench outside the old lady's door.

I left school at fourteen, and through the help of an old friend of my father's, obtained a clerkship in the London & North-western Railway at Euston. My salary was twenty-six pounds a year, with an annual rise of ten pounds. But that first year, owing to a general revision of fares, over-time was to be had for the asking. Twopence halfpenny an hour it worked out, in my case, up till midnight, and fourpence an hour afterwards. So that often I went home on Saturday with six or seven shillings extra in my pocket. My Aunt Fan had died. I fancy the "property" at Notting Hill had disappeared; but my sister had won examinations and was in a good situation, so that our days were of peace, if not of plenty.

Lunches were my chief difficulty. There were, of course, coffee shops, where one quaffed one's cocoa at a penny the half pint; and "doorsteps"—thick slices of bread smeared plentifully with yellow grease supposed to be butter—were a halfpenny each. But if one went further, one ran into money. A haddock was fivepence, Irish stew or beef-steak pudding sixpence. One could hardly get away under ninepence, and then there was a penny for the waitress. There was a shop in the

Hampstead Road where they sold meat pies for twopence and fruit pies for a penny, so that for threepence I often got a tasty if not too satisfying lunch. The pies were made in little shallow dishes. With one deft sweep of the knife, the woman would release it from its dish, and turning it upside down, hand it to you on a piece of paper; and you ate it as you walked along the street or round some quiet corner, being careful to dodge the gravy. It was best to have with one an old newspaper of one's own. Better still, from a filling point of view, would be half a pound of mixed sweet biscuits; while in the summer time a pound of cherries made a pleasant change. Some of the fellows brought their lunch with them and ate it in the office, but I was always fond of mooning about the streets, looking into the shop windows, and watching the people.

In my parents' time, among religious people, the theatre was regarded as the gate to Hell. I remember a tremulous discussion one evening at Finchley. My sister had been invited by some friends to go with them to the theatre. My mother was much troubled, but admitted that times might have changed since she was young; and eventually gave her consent. After my sister was gone, my mother sat pretending to read, but every now and then she would clasp her hands, and I knew that her eyes, bent down over the book, were closed in prayer. My sister came back about midnight with her face radiant as if she had seen a vision. "Babel and Bijou" I think had been the play, at Covent Garden. It was two o'clock in the morning before she had finished telling us all about it, and my mother had listened with wide-open eyes; and when my sister suggested that one day she must adventure it, she had laughed and said that perhaps she would. Later on, my sister and I went together to the pit of the Globe with an order I had bought for sixpence from a barber in Drummond Street. He was given them in exchange for exhibiting bills, and the price varied according to the success or otherwise of the play. Rose Massey and Henry Montague were the "stars." I forget what the play was about. It made my sister cry; and there were moments when I found it difficult to keep my anger to myself. Rose Massey remains in my memory as a very beautiful woman. I bought her photograph the next day for ninepence, and for years it stood upon my mantelpiece.

My mother died the following year. My sister was away up north, and we were alone together in the house. It came at eventide.

Chapter III

RECORD OF A DISCONTENTED YOUTH

The two or three years following my mother's death remain in my memory confused and disjointed. The chief thing about them was my loneliness. In the day time I could forget it, but when twilight came it would creep up behind me, putting icy hands about me. I had friends and relations in London who, I am sure, would have been kind; but my poverty increased my shyness: I had a dread of asking, as it were, for pity. I seem to have been always on the move, hoping, I suppose, to escape from solitude. I remember a house in Camden Town, across a square and down a long, silent street. There were other lodgers on the floors below. I could hear their muffled voices as I climbed the stairs. A man hanged himself in one of the back rooms. His body was not discovered until the Saturday morning, when the landlady came round for her rents. I had heard a sound one evening, when passing the door, as of a man hammering on the wall with his hands—maybe it was his stockinged feet. But it was not etiquette to be inquisitive about one's neighbours. There was a ridiculous little house off the Malden Road that was called "The Castle," with a circular tower and arched windows and battlemented walls. It had been built by an old German, a widower, who lived in the basement. Once he had been prosperous, and with his family had occupied the whole of it. I had the top chamber in the tower. For some things it was convenient. I could lie in bed in the centre of the room and reach everything I wanted. Then there was Nelson Square the other side of Blackfriars' Bridge. Will Owen, the artist, once lived in Nelson Square. We compared notes, and decided it must have been the same house. The little landlady, always scant of breath, had been an actress. A law-writer and his wife had the front attic. Often he would work all night, coughing incessantly. I got used to it after a time. It was so incessant that it seemed to be a part of the night. At one time I had a bed-sitting room in Thanet Place, a narrow *cul-de-sac*, opposite old Temple Bar. Lloyds' Bank now stands upon the site. The landlord was a retired engine driver. He and his wife lived on the ground floor. He was a choleric man, belonging to the Strict Baptists. They had a chapel just across the Strand in Clare Market. Our First Floor was a quiet, thick-set young man, with curly hair. I used to meet him now and then upon the stairs. He had a German accent, and was always pleasant-spoken. But one night he came home hilarious, bringing friends with him. There was popping of corks, and laughter, and singing of songs. After a while, I heard our landlord shouting up the stairs in stentorian tones: If First Floor's rubbishy friends were not immediately sent packing, and there wasn't immediate quiet, First Floor was going to be shot out into the street, then and there, and all his belongings thrown after him. Our landlord was a sturdy old fellow, apt in moments of excitement to be a retired engine driver first and a Strict Baptist afterwards. Undoubtedly he would have done his best to carry out his threat, had not First Floor meekly apologized and promised compliance. There followed a murmur of subdued voices, a muffled trampling of feet upon the stairs, and then the door closed softly. Next morning, on my way out, the landlord beckoned me into his room.

"You heard the row last night?" he said.

I owned up that, leaning over the banisters in my nightshirt, I had been an interested listener.

"Read that," he said, handing me a newspaper and pointing to a paragraph. He was chuckling.

It seemed the night before there had been a "Sensational Incident" at the Aquarium. A gentleman named Samson, well known as a lifter of weights, a snapper of chains, and a breaker of bars of iron, had long claimed to be the "strongest man in the world." Half-way through the performance, a young man in the audience had risen up and challenged Samson's claim. The audience, scenting sport, had insisted on immediate contest. The challenger had mounted the stage: stripped of unnecessary garments, had exhibited the muscles of a Hercules; and had easily beaten poor Samson at his own game. Asked for his name, had given it as Mr. Eugen Sandow.

"Next time Mr. Eugen Sandow brings a few friends home with him for a little jollification, perhaps I won't throw him out into the street," remarked our landlord.

"Provided that is, of course," he added, "that they don't make too much noise."

Loneliness still dwelt with me. I remember one Christmas day. It was my own fault. I had received invitations, kindly meant and kindly worded. But into one I had read patronage and into another compassion; and had answered stiffly, regretting "prior engagements." To escape from myself on the actual day, I had applied for a pass to Liverpool. We railway clerks were allowed four a year. I took an early train from Euston, arriving at Lime Street a little after twelve. A chill sleet was falling. I found a coffee shop open in a street near the docks, and dined there off roast beef and a whity-brown composition that they called plum pudding. Only one other table was occupied: the one farthest from the door. A man and woman sat there who talked continuously in whispers with their heads close together: it was too dark to see their faces. It appeared from the next day's papers that an old man had been murdered in a lonely inn on the Yorkshire wolds; and that a man and a woman had been arrested at Liverpool. There was nothing to support it, but the idea clung to me that I had dined with them on Christmas day. To fill out the time, I took a slow train back that did not reach London till past ten o'clock. The sleet had turned to snow, and the streets were strangely empty. Even the public-houses looked cheerless.

It was during this period that I set myself to learn the vices. My study of literature had impressed it upon me that without them one was a milksop, to be despised by all true men, and more especially by all fair women. Smoking, I had begun at school, but from cowardice had given it up. I take it the race has by now acquired smoking as an hereditary accomplishment. Your veriest flapper, nowadays, will enjoy her first cigarette. It was less in our blood when I was a boy. For the first few months, I found it wiser to smoke in the open, choosing quiet by-streets, so that if one scored a failure it was noticed by only a few. But with pluck and perseverance one attains to all things—even to the silly and injurious habit of pumping smoke into one's heart and liver.

With the drink I had yet greater difficulty. I commenced, perhaps ill-advisedly, with claret. It cost twopence-halfpenny the glass at a "Cave" near to the Adelphi arches. I used to sip it with my eyes shut: the after results suggesting to me that the wine St. Paul recommended to Timothy for his stomach's sake must have been of another vintage. Later on, silencing my conscience with the plea of economy, I substituted porter at three halfpence the half-pint. It was nastier, if anything, than the claret; but one gulped it down, and so got it over quicker. A fellow clerk at Euston, who had passed through similar ordeals, recommended me to try port. At Shortt's in the Strand, one got a large glass for threepence with a bun thrown in. But for Mr. Shortt, I might have been a teetotaller to this day. I would advise any boy of mine to disregard Doctor Johnson's dictum, and start straight away with port. He will save himself much suffering. From port I worked up through cider to bottled beer. Eventually, I came to drink even whisky without a shudder. The Chancellor of the Exchequer tells me that drinking during the last fifty years has increased. I feel sure there must be something he has overlooked. When I was a youngster, every corner house in London was a pub. Omnibuses did not go east or west: they went from one public-house to another. After closing time, one stopped to stare at a sober man, and drunken children were common. For recreation, young bloods of an evening would gather together in groups and do a mouch "round the houses." To be on a footing of familiarity with a barmaid was the height of most young clerks' ambition. Failing that, to be entitled to address the pot-boy by his Christian name conferred distinction.

For the more sentimentally inclined, there was Oxford Street after the shops were closed. You caught her eye; and if she smiled you raised your hat and felt sure you had met her the summer before at Eastbourne— Eastbourne, then, was the haunt of the *haut ton*. All going well, you walked by her side to the Marble Arch; and maybe on a seat in the park you held her hand. Sometimes trouble came of it: and sometimes wedding-bells and—let us hope—happiness ever after. Most often, nothing further; just a passing of shiplets in the night. Myself, I had but poor success. My shyness handicapped me. I would take the lady's preliminary rebuff, her icy suggestion that I had made a mistake, as final dismissal; and would shrink back scarlet into the shadows.

Of vice that does not have to be acquired, I would speak if I thought that to any it would be of use. But, I take it, there is nothing to be done. Each lad must "dree his own wierd." Nature and civilization are here, as elsewhere, at cross purposes: and not all the problems are soluble. Evolution may work cure. A thousand generations hence, the years between puberty and marriage may not be the fearsome thing they are to the young men of this day. The only suggestion I can make is that the writers of our stories should harp less upon sexuality: though at present there appears no sign of their doing so: and that among older men there should be less lewdness of talk and jest. In my schooltime, quite little boys would whisper to each other "smutty" stories: they must have heard them from their elders. I do not speak as a prude. Some of the best and kindest men I have met have been grave sinners in this respect. But knowing how hard put to it a young man is to keep his thoughts from being obsessed by sexual lust, to the detriment of his body and his mind, I would that all men of good-feeling treated this deep mystery of our nature with more reverence. I think it would help.

A youngster whose acquaintance I had made, a clerk in the city, had gone upon the stage. He made his first appearance at the old Camden Town Theatre, opposite the Britannia. It was burnt down the following year. I was lodging off the Maiden Road, at the time, and was awakened by the glare upon my window. I dressed and hastened out. Each street was pouring forth its throng. It was the first time the inhabitants of Camden Town had shown any interest in the place. His example had inspired me. Literature was still my goal, but, of course, I should write plays; and stage experience would be useful. Charley (I forget his surname) introduced me to "agents," some of them fat and not too clean. One of them, I suppose, must eventually have done the trick. I remember selling a ring that had been my father's, and wandering through endless corridors in Somerset House, trying to find the room where they stamped agreements. After the first two months, I was to be paid a salary "according to ability." I remember the phrase because, when the time came and I showed the manager my contract to remind him, he said it was absurd—that no theatre in London could afford it; but that if half a quid a week would be of any use to me I could have it. He wasn't a bad sort. His name was Murray Wood. He was the husband of Virginia Blackwood, a minor star who specialized in Dickens. We had opened at Astley's, just over Westminster Bridge, a huge barn of a place, used during the winter as a circus. I had not left Euston. I was in the advertising department, and my work was mainly going about London, seeing that bills and time-tables were properly exhibited. I could take time off for rehearsals and make it up without anybody knowing or caring. "Dolly Varden" and "Little Nell" were our first two productions; and then came "Lost in London." I played a wicked swell, which necessitated a dress suit. I bought one in Petticoat Lane on a Sunday morning for ten shillings. For years, Petticoat Lane "turned me out," as the phrase goes; and at no period of my life have I been so well dressed. I always dealt at the same stall; and I think the old Sheeny took a liking to me. If I hadn't the price about me, he would take five shillings down

and trust me for the balance. "And if anybody wanth to
know your tailor," he said to me on one occasion, "you
can tell 'em that ith Mr. Poole of Thavile Row." And I
believe it was. Later, we produced an Irish play by
Manville Fenn. I played a policeman. We came across a
gentleman lying in a wood. My superior officer—who
was also the hero—wanted to know whether it was alive
or dead. I ought to have knelt down, and after careful
scrutiny pronounced that life was extinct, and had in my
opinion been so for some considerable time. Instead of
all which, on the second night, it came to me to just lean
forward, take one satisfying sniff, and answer laconically,
"Dead." It got the laugh of the evening. The stage
manager was furious; but Fenn, who was watching from
the wings, said it didn't matter; and wrote me in some
extra lines. We finished our season with "Mazeppa." I
played three parts—a soldier, a shepherd, and a priest,
and they talked so much alike that I had to look at my
clothes to make sure which I was. Lisa Weber played
Mazeppa. She was a magnificent creature, and in her
riding costume was the nearest thing to nature that up
till then had been seen upon the London stage.
Nowadays she would have attracted no attention. Our
ninepenny pit was converted into six shilling stalls, and
money was turned away every night. Murray Wood,
good soul, raised my salary to thirty shillings a week.

Our season at Astley's came to an end in November:
to make room for Lord George Sanger and his circus. I
chucked the North-western Railway, and joined a
touring company. My sisters were much troubled. At

Euston, I was earning seventy pounds a year, and I might become general manager. I pointed out to them that, instead, I might become London's leading actor with a theatre of my own. But they only cried. We opened at Torquay on Boxing day with a farce, a two-act drama and a pantomime. I had assumed the name of Harold Crichton, and our chief comedian turned out to be Haldane Crichton, who afterwards became a lessee of theatres; and had for daughter Madge Crichton. I think she is now in America. We were assumed to be brothers, and he took an interest in me, and taught me dancing and tumbling. I had to leap through flaps, and sometimes there was a mattress on the other side to catch me, and sometimes there wasn't; and arriving on the stage by way of a star trap calls for nerve and a thick skull. Haldane thought I had the makings of a clown in me, but my own ambition was rather towards the legitimate. After Torquay, we travelled round the south with what would now be termed repertory. Often, during the evening's performance, I would be handed my part in a piece to be played the next night. For one play I remember we had three rehearsals.

"What do they think we are," grumbled our first old man, "a pack of sanguinary amateurs?"

Altogether, I was on the stage three years. Occasionally, I obtained a short London engagement: at the old Surrey under the Conquests; at the Brit, and the Pav. Then, as now, the West End, to those without money or influence, lay behind a closed door. Most of my time I spent in the provinces. The bogus manager was our haunting fear. So long as he was making money, salaries were paid: they varied from a pound to fifty shillings. If the luck changed, the manager would disappear—generally on a Friday evening during the performance. Leaving their baskets with their landladies, the company would get back to their homes as best they could. Often they would have to tramp, begging their way by the roadside. Nobody complained: everybody was used to it. Sometimes a woman would cry. But even that was rare. There were one-night companies that played in Town halls, Institutes, Assembly Rooms and such like. Here thirty shillings a week would be the maximum salary—when you got it. "The shilling a nighters," we were called. If one could not secure a night's lodging for a shilling, paid in advance, one went without. In summer, one hunted for an out-of-the-way corner, or climbed the railings and slept in the church porch. In winter time, we would club together and, bribing the door-keeper, would sleep in the dressing-rooms, when there were any; and if not, upon the stage. Now and then, of course, one struck a decent company and then one lived bravely, sleeping in beds, and eating rabbit pie on Saturday.

Though I say it myself, I think I would have made a good actor. Could I have lived on laughter and applause, I would have gone on. I certainly got plenty of experience. I have played every part in "Hamlet" except Ophelia. I have doubled the parts of Sairey Gamp and Martin Chuzzlewit on the same evening. I forget how the end came. I remember selling my wardrobe in some town up north, and reaching London with thirty shillings in my pocket. Fortunately the weather was mild and I was used to "sleeping rough," as they call it in the country. The difficulty, of course, in London was to dodge the police. On wet nights I would have to fork out ninepence for a doss-house. The best I ever struck was one half-way up Pentonville Hill, where they gave you two blankets; but one had to be early for that. Literary gents have always been much given to writing of the underworld. I quite agree there must be humour and pathos and even romance to be found there; but you need to be outside it to discover its attractions. It was a jungle sort of existence. Always we slept with everything belonging to us, even to our leaky boots, underneath our pillows; and would start up with our hands clenched if a mouse crept across the floor. Round the common frying-pan, where we cooked our breakfast, when it ran to it, we stood on guard, ready to defend our skimpy rasher or our half-starved-looking bloater, if need be, with our lives. The old and feeble fared badly. The janitor was supposed to keep order; but among the outcast there is one law for the strong and another for the weak; and always there would be some hefty bully with whom it was best to make terms. By luck I came across a chum, one with whom I had gone poaching when a boy. He, too, had fallen upon evil days, and had taken to journalism. He was now a penny-a-liner—or to be exact, a three-half-penny-a-liner. He took me round with him to police courts and coroners' inquests. I soon picked it up. Often I earned as much as ten shillings a week, and life came back to me. I had my own apartment, furnished with a bed, a table and a chair, which also served for washstand, together with a jug and basin. But after the doss-house it was luxury. Sometimes a theatre order came my way. I remember Charles Matthews and Madame Vestris at the Royalty; and Irving's first appearance in "The Bells," at the old Lyceum under Mrs. Bateman's management. Phelps was playing at Sadler's Wells, and "Madam Angot," at the Philharmonic, opposite the Angel, was being whistled all over the town. There were hangings in the courtyard at Newgate. You could see them over the wall from the windows of the houses opposite. There was a coffee shop in the Old Bailey, where, for half a crown, they let you climb up on the roof. I found out how to make "flimsy" more saleable by grafting humour on to it: so that sub-editors would give to mine a preference over more sober, and possibly more truthful records. There was a place in Fleet Street called "The Codgers' Hall," where over pipes and pewter pots we discussed Home Rule, Female Suffrage, Socialism and the coming Revolution. Gladstone had raised the Income Tax to eight-pence and those of us who took things seriously foresaw the ruin of the country. Forster brought in compulsory education, and the danger was that England would become too intellectual. One evening, an Irishman threw a water-bottle at my head: what it was doing there still remains to me unexplainable. I ducked just in time, and it caught a Nihilistic gentleman on the side of the head. For the next ten minutes it was anybody's fight; but eventually we all made friends, and joining hands, sang "Auld Lang Syne." I took up shorthand at this period. Dickens had started his career as a Parliamentary reporter. It seemed to me I could not do better than follow in his footsteps. I attended public meetings, and on Sundays took down sermons. Spurgeon was a good man. You could hear every word he said. I remember the Sunday morning when he began by mopping his brow, and remarking that it was "damned hot."

I grew tired of penny-a-lining. Had I been of a saving disposition it might have worked out better. One week, I would earn two pounds—another week three. And then, by some peculiar economic law I could never understand, my expenditure would be precisely that same sum. The following week, my takings might total only a few shillings. How could a gentleman live! The work necessitated constant running about—hurrying here and there. I recall the idea I formed of what would constitute competence, beyond which a man need take no thought: it was, whenever one was tired or bored, to be able to jump upon a 'bus, indifferent as what the fare might be.

I tried school-mastering. One did not in those days have to be possessed of diplomas and certificates. I obtained an assistant mastership at a Day and Boarding School in the Clapham Road. English and mathematics were my department. But it seemed to include most things: my chief, a leisurely old gentleman, confining himself to the classics and theology. My duties included also "general supervision" of the boarders, the teaching of swimming and gymnastics, and of proper deportment during our daily walk round Clapham Common, and at church on Sundays. It was up to me to see that each boy did really drop his threepenny bit into the bag; but I have the suspicion that one or two of them, occasionally, may have been too clever for me. I had to wear gloves and a top hat; and once a week I had an evening out. The house-and parlour-maid, combined, a jolly little thing, only laughed at me. "Now you know what it's like," she said, "and when you're married you can tell your wife." Things have changed since then, I am informed. I stuck it for a term. My shorthand had suffered for want of practice. The House of Commons' gallery loomed distant. I answered advertisements. For secretarial work my shorthand was sufficient. I could have been secretary to Herbert Spencer. A friend in London to whom he had deputed the business, tested and approved me. I was to have gone down to Brighton the next week. I was eager and excited. But my sister, when I told her, was heartbroken. The stage had been a long way towards perdition, and journalism a step further. After Herbert Spencer, what hope could remain for my salvation? During my days of evil fortune, I had hidden myself from friends and relatives; writing lying letters from no address. I had caused her much suffering, I knew, and shrank from inflicting another blow. I saw Herbert Spencer's friend—I forget his name—and told him. He laughed, but was sure that Mr. Spencer would think that I had done right. So, instead, I became secretary to a builder in the north of London. He was a wonderful old fellow. He could neither read nor write;

but would think nothing of undertaking a ten-thousand-pound contract. He had invented an hieroglyphic that his bank accepted as his signature. He would write it with the pen grasped firmly in his fist and, after each completion, would pause and take a deep breath. His memory was prodigious. Until I came, he had kept no accounts whatever. Every detail of his quite extensive business had its place in his head; and according to common report no one had ever succeeded in doing him out of a halfpenny. I tried to reform him. At first he was grateful; but after a time grew worried and dejected. Until one Saturday, he planked down five weeks' wages in front of me and, assuring me of his continued friendship, begged me as a personal favour to take myself off. My next job was with a firm of commission agents. People in India—white or coloured it mattered not—sent us orders, accompanied by cheques; and we got the things and packed them into tin-lined cases and despatched them. The idea suggested in our advertisement was that we possessed a staff of expert buyers, rich in knowledge and experience: but I did most of it. I bought for far-off ladies their dresses, boots, and underwear, according to accompanying measurements. I matched their hair and chose their birthday presents for their husbands—at least, so one hopes. I selected wines and cigars for peppery old Colonels—I take it they were peppery. I judged what guns would be most serviceable to them for tiger-shooting or for hippopotami; and had saddles made for them under my own eye. It was interesting work. I felt myself a sort of universal uncle; and honestly I did my best. I was sorry when my employer left suddenly for South America. From there I went to a firm of Parliamentary agents. Society is fearfully and wonderfully contrived. It is calculated that out of every apple, between the time it leaves the tree and is finally eaten, eleven people got a bite. When public necessity requires that a new railway line should be constructed, a new tramway laid, or a new dock built, Parliamentary sanction must very properly be obtained. This might be a simple affair. The promoters might present their case before three or four intelligent members of the House of Lords, and the needful business be at once set going. But then nobody would get anything out of it; excepting only those that did the work and the people who would benefit by the result of their enterprise. This would never do. What would become of the parasites? Opposition must be whipped up. Somehow or another, briefs must be found, marked anything up to a thousand guineas, for half-a-dozen eminent K.C.'s. The case must be argued for a couple of years, providing bills of costs for half-a-dozen Parliamentary firms, fees and expenses for expert advisers, engineers, surveyors, newspaper men. When everyone has gorged his fill and new prey is in sight, it can suddenly be discovered that really, as a matter of fact, there is nothing whatever to be said against the scheme—and never was. Maybe a hundred thousand pounds or so has been added to the cost of it. The affair ends in a dinner where everybody proposes a vote of thanks to everybody else, and thanks God for the British Constitution.

Later, I drifted to a solicitor's office. Memoirs of any old family solicitor should make good reading. Almost in every dust-covered, black tin box there lurks a story. Now and again I would open one, re-arrange its contents. Bundles of old faded letters; fly-blown miniatures and photographs. Purchase of Harlowe Manor, together with adjoining lands, April 1832. Draft mortgage. Foreclosed 11.8.'69. Cosgrove *v.* Cosgrove and Templeton, with note as to custody of children. Ellenby dec^d.—provision for Laura and two children secured under separate deed. Crown v. Manningham, with cutting from *The Morning Post* describing scene in Court. A will enclosing an advertisement for one Munroe George Hargreaves, and across it in red ink "Never discovered." And so on. Slowly I would close the lid. The shadowed shapes I had unloosed would fade into their hiding-place.

"Ouida" was one of our clients. Once a year, she would leave her beloved Florence to spend a few weeks in London. Her books earned her a good income, but she had no sense of money. In the course of a morning's stroll she would, if in the mood, order a thousand pounds' worth of goods to be sent to her at the Langham Hotel. She never asked the price. She was like a child. Anything that caught her fancy she wanted. Fortunately for herself, she always gave us as a reference. I would have to go round and explain matters. One or two of the less expensive articles we would let her have. She would forget about the others.

I remember having to answer an inquiry as to whether Alfred Harmsworth was likely to prove a desirable tenant for a room in Chancery Lane at thirty pounds a year. My instructions were to reply "guardedly." But it turned out all right. It was there he started *Answers*.

We had a client, the Lord Lieutenant of a Welsh county. One day, in Pembroke, he saw a little fisher girl. He took her up on his shoulder and carried her to her home. He arranged with her parents that she should be sent abroad to school; and when she was eighteen he would marry her. The programme was carried out, but it proved an unhappy marriage. He was nearly fifty by then and, as may be guessed, a somewhat eccentric person. He died a few years afterwards, leaving her two thousand a year, provided she never remarried. She was a handsome young woman, and solved the problem by going out to America with a cousin, a young sailor. Only instead of her taking his name, he took hers.

I remember another will case that would have made good drama. The characters were an elderly clerical gentleman who had just come into some property, and a vamp—to use the modern slang. But what made the play remarkable was the lady who played the vamp. She was a woman of over forty, a devoted wife and mother. It was love of her children, I take it, that prompted her. The elder boy was at Oxford, and the younger at Sandhurst. But how to keep them there had long been her difficulty. They met first in our waiting-room, and got into conversation. The progress of the affair I could only guess; though I observed that later on their appointments always happened to coincide, to within half-an-hour or so; and invariably they left together. This had been going on for about a year when, one morning early, a slatternly girl brought a note to the office. My chief had not arrived, and I opened the letter. It was from the old gentleman—a shaky scrawl in pencil, begging someone for God's sake to come at once to an address off the Euston Road. A postscript explained that he was known there by the name of Wilson. I jumped into a cab and was soon there. I found him lying in bed in a comfortably furnished room on the first floor. He was evidently most desperately ill. He could speak only in a whisper.

"She got me last night," he said, "to sign a will. She had a couple of witnesses outside the door. It leaves her nearly everything. I must have been mad. When I woke this morning she was gone. She has taken it with her."

I sought to comfort him by the assurance that such a will could easily be set aside—that she would not dare to defend it.

"You don't know her," he said. "Besides, my wife will sacrifice herself rather than drag my name into the mud. She is reckoning on that."

"What's the matter with you?" I asked him.

"Heart," he managed to answer. "She excited me on purpose, I am sure of it. I am dying."

I told him his only chance was to keep calm. A hansom was the quickest thing in London in those days; but I seemed to be hours getting back to the office. My chief rushed off a four-line will, leaving everything the man possessed to his wife, and expressly cancelling the will made the day before. He was in great pain when we got back, but was just able to sign. And then I went for a doctor. He died in the evening. The lady changed her solicitors. I met her years afterwards, at a reception at the Foreign Office. She remembered me, and was most gracious. She had grown grey, but was still a handsome woman.

All this time I had been writing stories, plays, essays. But it was years before anything came of it.

Chapter IV

MY FIRST BOOK, AND OTHERS

My first book! He stands before me, bound in paper wrapper of a faint pink colour, as though blushing all over for his sins. "On the Stage—and Off. By Jerome K. Jerome" (the K very large, followed by a small j; so that by many the name of the author was taken to be Jerome Kjerome). "The Brief Career of a would-be Actor. One shilling nett. Ye Leadenhall Press. London. 1885."

He was born in Whitfield Street, Tottenham Court Road, in a second floor back overlooking a burial ground. The house is now a part of Whitfield's Tabernacle. A former tenant of the room—some young clerk like myself, I guessed him to be—had been in love with a girl named Annie. The bed was in a corner, and, lying there, he had covered the soot-grimed wall-paper with poetry to her—of sorts. It meandered in and out among Chinese temples, willow-trees and warriors. One verse I remember ran:

"Oh, Annie fair, beyond compare, To speak my love I do not dare. Oh, cruel Fate that shakes her head, And tells me I'm too poor to wed."

Being directly opposite the pillow, it greeted me each morning when I opened my eyes. It was applicable to my own case also, and had a depressing effect upon me.

I had tried short stories, essays, satires. One—but one only—a sad thing about a maiden who had given her life for love and been turned into a water-fall, and over the writing of which I had nearly broken my heart, had been accepted by a paper called *The Lamp*. It died soon afterwards. The others, with appalling monotony, had been returned to me again and again: sometimes with the Editor's compliments and thanks, and sometimes without: sometimes returned with indecent haste, seemingly by the next post; sometimes kept for months—in a dustbin, judging from appearances. My heart would turn to lead whenever the dismal little slavey would knock at the door and enter with them. If she smiled as she handed me the packet, her thumb and finger covered with her apron so as not to soil it, I fancied she was jeering at me. If she looked sad, as more often she did, poor little overworked slut, I thought she was pitying me. I shunned the postman when I saw him in the street, feeling sure he knew my shame. I wonder if the smart journalists who make fun in the comic papers of the rejected contributor have ever been themselves through that torture-chamber.

By luck, my favorite poet, just then, was Longfellow. It has become the fashion to belittle him. Perhaps all his verse does not reach the level of, say, "The Building of the Ship." But even Wordsworth nods. To youth, face to face with giants, he will long remain a helpful voice. Some two years before, on a sudden impulse, I had written him a long rigmarole of a letter, pouring out my troubles to him, addressing it simply to Henry

Wadsworth Longfellow, America; and had received an answer proving to me that he understood my case exactly and knew all about me. Always when things were at their worst, or nearly so, I would go to him for comfort; and one evening, crouching over my small fire, I struck the poem beginning:

"By his evening fire the artist Pondered o'er his secret shame;"

I had the feeling that Longfellow must have been thinking about me. And when I read the last two lines:

"That is best which lieth nearest; Shape from that thy work of art,"

it came to me that Longfellow was telling me not to bother about other people's troubles—those of imaginary maidens turned into waterfalls, and such like—but to write about my own. I would tell the world the story of a hero called Jerome who had run away and gone upon the stage; and of all the strange and moving things that had happened to him there. I started on it that same evening, and in three months it was finished. I hunted up an old actor named Johnson—the oldest actor on the boards, he boasted himself; and he certainly looked it. He had played with Edmund Kean, Macready, Phelps and Booth, not to mention myself. We had been at Astley's together, during the run of "Mazeppa." It had fallen to our lot, in the third act, to unbind Lisa Weber from the exhausted steed, and carry her across the stage. I took her head and old Johnson her heels. She was what Mr. Mantalini would have called a demmed fine woman, weighing, I should think, some fourteen stone; and during the journey she would pour out blood-curdling threats as to what she would do to both or either of us if we dropped her. Old Johnson lost his temper one night: "Oh, come on, young 'un," he called out to me in a loud whisper, "let's chuck her into the orchestra." He began to heave his end. She kept quiet after that. He was now with Wilson Barrett at the old Princess's. I used to wait for him at the stage door, and we would adjourn to a little tavern in Oxford Market. It really was a market in those days, with wooden booths all round, and stalls in the centre; where now stands Oxford Mansions. He would look over my MS. to see that I had made no blunders; and the anecdotes and stories that he told me would have made a rattling good book of themselves. I meant to write it. But he died before we had completed it.

For a workroom I often preferred the dark streets to my dismal bed-sitting-room. Portland Place was my favourite study. I liked its spacious dignity. With my note-book and a pencil in my hand, I would pause beneath each lamp-post and jot down the sentence I had just thought out. At first the police were suspicious. I had to explain to them. Later they got friendly; and often I would read to them some passage I thought interesting or amusing. There was an Inspector—a dry old Scotchman who always reached Langham church as the clock struck eleven: he was the most difficult. Whenever

I made him laugh, I went home feeling I had done good work.

When finished, it went the round of many magazines. I think I sent it first to *The Argosy*, edited by Mrs. Henry Wood. But the real editor was a little fat gentleman named Peters. He ran also *The Girls' Own Paper*, for which he wrote a weekly letter signed "Aunt Fanny," giving quite good advice upon love, marriage, the complexion and how to preserve it, how to dress as a lady on fifteen pounds a year—all such-like things useful for girls to know. A kindly old bachelor. I came to know him. He lived in a dear little cottage in Surrey and was a connoisseur of port wine. George Augustus Sala, then editing *Temple Bar*, next had a chance of securing it. He wrote me that himself he liked it, but feared it was not quite the thing for family reading. Sala, also, was a connoisseur of port wine. He had a nose about which, like Cyrano de Bergerac, he was touchy. He brought a libel action once against a man who had made some chaffing remark about it at a public dinner. Sala was a brilliant talker, provided he had the table to himself. I remember a dinner-party in Harley Street at which a young doctor, unacquainted with Bohemia, and before poor Sala had got into his stride, started a story of his own. It was an interesting story, and he followed it up with another. The conversation became general. When at last we remembered Sala, we discovered he had gone home.

Afterwards I tried *Tinsley's Magazine*. I never found old Tinsley at his office, but generally at a favourite little place of his near by. Prohibition was not then within the range of practical politics, as Mr. Gladstone would have put it; and the editorial fraternity had not begun to even think about it. I remember the first man who ordered tea and toast at the Savage Club. The waiter begged his pardon, and the man repeated it. The waiter said "Yes, Sir," and went downstairs and told the steward. Fortunately the steward was a married man. His wife lent her teapot, and took charge of the affair. It was the talk of the club for a fortnight. Most of the members judged it to be a sign of the coming decline and fall of English literature.

Eventually, despairing of the popular magazines, I sent it to a penny paper called *The Play*, which had just been started; and four days later came an answer. It ran:

"Dear Sir, I like your articles very much. Can you call on me to-morrow morning before twelve? Yours truly, W. Aylmer Gowing. Editor, *The Play*."

I did not sleep that night.

Aylmer Gowing was a retired actor. As "Walter Gordon," he had been leading juvenile at the Haymarket Theatre under Buckstone. "Gentleman Gordon," Charles Mathews had nicknamed him. He had married well, and ran *The Play* at a yearly loss because he could not bear to be unconnected with his beloved stage. His wife, a little bird-like woman, wrote poetry for it. They lived in a pretty little house in Victoria Road, Kensington. He was the first "editor" who up till then had seemed glad to see me when I entered the room. He held out both hands to me, and offered me a cigarette. It all seemed like a dream. He told me that what he liked about my story was that it was true. He had been through it all himself, forty years before. He asked me what I wanted for the serial rights. I was only too willing to let him have them for nothing, upon which he shook hands with me again, and gave me a five-pound note. It was the first time I had ever possessed a five-pound note. I could not bear the idea of spending it. I put it away at the bottom of an old tin box where I kept my few treasures: old photographs, letters, and a lock of hair. Later, when the luck began to turn, I fished it out, and with part of it, at a secondhand shop in Goodge Street, I purchased an old Georgian bureau which has been my desk ever since.

Aylmer Gowing remained always a good friend to me. Once a week, when he was in town, I dined with him. I guess he knew what a good dinner meant to a youngster living in lodgings on twenty-five shillings a week. At his house I met my first celebrities: John Clayton, the actor, with his wife, a daughter of Dion Boucicault. Poor Clayton! I remember a first night at the Court Theatre when he had to play the part of an adoring husband whose wife has run away. The thing had happened to him that very afternoon. We thought he would break down, but he played it out to the end;

and then went back to his empty house. Old Buckstone, Mrs. Chippendale, Palgrave Simpson, the dramatist, were among others. Palgrave Simpson had a great beaked nose and piercing dark eyes. He always wore a long cloak and a slouch hat; and one fifth of November arrived at the Garrick Club followed by a crowd of cheering urchins, who thought Guy Fawkes had come to life again. Mrs. Chippendale was a very stout lady. I remember a revival of "Homeward Bound" at the Haymarket in which she gained the biggest laugh of the evening. She was wandering about the deck of the ship, carrying a ridiculous little camp stool; but as she carried it behind her nobody could see it. "Looking for a seat, dear?" asked old Buckstone, who was playing her husband. "Got a seat," she answered, "looking for somewhere to put it."

All my new friends thought it would be easy to find a publisher for the book. They gave me letters of introduction. But publishers were just as dense as editors had been. From most of them I gathered that the making of books was a pernicious and unprofitable occupation for everybody concerned. Some thought the book might prove successful if I paid the expense of publication. But, upon my explaining my financial position, were less impressed with its merits. To come to the end, Tuer of the Leadenhall Press offered to publish it on terms of my making him a free gift of the copyright. The book sold fairly well, but the critics were shocked. The majority denounced it as rubbish and, three years later, on reviewing my next book, "The Idle Thoughts of an Idle

Fellow," regretted that an author who had written such an excellent first book should have followed it up by so unworthy a successor.

I think I may claim to have been, for the first twenty years of my career, the best abused author in England. *Punch* invariably referred to me as "'Arry K'Arry," and would then proceed to solemnly lecture me on the sin of mistaking vulgarity for humour and impertinence for wit. As for *The National Observer*, the Jackdaw of Rheims himself was not more cursed than was I, week in, week out, by W. S. Henley and his superior young men. I ought, of course, to have felt complimented; but at the time I took it all quite seriously, and it hurt. Max Beerbohm was always very angry with me. *The Standard* spoke of me as a menace to English letters; and *The Morning Post* as an example of the sad results to be expected from the over-education of the lower orders. At the opening dinner of the Krasnapolski restaurant in Oxford Street (now the Frascati), I was placed next to Harold Frederick, just arrived from America. I noticed that he had been looking at me with curiosity. "Where's your flint hammer?" he asked me suddenly. "Left it in the cloak-room?" He explained that he had visualized me from reading the English literary journals, and had imagined something prehistoric.

F. W. Robinson, the novelist (author of "Grandmother's Money"), was my next editor. He had just started a monthly magazine called *Home Chimes*. I sent him the first of my "Idle Thoughts," and he wrote me to come and see him. He lived in a pleasant old house in leafy Brixton, as it might have been called then; and I had tea with him in his fine library, looking out upon the garden. It was wintry weather, and quite a large party of birds were feeding on a one-legged table just outside. Every now and then, one of them would come close up to the window and scream; and then Robinson, saying "Excuse me, a minute," would cut a slice of cake and take it out to them. He liked my essay, he told me; there was a new note in it; and it was arranged that I should write him a baker's dozen.

Swinburne, Watts-Dunton, Doctor Westland Marston and his blind son Philip, the poet, Coulson Kernahan, William Sharp, Coventry Patmore, Bret Harte, and J. M. Barrie, were among my fellow contributors to *Home Chimes*. Barrie has left it on record that his chief purpose in coming to London was to see with his own eyes the editorial office from which *Home Chimes* was broadcasted to the world. He had been disappointed to find it up two flights of stairs in a narrow lane off Paternoster Row. He had expected that, if only as a result of his own contributions, Robinson would have been occupying more palatial premises.

Barrie was an excellent after-dinner speaker, on the rare occasions when he could be induced to overcome his shyness. His first attempt, according to his own account, was at a students' dinner given to Professor Blackie in Glasgow. Blackie had accepted on the express condition that there was to be no speech-making—a thing he could not abide. After the dinner, by way of a rag, Barrie, who was unaware of the stipulation, was half bullied, half flattered into getting on his legs and proposing the Professor's health. For the first minute and a half the Professor stared at him, voiceless with amazement. When Barrie came to this being the proudest moment of his life and so forth, Blackie sprang from his chair and turned upon him like a roaring lion. Denouncing him as the offspring of Satan out of Chaos, and the whole remainder of the company as fit only for the hangman's rope, he strode out of the room. Barrie, more dead than alive, sat down and tried to think of a prayer; but as the evening wore on, surrounded by hilarity, recovered his spirits. Toasts and speeches became the order of the evening, and somewhere near to midnight, Barrie—this time of his own volition—rose to add his contribution to the general happiness. Meanwhile the Professor, reflecting in the calm of his own study that perhaps he had been severe towards his youthful hosts, determined to return and make it up with them. He arrived at the moment when Barrie, warming to his work, was just beginning to be eloquent. The Professor gave one look round the room and then threw up his hands.

"Great God, if the chiel is na' at it still," he exclaimed, and plunged back down the stairs.

Robinson could not afford to pay any of us much. I think I had a guinea apiece for my essays; and the bigger men, I fancy, wrote more for love of Robinson than thought of pelf. In those days, there was often a fine friendship between an editor and his contributors. There was a feeling that all were members one of another, sharing a common loyalty. I tried when I became an editor myself to revive this tradition; and I think to a great extent that I succeeded. But the trusts and syndicates have now killed it. One hands one's work to an agent. He sells it for us over his counter at so much a thousand words. That is the only interest we have in it. Literature is measured to-day by the yard-stick. The last time I was in America, one newspaper was inviting the public from every hoarding to read: "Our great new dollar-a-word story." I don't know who the author was, the advertisement did not mention his name. "It must be a fine story, that!" one heard the people saying. Myself, the highest figure I have ever reached is ten cents. But even so, my conscience has had much trouble in holding up its end. Every time that in going over the manuscript I have knocked out a superfluous adjective or a quite unnecessary pronoun, I have groaned, thinking to myself: "There goes another fourpence"—or fivepence, according to the rate of exchange.

It is a pernicious system, putting an unfair strain upon a family man. One's heroine is talking much too much. It is not in keeping with her character. It does not go with her unfathomable eyes. Besides, she's said it all before in other words, the first time that she met him. From a literary point of view, it ought to all come out. The author seizes his blue pencil; but the husband and father stays his hand. "Don't stop her," he whispers, "let her rip. That passionate outpouring of her hidden soul that you think so unnecessary is going to pay my water-rate."

I called my sheaf of essays "The Idle Thoughts of an Idle Fellow"; and again the Leadenhall Press was my publisher. The book sold like hotcakes, as the saying is. Tuer always had clever ideas. He gave it a light yellow cover that stood out well upon the bookstalls. He called each thousand copies an "edition" and, before the end of the year, was advertising the twenty-third. I was getting a royalty of twopence halfpenny a copy; and dreamed of a fur coat. I am speaking merely of England. America did me the compliment of pirating the book, and there it sold by the hundred thousand. I reckon my first and worst misfortune in life was being born six years too soon: or, to put it the other way round, that America's conscience, on the subject of literary copyright, awoke in her bosom six years too late for me. "Three Men in a Boat" had also an enormous sale in America—from first to last well over a million. Putting aside Henry Holt, dear fellow, who still sends me a small cheque each year, God's Own Country has not yet paid me for either book.

Writing letters to *The Times*, according to Barrie, is—or was in our young days—the legitimate ambition of every Englishman. Barrie was lodging in a turning out of Cavendish Square, and I was in Newman Street near by. I confided to him one evening that the idea had occurred to me to write a letter to *The Times*. It seemed to me a handy way of keeping one's name before the public.

"They won't insert it," said Barrie.

"Why not?" I demanded.

"Because you're not a married man," he answered. "I've been studying this matter. I've noticed that *The Times* makes a specialty of parents. You are not a parent. You can't sign yourself 'Paterfamilias,' or 'Father of Seven'—not yet. You're not even 'An Anxious Mother.' You're not fit to write to *The Times*. Go away. Go away and get married. Beget children. Then come and see me again, and I'll advise you."

We argued the matter. Barrie, by the bye, sat down and wrote an article on the subject after I was gone. But I was not to be disheartened, I waited for the Academy to open. As I expected, a letter immediately appeared on the subject of "The Nude in Art." It was a perennial topic in the 'eighties. It was signed "British Matron." I forget precisely what I said. It had to be something to attract attention. My argument was, that the real Culprit was God Almighty. I agreed with "British Matron" that no healthy man or woman—especially woman—was fit to be seen: but pointed out to her that in going for the mere delineator she was venting her indignation on the wrong party. I signed the letter with my name in full; and *The Times*, contrary to Barrie's prediction, inserted it.

In the Victorian Age, no respectable citizen mentioned God, except on Sunday. I awoke the next morning to find myself famous—or infamous, I should perhaps say. My only relation worth a penny did say it, and there was an end of that. I didn't mind. I had heard my name spoken in an omnibus. I was a public character.

To subsequent letters of mine *The Times* was equally kind. I wrote upon the dangers of the streets—dogs connected to old ladies by a string; the use of the perambulator in dispersing crowds; the rich man's carpet stretched across the dark pavement and the contemplative pedestrian. I advised "Paterfamilias" what to do with his daughters. I discussed the possibility of living on seven hundred a year. *The Times*, in an editorial, referred to me as a "humorist." I feel the writer meant to be complimentary; but by later critics the term has generally been hurled at me as a reproach.

I was still a literary man only in the evening. From ten to six I remained a clerk. At the time, I was with a solicitor named Hodgson in Salisbury Street, Adelphi, where now the Hotel Cecil stands. I would buy a chop or a steak on my way home and have it fried with my tea. The London lodging-housekeeper has but one culinary utensil—a frying-pan. Everything goes in to it, and everything comes out of it tasting the same. Then, the table cleared, I would get to my writing. My chief recreation was theatre-going. I got the first-night habit. For great events, such as an Irving production at the

Lyceum or a Gilbert and Sullivan opera, this meant a wait of many hours, ending in a glorious scrimmage, when at last the great doors creaked, and the word ran round "They're opening." First nights were generally on a Saturday. I would leave the office at two, and after a light lunch, take up my stand outside pit or gallery entrance, according to the state of the exchequer. With experience, some of us learned the trick of squirming our way past the crowd by keeping to the wall. The queue system had not yet been imported. It came from Paris. We despised the Frenchies for submitting to it. Often, arriving only a few minutes before opening time, have I gained a front seat. Looking behind me at poor simple folk who had been waiting all the afternoon, my conscience would prick me. But such is the way of the world, and who was I to criticise my teachers?

We regular "First Nighters" got to know one another. And to one among us, Heneage Mandell, occurred the idea of forming ourselves into a club where, somewhere out of the rain, we could discuss together things theatrical, and set the stage to rights.

That was the beginning of The Playgoers' Club, which gained much notoriety; and is still, I believe, going strong: though no longer the terror to hide-bound managers and unjust critics that it was in the days of its youth. We met at a coffee shop in Hollywell Street, a shady thoroughfare of old half-timbered houses and dust-grimed shop-windows where, jumbled together, were displayed oil paintings "after" Correggio, Teniers, and others; dilapidated jewellery; moth-eaten garments; and prominent—but not too prominent—among the rubbish, books and photographs of salacious suggestion, with intimation that matter even more "curious" might be inspected within. In Hollywell Street stood the old Opera Comique, where the earlier Gilbert and Sullivan's operas were produced; as also the Globe Theatre, in which first "The Private Secretary," and afterwards "Charley's Aunt" both ran for over a thousand nights—a long run in those days; while in Wych Street, round the corner, was the old Olympic, where I first fell in love with Marion Terry. Wych Street led into Clare Market, a region of adventure. All have been swept away. The stately Law Courts stand there now, proclaiming virtue; and wickedness has sought—and found, one takes it— new quarters.

Addison Bright was our first president. He was a small man with a magnificent head. It was said of him that no one could be as clever as he looked. But he got very near it. He shared a studio with Bernard Partridge, the artist, in a street near the Langham Hotel. It was reception-room, dining-room, kitchen and bedroom combined. There were great gatherings there of youthful wit and wisdom. I had a deep affection for Addison Bright. Why he never went upon the stage I cannot understand: he was a wonderful actor. He could read a play to a manager better than the author could himself; and this led to his becoming a theatrical agent. It was a new idea, then. All we younger dramatists were his clients.

All this, however, belongs to another chapter. I speak of the Playgoers' Club here because it led to my writing "Stageland." Heneage Mandell, the founder of the club, was connected with a firm of printers, and persuaded his chief to start a paper called *The Playgoer*. Poor Heneage died not long afterwards, and the paper came to an end. I seem to have written the editorial notes—or some of them. I had forgotten this, until glancing through them the other day. I must have been a bit of a prig, I fear. I trust I have outgrown it, but one can never judge oneself. I see that in one number I lecture Marie Tempest and a gentleman named Leslie from a very superior height, pointing out to them the internal satisfaction to be obtained by always wearing the white flower of a blameless life. Also I come across a paragraph censoring the conceit of one, Robert Buchanan, for thinking the public likely to be interested in his private affairs.

It was in *The Playgoer* that "Stageland" first appeared. The sketches were unsigned, and journals that had been denouncing me and all my works as an insult to English literature hastened to crib them. Afterwards Bernard Partridge illustrated them, and we published them in partnership at our own risk. It proved to me that publishing is quite an easy business. If I had my time over again, I would always be my own publisher.

Bernard Partridge, at five-and-twenty, was one of the handsomest men in London. I have not seen him for many years. A thing came between us that spoilt our friendship. But this again belongs elsewhere, and I content myself, here, with saying that he was right and I was wrong. Into "Stageland" he put some of the best work he has ever done. For the Hero he drew himself, and Gertrude Kingston sat for the Adventuress.

The book was quite a success. They were the palmy days of the old Adelphi. Sims and Pettitt, Manville Fenn, Augustus Harris, Arthur Shirley, Dion Boucicault and H. A. Jones were all writing melodrama. The Stage Hero, his chief aim in life to get himself accused of crimes he had never committed; the Villain, the only man in the play possessed of a dress suit; the Heroine, always in trouble; the Stage Lawyer, very old and very long and very thin; the Adventuress, with a habit of mislaying her husbands; the Stage Irishman, who always paid his rent and was devoted to his landlord; the Stage Sailor, whose trousers never fitted him—they were well-known characters. All now are gone. If Partridge and myself helped to hasten their end, I am sorry. They were better—more human, more understandable—than many of the new puppets that have taken their place.

I see from old letters that I was studying at this period to become a solicitor. Not that I had any thought of giving up literature. I would combine the two. If barristers—take, for example, Gilbert and Grundy—wrote plays and books, why not solicitors? Besides, I had just married. A new sense of prudence had come to me: "Safety first," as we say now. I was with a Mr. Anderson Rose in Arundel Street, Strand. He had a fine collection of china and old pewter, and was a well-known art collector. Sandys' portrait of Mrs. Anderson Rose, his mother, made a sensation when it was first exhibited; and is still famous. He was a dear old gentleman. In the office, we all loved him. And so did his clients, until soon after his death, when their feelings towards him began to change. I fancy Granville Barker must have known him, or heard of him; and used him for "The Voysey Inheritance."

His death put an end to my dream of being a lawyer. He had been kindness itself to me in helping me, and had promised to put work in my way. I decided to burn my boats, and to devote all my time to writing. My wife encouraged me. She is half Irish, and has a strain of recklessness.

Chapter V

THE WHEELS OF CHANGE

When I was a boy, a stage-coach started each morning (Sundays excepted) from an old inn off the Minories. Not the shining band-box of the coloured print, with its dancing horses, its jolly coachman, and its dandy guard, but a heavy lumbering vehicle drawn by four shambling horses, all of a different size, driven by a rheumaticy old curmudgeon, who had to be hoisted on to his seat, and his whip handed up to him afterwards. It went through Ongar and Epping, but its final destination I forget. To many of the smaller towns round London the railway had not then penetrated; and similar relics set out each morning from other ancient hostelries. Carriers' carts were common everywhere, connecting London with what are now its nearer suburbs, but which were then outlying villages. A row of them stood always in the middle of the Whitechapel Road, opposite St. Mary's church. They were covered with a hood, and had a bench for passengers along each side, and a little window at the back. For those in a hurry who could afford the price, post chaises were still to be hired, with top-hatted postillions and horses with bells that galloped over the cobbles. Respectable people—especially publicans—kept a gig; and sporting old ladies, on visits to their bankers or solicitors, would drive themselves into the city behind their own fat ponies.

The bicycle had not yet arrived: though nearly every afternoon an odd old fellow used to ride down Mare Street, Hackney, on a tricycle he had made for himself. In wet weather, he carried an umbrella over his head with one hand, and steered with the other. He was quite a public character, and people used to wait about to see him pass. The first bicycles were nicknamed "spiders." The front wheel was anything from fifty to sixty inches in diameter and was joined to a diminutive back wheel by a curved steel bar, shaped like a note of interrogation. Their riders had to be youths of skill and courage, or woe betide them. They wore tight-fitting breeches and short jackets that ended at the waist. Your modern youngster on his grimy "jig-pig" with his padded legs, his bulging mackintosh, his skull-cap and his goggles, goes further and faster, I admit; but his slim grandfather, towering above the traffic on his flashing wheel, was a braver sight for gods and girls.

It was my nephew, Frank Shorland, who first rode a safety bicycle in London. A little chap named Lawson claimed to have invented it. He became a company promoter, and later retired to Devonshire. A cute little chap. The luck ran against him. It was he who first foresaw the coming of the motor, and organized that first joy ride from the Hotel Metropole to Brighton in 1896. Young Frank was well known as an amateur racer. He believed in the thing the moment he saw it, and agreed to ride his next race on one. He was unmercifully chaffed by the crowd. His competitors, on their tall, graceful "spiders," looked down upon him, wondering and amazed. But he won easily, and from that day "spiders" went out of fashion; till they came to be used only by real spiders for the spinning of their webs.

The coming of the "safety" made bicycling universally popular. Till then, it had been confined to the young men. I remember the bitter controversy that arose over the argument: "Should a lady ride a bicycle?" It was some while before the dropped bar was thought of, and so, in consequence, she had to ride in knickerbockers: very fetching they looked in them, too, the few who dared. But in those days a woman's leg was supposed to be a thing known only to herself and God. "Would you like it, if your sister showed her legs? Yes, or no?" was always the formula employed to silence you, did you venture a defence. Before that, it had been: "Could a real lady ride outside an omnibus?" or "Might a virtuous female ride alone in a hansom cab?" The woman question would seem to have been always with us. The landlady of an hotel on the Ripley Road, much frequented then by cyclists, went to the length of refusing to serve any rider who, on close inspection, turned out to be of the feminine gender; and the Surrey magistrates supported her. The contention was that a good woman would not—nay, could not—wear knickerbockers, "Bloomers" they were termed: that, consequently, any woman who did wear bloomers must be a bad citizeness: in legal language, a disorderly person, and an innkeeper was not bound to serve "disorderly characters." The decision turned out a blessing in disguise to the cycling trade. It stirred them to invention.

To a bright young mechanical genius occurred the "dropped bar." A Bishop's wife, clothed in seemly skirts, rode on a bicycle through Leamington.

Bicycling became the rage. In Battersea Park, any morning between eleven and one, all the best blood in England could be seen, solemnly peddling up and down the half-mile drive that runs between the river and the refreshment kiosk. But these were the experts—the finished article. In shady by-paths, elderly countesses, perspiring peers, still in the wobbly stage, battled bravely with the laws of equilibrium; occasionally defeated, would fling their arms round the necks of hefty young hooligans who were reaping a rich harvest as cycling instructors: "Proficiency guaranteed in twelve lessons." Cabinet Ministers, daughters of a hundred Earls might be recognized by the initiated, seated on the gravel, smiling feebly and rubbing their heads. Into quiet roads and side-streets, one ventured at the peril of one's limbs. All the world seemed to be learning bicycling: sighting an anxious pedestrian, they would be drawn, as by some irresistible magnetic influence, to avoid all other pitfalls and make straight for him. One takes it that, nowadays, the human race learns bicycling at an age when the muscles are more supple, the fear of falling less paralyzing to the nerves. Still occasionally, of an early morning, one encounters the ubiquitous small boy, pursuing an erratic course upon a wheel far and away too high for him—borrowed without permission, one assumes, from some still sleeping relative. With each revolution, his whole body rises and falls. He seems to be climbing some Sisyphian staircase. But one feels no anxiety. One knows that by some miracle he will, at the last moment, succeed in swerving round one; will shave the old lady with the newspapers by a hair's breadth; will all but run over the dog; and disappear round the corner. Providence is helpful to youth. To the middle aged it can be spiteful. The bicycle took my generation unprepared.

In times of strike, there emerges the old hansom. Its bony horse must be twenty years older, but looks much the same. Its driver has grown grey and harmless; thanks you for a shilling over his fare, and trots away. Once, he was both the terror and the pride of London town. Nervous old ladies and gentlemen, on their way home to genteel suburbs, would ride in fear and trembling, wondering what he would say—or do—to them if they failed immediately to satisfy his exorbitant demand. Young men, with sweethearts, would furtively count their change, trying to guess how much it would cost them to silence his loud-mouthed sarcasm. Myself, I discovered that there was but one way of teaching him Christian behaviour; and that was by knowing more bad language than he had ever learnt, and getting it in first. How could he know that I had slept in doss-houses, shared hay-ricks with tramps? I had the further advantage over him of being able to add vituperation both in French and German. Outclassed, he would whip up his horse, glad to escape. But not all had my gift of tongues. The late Weedon Grossmith had recourse to guile. He had found a charming place called "The Old House" at Canonbury. But it was far from theatre-land;

and Weedon's difficulty was getting home at nights. From the Strand to Canonbury was what the drivers used to call "collar work." The horse had the work. The driver had the extra tip. Weedon was willing to pay in reason, but the old hansom-cab driver was a born bully: especially when dealing with a smallish gentleman in a lonely *cul-de-sac*. So instead of giving the address of his own front gate, Weedon always gave the address of a house near by that happened to be next to a police station. The constable on duty—not perhaps entirely forgotten on his birthday and other anniversaries— would stroll up as Weedon Grossmith jumped out. The cabman would accept his fare, plus a respectable addition, with a pleasant "Thank you, sir"; and wishing Weedon and the constable good-night, drive off. And all was peace.

It was a picturesque vehicle, the old hansom: there was that to be said for it. George Augustus Sala, a bright young journalist, on the staff of *The Daily Telegraph*, called it the London Gondola. And the bright young journalists of Venice wrote of their own Gondola, I doubt not, as the Venetian Hansom. But to ride in, they were the most uncomfortable contrivances ever invented. To get into them, you grabbed at two handles, one jutting out from the splash board and the other just over the wheel, and hauled yourself up on to a small iron step. If the horse made a start before you got further, you were carried down the street in this position, looking like a monkey on a stick. If you had not secured a firm hold, you were jerked back into the gutter, and the cab went on without you: which was safer, but even less dignified. Getting out was more difficult. A false step landed you on all fours, and your aunt or your sister, or whatever it might happen to be, stepped on you. To enter or alight without getting your hat knocked off by the reins was an art in itself. The seat was just big enough for two. It was high, and only long ladies could reach the floor. The others bobbed up and down with their feet dangling. The world always thought the worst, but as often as not, one put one's arm round her purely to prevent her from slipping off. There was a trap door in the roof. Along dim-lit roads, one noticed the cabman holding it open, and driving with his head bent down. A folded window could be let down by the driver to protect you from the rain. It was called the guillotin. That was another thing that always knocked your hat off: and then it hit you on the head. Most people chose the rain. If by any chance the horse slipped—and he was the sort of horse that made one wonder how it was that he stood up—then the "apron" doors would fly open and you would be shot out into the road—minus, of course, your hat. Another experience that could happen to you in a hansom was the breaking of the belly-band; and then the whole thing tilted up; and you lay on your back with your legs in the air and no possibility, if you were a lady, of getting at your skirts. As they had fallen, so they must abide; her only hope being that all such things as had now become visible were seemly. There was nothing to catch hold of—nothing by which one could regain one's feet. There one had to lie till the driver had extricated himself, and with the help of the hilarious crowd, had brought the cab back to the horizontal. Then you crawled out, and distributed shillings; and walked home, without your hat.

I have no regrets for the passing of the hansom.

The old two-horse 'bus, one is glad has disappeared, if only for the sake of the horses. It had straw inside and a little oil lamp that made up in smell what it lacked in illuminating power. It carried twelve inside, and fourteen out—ten on the knife-board, and two each side of the driver. The seats by the driver were reserved for acrobats. You caught a swinging strap and sprang on to the hub of the front wheel, leapt from there on to the trace-pin and then with a final bound gained the foot-board. The "knife-board" was easier of attainment. You climbed up a fixed ladder, the rungs a foot apart. The only real danger was from the man above you. If he kicked out you were done. There was no bell. Passengers stopped the 'bus by prodding the conductor with their umbrellas. The driver wore a mighty coat with flapping capes, and wrapped a rug round his legs before strapping himself to his seat. He was a genial soul, not above accepting a cigar, and had a tongue as clever as his hands. Wit and sarcasm dropped from him as he drove. The motor has silenced the humour of the streets.

I cannot help fancying that London was a cosier place to dwell in, when I was a young man. For one thing, it was less crowded. Life was not one everlasting scrimmage. There was time for self-respect, for courtesy.

For another thing, one got out of it quicker. On summer afternoons, four-horse brakes would set out for Barnet, Esher Woods, Chingford and Hampton Court. One takes now the motor 'bus, and goes further; but it is through endless miles of brick and mortar. And at the end, one is but in another crowd. Forty years ago, one passed by fields and leafy ways, and came to pleasant tea gardens, with bowling greens, and birds, and lovers' lanes.

Of a night time, threepenny 'buses took us to Cremorne Gardens, where bands played, and we danced and supped under a thousand twinkling lights. Or one walked there through the village of Chelsea, past the old wooden bridge. Battersea Park was in the making, and farm lands came down to the water's edge. The ladies may not all have been as good as they were beautiful; but somehow the open sky and the flowing river took the sordidness away. Under the trees and down the flower-bordered paths, it was possible to imagine the shadow of Romance. The Argyll Rooms, Evans' and others were more commonplace. But even so, they were more human—less brutal than our present orgy of the streets. Fashion sipped its tea, and stayed to dinner, at the lordly "Star & Garter," and drove home in phaeton or high dog-cart across Richmond Park and Putney Heath. The river was a crowded highway. One went by steamer to "The Ship" at Greenwich, for its famous fish dinner, with Mouton Rothschild at eight and six the bottle. Or further on, to "The Falcon" at Gravesend, where the long dining-room looked out upon the river, and one watched the ships passing silently upon the evening tide. On Sundays, for half a crown, one travelled to Southend and back. Unlimited tea was served on board, with prawns and watercress, for ninepence. We lads had not spent much money on our lunch, but the fat stewardess would only laugh as she brought us another pile of thick-cut bread and butter. I was on the "Princess Alice" on her last completed voyage. She went down the following Sunday, and nearly every soul on board was drowned. So, also, I was on the last complete voyage the "Lusitania" made from New York. They would not let us land at Liverpool, but made us anchor at the mouth of the Mersey, and took us off in tugs. We were loaded up to the water line with ammunition. "Agricultural Machinery," I think it was labelled. Penny Gaffs were common. They were the Repertory Theatre of the period. One sat on benches and ate whelks and fried potatoes and drank beer. "Sweeney Todd, the Barber of Fleet Street," was always a great draw, though "Maria Martin, or The Murder in the Red Barn," ran it close. "Hamlet," cut down to three-quarters of an hour, and consisting chiefly of broad-sword combats, was also popular. Prize fights took place on Hackney marshes, generally on Sunday morning; and foot-pads lurked on Hampstead Heath. Theatre patrons had no cause to complain of scanty measure. The programme lasted generally from six till twelve. It began with a farce, included a drama and an opera, and ended up with a burlesque. After nine o'clock, half prices were charged for admission. At most of the bridges one paid toll. Waterloo was the cheapest. Foot passengers there were charged only a halfpenny. It came to be known as the Scotchman's bridge. The traditional Scotchman, on a visit to a friend in London, was supposed to have been taken everywhere and treated. Coming to Waterloo Bridge, his host put his hand in his pocket, as usual, to draw out the required penny. The Scotchman with a fine gesture stepped in front of him. "My turn," said the Scotchman. Before the Aerated Bread Company came along, there were only three places in London, so far as I can remember, where a cup of tea could be obtained: one in St. Paul's Churchyard, another in the Strand called the Bun Shop, and the third in Regent Street at the end of the Quadrant. It was the same in New York when I first went there. I offered to make Charles Frohman's fortune for him. My idea was that he should put down five thousand dollars, and that we should start tea shops, beginning in Fifth Avenue. I reckon I missed being a millionaire. Gatti's in the Strand first introduced ices into London. Children were brought up from the country during the holidays to have a twopenny ice at Gatti's. It was at the old Holborn Restaurant that first one dined to music. It was held to be Continental and therefore immoral; and the everlasting woman question rose again to the surface: could a good woman dine to the accompaniment of a string band?

As a matter of fact, it didn't really matter in those days. A giddy old aunt from the country would sometimes clamour to be taken out, but "nice" women fed at home. At public dinners, a gallery was set aside for them. They came in—like the children—with the dessert; and were allowed to listen to the speeches. Sometimes they were noticed, and their health drunk. The toast was always entrusted to the comic man, and responded to by the youngest bachelor: supposed to be the nearest thing to a lady capable of speech. In all the best houses there was a "smoking-room" into which the master of the house, together with his friends, when he had any, would retire to smoke their pipes or their cigars. Cigarettes were deemed effeminate. A popular writer in 1870 explained the victory of Germany over France by pointing out that the Germans were a pipe-smoking people, while the French smoked cigarettes. If there wasn't any smoking-room he smoked in the back kitchen. After smoking, and before rejoining the ladies, one sucked a clove. It was said to purify the breath. I remember, soon after the Savoy Hotel was opened, a woman being asked to leave the supper-room for smoking a cigarette. She offered to put it out; but the feelings of the other guests had been too deeply outraged; forgiveness, it was felt, would be mere weakness. A gentleman, seen in company with a woman who smoked, lost his reputation.

Only mansions boasted bathrooms. The middle-classes bathed on Saturdays. It was a tremendous performance, necessitating the carrying of many buckets of water from the basement to the second floor. The practical-minded, arguing that it was easier for Mohammed to go to the mountain, took their bath in the kitchen. There were Spartans who professed themselves unhappy unless they had a cold "tub" every morning. The servants hated them. It was kept under the bed, and at night time was hauled out, and left ready for him with a can of water. It was shaped like a wide shallow basin, and the water just covered your toes. You sat in it with your legs tucked up and soused yourself with the sponge. The difficulty was emptying it. You lifted it up and staggered about with it, waiting for the moment when the waters should grow calm and cease from wobbling. Sometimes you succeeded in pouring it into the pail without spilling half of it on to the floor, and sometimes you didn't. It was the Americans who introduced baths into England. Till the year of Jubilee, no respectable young lady went out after dusk unless followed by the housemaid. For years the stock joke in *Punch* was ankles. If a lady, crossing the road, lifted her dress sufficiently high to show her ankles, traffic became disorganized. Crowds would collect upon the curb to watch her. The high-minded turned their eyes the other way. But the shameless—like Miss Tincklepot's parrot— would make no bones about "having a damn good look." There came a season when Fashion decreed that skirts should be two inches from the ground; and *The Daily Telegraph* had a leader warning the nation of the danger of unchecked small beginnings. Things went from bad to worse. A woman's club was launched called "The Pioneers." All the most desperate women in London enrolled themselves as members. Shaw, assumed to be a feminist, was invited to address them. He had chosen for his text, Ephesians, fifth chapter, twenty-second verse, and had been torn limb from limb, according to the earlier reports. And *The Times* had a leader warning the nation of the danger, should woman cease to recognize that the sphere of her true development lay in the home circle. Hardly a year later, female suffrage for unmarried women householders in their own right was mooted in the House of Commons, and London rocked with laughter. It was the typewriter that led to the discovery of woman. Before then, a woman in the city had been a rare and pleasing sight. The tidings flew from tongue to tongue, and way was made for her. The right of a married woman to go shopping by herself, provided she got back in time for tea, had long been recognized; and when Irving startled London by giving performances on Saturday afternoons ("*matinées*" they came to be called) women, unattended by any male protector, were frequently to be noticed in the pit.

The telephone was hailed as a tremendous advance towards the millennium. The idea then current was that, one by one, the world's troubles were disappearing. But for a long while, it saved time and temper to take a cab and go round and see the man. Electric lighting was still in the experimental stage; and for some reason got itself mixed up with Bradlaugh and atheism: maybe, because it used to go out suddenly, a phenomenon attributed by many to the wrath of God. A judge of the High Court was much applauded for denouncing it from the Bench, and calling for tallow candles. A wave of intellectuality passed over England in the later 'eighties. A popular form of entertainment was the Spelling-Bee. The competitors sat in rows upon the platform, while the body of the hall would be filled with an excited audience, armed with dictionaries. Every suburb had its amateur Parliament, with real Liberals and Conservatives. At Chelsea, where we met over a coffee shop in Flood Street, we had an Irish party, which was always being "suspended": when it would depart, cursing us, to sing the "Marseillaise," and "The Wearin' of the Green," in the room below. Rowdy young men and women—of the sort that nowadays go in for night clubs and jazz dancing—filled the ranks of the Fabian Society; and revelled in evenings at Essex Hall. They argued with the Webbs, and interrupted Shaw. Wells had always plenty to say, but was not an orator. He would lose his head when contradicted, and wave his arms about. Shaw's plays always led to scenes on the first night. At "Widowers' Houses," there was a free fight in the gallery. Shaw made a speech that had the effect of reconciling both his friends and enemies in a united desire to lynch him. The Salvation Army came as a great shock to the Press. It was the Salvation Army's "vulgarity," its "cheap sentiment" that wounded the fine feelings of Fleet Street. Squire Bancroft was the first citizen of credit and renown to champion the Salvation Army. Fleet Street rubbed its eyes. It had always thought the Bancrofts so respectable. But gradually the abuse died down.

Soho, when I was a young man, was the haunt of revolutionaries. I came to know a few of them. When the revolutionary is not revolutionizing, he loves a sentimental song, or a pathetic recitation: will accept the proffered cigar and grow reminiscent over a tenpenny bottle of *vin ordinaire*. What I admired about them was their scorn of all pretences. Fourpence laid out at any barber's in the neighbourhood might have put the police off the scent. They despised such subterfuge. Their very trousers were revolutionary. Except on the legs of the conspirators' chorus in "Madame Angot," one never saw the like. I thought, at times, of suggesting to them that they should wear masks and carry dark lanterns. I believe, if I had done so, it would have appealed to them. It could have made no practical difference; and would have added a final touch of picturesqueness.

A little while before the war, I renewed acquaintance with the Russian revolutionary, this time at the house of Prince Kropotkin, in Brighton. Prince Kropotkin himself was a kindly, dapper little gentleman of aristocratic appearance, but his compatriots, who came to visit him, there was no mistaking. The sight of them, as they passed by, struck terror to the stoutest hearts of Kemp Town. There was one gentleman with a beard down to his waist and a voice that shook the ornaments upon the mantelpiece. He belonged to a new religious sect that held it wrong, among other things, to destroy house flies; but was less scrupulous, I gathered, regarding the existence of the *petite bourgeoisie*. Alas! even the best of us are not always consistent. During the war, I have listened to members of humanitarian societies chortling over the thought that German babies were being starved to death.

I fancy the At Home has died out. Anyhow one hopes so. It was a tiresome institution. Good women had a special afternoon: "At Home every Thursday."

Sometimes it was every other Thursday, or every first Friday, or third Monday. One's brain used to reel, trying to remember them. Most often, one turned up on the wrong day. Poor ladies would remain in all the afternoon, sitting in the drawing-room in all their best clothes, surrounded by expensive refreshments; and not a soul to speak to. In my mother's day, the morning was the fashionable time for calls. There were always cake and biscuits in a silver basket, and port and sherry on the side-board. They used to talk about the servants, and how things were going from bad to worse.

Douglas Sladen was the most successful At Home giver that I ever knew. Half "Who's Who" must have come to his receptions at Addison Mansions from ten-thirty to the dawn. He had a wonderful way when he introduced you of summarizing your career, opinions, and general character in half-a-dozen sentences, giving you like information concerning the other fellow—or fellowess. You knew what crimes and follies to avoid discussing, what talents and virtues it would be kind to drag into the conversation.

Science informs us that another Glacial period is on the way—that sooner or later the now temperate zone will again be buried under ice. But, for the moment, we would seem to be heading the other way. Snow-drifts in the London streets were common in my early winters. Often the bridges were impassable, till an army of sweepers had cleared a passage. I have watched the sleighs, with their jingling bells, racing along the

Embankment. One year, we had six weeks of continuous skating. There was quite a fair on the Serpentine, and a man with a dog crossed the Thames on foot at Lambeth. Fogs were something like fogs in those days. One, I remember, lasted exactly a week. Gas flares roared at Charing Cross and Hyde Park Corner. From the other side of the road they looked like distant lighthouses. Link-boys, waving their burning torches, plied for hire; and religious fanatics went to and fro, invisible, proclaiming the end of the world.

On a morning in 1896, a line of weird-shaped vehicles, the like of which London had never seen before, stood drawn up in Northumberland Avenue outside the Hotel Metropole. They were the new horseless carriages, called automobiles, about which we had heard much talk. Lawson, a company promoter, who claimed to have invented the safety bicycle, had got them together. The law, insisting that every mechanically propelled vehicle should be preceded by a man carrying a red flag, had expired the day before; and at nine o'clock we started for Brighton. I shared a high two-seater with the editor of a financial journal, a gentleman named Duguid. We were fifth in the procession. Our driver, a large man, sat perched up on a dicky just in front of us, and our fear throughout the journey was, lest he should fall backwards, and bury us. An immense crowd had gathered, and until we were the other side of Croydon it was necessary for mounted police to clear a way for us. At Purley the Brighton coach overtook us, and raced us into Reigate. By the time we reached Crawley, half our number had fallen out for repairs and alterations. We were to have been received at Brighton by the Mayor and Corporation and lunched at the Grand Hotel. The idea had been that somewhere between twelve and one the whole twenty-five of us would come sweeping down the Preston road amid enthusiastic cheers. It was half-past three before the first of us appeared. At lengthening intervals some half-a-dozen others straggled in (Duguid and myself were, I think, the last), to be received with sarcasm and jeers. We washed ourselves—a tedious operation—and sat down to an early dinner. Little Lawson made a witty speech. All the Vested Interests of the period—railway companies; livery stable keepers, and horse dealers; the Grand Junction Canal; the Amalgamated Society of Bath-chair Proprietors, and so forth, were, of course, all up in arms against him. One petition, praying Parliament to put its foot down upon the threatened spoiling of the countryside, was signed "Friends of the Horse." It turned out to be from the Worshipful Company of Whipmakers. Some credit is due to the motorists of those days. It was rarely that one reached one's destination. As a matter of fact, only the incurable optimist ever tried to. The common formula was: "Oh, let's start off, and see what happens." Generally, one returned in a hired fly. Everywhere along the country roads, one came across them: some drawn up against the grass, others helplessly blocking the way. Beside them, dejected females sitting on a rug. Underneath, a grimy man, blaspheming: another running round and treading on him. Experienced wives took their knitting and a camp stool. Very young men with a mechanical turn of mind got enjoyment out of them, apparently. At the slightest sign of trouble, they would take the whole thing to pieces, and spread it out upon the roadside. Some cheerful old lady, an aunt presumably, would be grovelling on her hands and knees, with her mouth full of screws, looking for more. Passing later in the evening, one would notice the remains piled up against the hedge with a lantern hung on to it. At first, we wore masks and coloured goggles. Horses were terrified when they met us. We had to stop the engine and wait. I remember one old farmer with a very restive filly. Of course we were all watching him. "If you ladies and gentlemen," he said, "wouldn't mind turning your faces the other way, maybe I'd get her past."

They were of strange and awful shapes, at the beginning. There was one design supposed to resemble a swan; but, owing to the neck being short, it looked more like a duck: that is, if it looked like anything. To fill the radiator, you unscrewed its head and poured the water down its neck; and as you drove the screw would work loose, and the thing would turn round and look at you out of one eye. Others were shaped like canoes and gondolas. One firm brought out a dragon. It had a red tongue, and you hung the spare wheel on its tail.

Flying-machines, properly speaking, came in with the war. We used to have balloon ascents from the Crystal Palace on fine Thursdays. You paid a guinea to go up and took your chance as to where you would come down. Most of them came home the next morning with a cold. Now the journey from London to Paris takes two hours. Thus the wheels go round; and to quote from a once popular poet: "Ever the right comes uppermost, and ever is justice done."

Chapter VI

MORE LITERARY REMINISCENCES

"Three Men in a Boat. To say nothing of the dog," I wrote at Chelsea Gardens, up ninety-seven stairs. But the view was worth it. We had a little circular drawing-room—I am speaking now as a married man—nearly all window, suggestive of a lighthouse, from which we looked down upon the river, and over Battersea Park to the Surrey hills beyond, with the garden of old Chelsea Hospital just opposite. Fourteen shillings a week we paid for that flat: two reception-rooms, three bedrooms and a kitchen. One was passing rich in those days on three hundred a year: kept one's servant, and sipped one's Hennessy's "Three Star" at four and twopence the bottle. I had known Chelsea Gardens for some time. Rose Norreys, the actress, had a flat there, and gave Sunday afternoon parties. She was playing then at the Court Theatre with Arthur Cecil and John Clayton. Half young Bohemia used to squeeze itself into her tiny drawing-room, and overflow into the kitchen. Bald or grey-headed they are now, those of them that are left. Bernard Partridge and myself were generally the last to leave. One could not help loving her. She was a strange spiritual little creature. She would have made a wonderful Joan of Arc. She never seemed to grow up. I was rehearsing a play at the Vaudeville Theatre, when a boy slipped into my hand the last letter I had from her. The boy never said whom it was from; and I did not open it till the end of the act, some two hours later. It was written in pencil, begging me to come to her at once. She had rooms in Great Portland Street in a house covered with ivy. A small crowd was round the door when I got there; and I learned she had just been taken away to Colney Hatch asylum. I never could bring myself to go and see her there. She had kind women friends—Mrs. Jopling Rowe, the artist, was one—who watched over her. I pray her forgiveness.

I did not intend to write a funny book, at first. I did not know I was a humorist. I never have been sure about it. In the Middle Ages, I should probably have gone about preaching and got myself burnt or hanged. There was to be "humorous relief"; but the book was to have been "The Story of the Thames," its scenery and history. Somehow it would not come. I was just back from my honeymoon, and had the feeling that all the world's troubles were over. About the "humorous relief" I had no difficulty. I decided to write the "humorous relief" first—get it off my chest, so to speak. After which, in sober frame of mind, I could tackle the scenery and history. I never got there. It seemed to be all "humorous relief." By grim determination I succeeded, before the end, in writing a dozen or so slabs of history and working them in, one to each chapter, and F. W. Robinson, who was publishing the book serially, in *Home Chimes*, promptly slung them out, the most of them. From the beginning he had objected to the title and had insisted upon my thinking of another. And half-way through I hit upon "Three Men in a Boat," because nothing else seemed right.

There wasn't any dog. I did not possess a dog in those days. Neither did George. Nor did Harris. As a boy I had owned pets innumerable. There was a baby water-rat I had caught in a drain. He lived most of his time in my breast pocket. I would take him to school with me; and he would sit with his head poking out between my handkerchief and my coat so that nobody could see him but myself, and look up at me with adoring eyes. Next to my mother, I loved him more than anybody in the world. The other boys complained of him after a time, but I believe it was only jealousy. I never smelt anything. And then there was a squirrel—an orphan—that I persuaded a white rabbit to adopt, until he bit one of his foster-brothers; and a cat that used to come to the station to meet me. But it never ran to a dog. Montmorency I evolved out of my inner consciousness. There is something of the dog, I take it, in most Englishmen. Dog friends that I came to know later have told me he was true to life.

Indeed, now I come to think of it, the book really was a history. I did not have to imagine or invent. Boating up and down the Thames had been my favourite sport ever since I could afford it. I just put down the things that happened.

A few years ago I took some American friends, who had been staying with me, to see Oxford. We had left the house at eight o'clock, and had finished up with the Martyrs' Memorial at a quarter to seven. Looking back, I cannot think of anything we missed. I had said good-bye to them at the railway station. They were going on to Stratford. I was too exhausted to remember I had left the motor at the Randolph. There was a train going in the opposite direction to Stratford; and caring about nothing else, I took it. Just as it was starting there shot in a liver-coloured dog, followed by three middle-aged and important-looking gentlemen. The dog, a Chow, took the seat opposite to me. He had a quiet dignity about him. He struck me as more Chinese than dog. The other three spread themselves about. The eldest, and most talkative, was a professor: anyhow that's what they called him; added to which, he looked it. The stoutest of the three I judged to be connected with finance. It appeared that if the "A.G. group" did not put up fourteen millions by Friday, he would have to go to town on Monday, and that would be a nuisance. I could not help overhearing and feeling sorry for him. At the period, I was worried over money matters myself. The third was a simple soul connected with Egyptology and a museum. I was dropping off to sleep, when the train gave a lurch, and the Professor suddenly said "Damn."

"Wish I'd never sat down on that corkscrew," remarked the Professor, while rubbing the place.

"If it comes to that," remarked the Financier, "there were one or two things that would have been all the better for your not sitting down upon them: tomatoes, for example."

I kept my eyes closed and listened. I learnt that, brain fagged and desiring a new thing, they had hit upon the idea of hiring a boat at Kingston and pulling up the river. They were in reminiscent mood, and it was clear they had had trouble with their packing. They had started with a tent. For the first two nights, they had slept in this tent—at intervals. The tent, it was evident, had shown no more respect for Philosophy and High Finance and Egyptology than for Youth and Folly. It had followed the law of its being; and on the third morning they had deliberately set fire to it and had danced round it while it burnt. They had bathed of mornings; and the Egyptologist, slipping on a banana rind, had dived before he intended and taken his pyjamas with him. They had washed their clothes in the river and afterwards given them away. They had sat hungry round hermetically sealed luxuries, having forgotten the tin-opener. The Chow, whose name it transpired was Confucius, had had a row with a cat, and had scalded himself with the kettle.

From all of which it would appear that anyone, who had thought of it, could have written "Three Men in a Boat." Likely enough, some troop of ancient Britons, camping where now the Mother of Parliaments looks down upon old Thames, listened amused while one among them told of the adventures of himself and twain companions in a coracle: to say nothing of the wolf. Allowing for variation in unimportant detail, much the same sort of things must have happened. And in 30,000 A.D.—if Earth's rivers still run—a boat-load of Shaw's "ancients" will, in all probability, be repeating the experiment with similar results, accompanied by a dog five thousand years old.

George and Harris were likewise founded on fact. Harris was Carl Hentschel. I met him first outside a pit door. His father introduced photo-etching into England. It enabled newspapers to print pictures, and altered the whole character of journalism. The process was a secret then. Young Carl and his father, locking the back kitchen door, and drawing down the blind, would stir their crucibles far on into the night. Carl worked the business up into a big concern; and we thought he was going to end as Lord Mayor. The war brought him low. He was accused of being a German. As a matter of fact he was a Pole. But his trade rivals had got their chance, and took it. George Wingrave, now a respectable Bank Manager, I met when lodging in Newman Street; and afterwards we chummed together in Tavistock Place, handy for the British Museum reading-room: the poor students' club, as it used to be called.

We three would foregather on Sunday mornings, and take the train to Richmond. There were lovely stretches then between Richmond and Staines, meadowland and cornfields. At first, we used to have the river almost to ourselves; but year by year it got more crowded and Maidenhead became our starting-point. England in those days was still a Sabbath-keeping land. Often people would hiss us as we passed, carrying our hamper and clad in fancy "blazers." Once a Salvation Army lass dropped suddenly upon her knees in front of us and started praying. Tennis, on Sundays, was played only behind high walls, and golf had not come in. Bicycling was just beginning. I remember the indignation of a village publican, watching some lads just starting for a Sunday outing. "Look at them," he said, "they'll gad about all day like wooden monkeys on a stick, and won't get home till after closing time. God forgive 'em."

Sometimes we would fix up a trip of three or four days or a week, doing the thing in style and camping out. Three, I have always found, make good company. Two grow monotonous, and four or over break up into groups. Later on we same three did a cycle tour through the Black Forest: out of which came "Three Men on the Bummel" ("Three Men on Wheels," it was called in America). In Germany it was officially adopted as a school reading-book. Another year we tramped the valley of the Upper Danube. That would have made an interesting book, but I was occupied writing plays at the time. It lingers in my memory as the best walk of all. We seemed to have mounted Wells' "Time Machine," and slipped back into the Middle Ages. Railways and hotels had vanished. Barefooted friars wandered, crook in hand, shepherding their flocks. Peering into the great barns, we watched the swinging of the iron flails. Yoked oxen drew the creaking wains. Outside the cottage doors, the women ground the corn between the querns. We slept in the great guest room side by side: tired men and women with their children, Jew pedlar, travelling acrobat. A knapsack on one's back and a stout staff in one's hand makes joyous travelling. Your modern motor-car, rushing through history in a cloud of dust, is for Time's rich slaves. Even on the old push bicycle one is too much in a hurry. One sees the beauty after one has passed. One wonders: shall one get off and go back? Meanwhile, one goes on: it is too late. On foot, one leans one's arms upon the gate: the picture has time to print itself upon the memory. One falls into talk with cheery tinker, brother tramp, or village priest. The pleasant byway lures our willing feet: it may lead to mystery, adventure. Another of our excursions was through the Ardennes. But that was less interesting, except for a strange combination of monastery and convent with a sign-post outside it offering accommodation for man and beast, where monks did the cooking, and nuns waited, and the Abbess (at least so I took her to be) made out the bill. It was in the 'nineties. If one asked one's way of the old folk, one spoke in French; but if of the young, one asked in German and was answered cheerfully. On the whole, one gathered that the peasants were nearer to Germany. It was in the towns that one found the French.

Subsequently Carl, busy climbing to that Mayorial chair, deserted; and Pett-Ridge, who may be said to have qualified himself by afterwards marrying a sister of Carl's, made our third. The only fault we found with him was that he never changed his clothes. Or if he did, it was to prove the truth of the French proverb: that the more things change, the more they remain the same. He would join us for a walking tour through the Tyrol or a tramp across Brittany, wearing the same clothes in which we had last seen him strolling down the Strand on his way to the Garrick Club: cut-away coat with fancy vest, grey striped trousers, kid boots buttoned at the side (as worn then by all the best people), spotless white shirt and collar, speckled blue tie, soft felt hat, and fawn gloves. I have tobogganed with Pett-Ridge amid the snows of Switzerland. I have boated with him. I have motored with him. Always he has been dressed in precisely those same clothes. He'll turn up at the Day of Judgment clothed like that: I feel sure of it. Possibly, out of respect to the Court, he will substitute a black tie.

We put up with him for the reason that he was—and always is—a most delightful companion. The worst one can say about his books is that they are not as good as his talk. If they were, we other humorists wouldn't have a look in.

"Three Men in a Boat" brought me fame, and had it been published a few years later would have brought me fortune also. As it was, the American pirate reaped a great reward. But I suppose God made him. Of course it was damned by the critics. One might have imagined— to read some of them—that the British Empire was in danger. One Church dignitary went about the country denouncing me. *Punch* was especially indignant, scenting an insidious attempt to introduce "new humour" into comic literature. For years, "New Humorist" was shouted after me wherever I wrote. Why in England, of all countries in the world, humour, even in new clothes, should be mistaken for a stranger to be greeted with brickbats, bewildered me. It bewildered others. Zangwill, in an article on humour, has written:

"There is a most bewildering habit in modern English letters. It consists in sneering down the humorist—that rarest of all literary phenomena. His appearance, indeed, is hailed with an outburst of gaiety; even the critics have the joy of discovery. But no sooner is he established and doing an apparently profitable business than a reaction sets in, and he becomes a by-word for literary crime. When 'Three Men in a Boat' was fresh from the press, I was buttonholed by grave theologians and scholars hysterically insisting on my hearing page after page: later on these same gentlemen joined in the hue and cry and shuddered at the name of Jerome. The interval before the advent of another humorist is filled in with lamentations on the decay of humour."

There is more in the article my vanity would like to quote, but my modesty forbids. If few writers have been worse treated by the Press, few can have received more kindness from their fellow-workers. I recall a dinner given me on the eve of my setting out for a lecturing tour through America. Barrie was in the chair, I think—anyhow in one of them. In the others were Conan Doyle, Barry Pain, Zangwill, Pett-Ridge, Hall Caine—some twenty in all. Everybody made a speech. I am supposed to be rather good at after-dinner speaking, but forgot everything I had intended to say that night. It all sounds very egotistical, but that is the danger of writing one's own biography.

I had got the habit of going about in threes. I wanted to see the Oberammergau Passion Play. The party was to have consisted of Eden Phillpotts, Walter Helmore, brother of the actor, and myself. Phillpotts and Helmore were then both in the Sun Insurance Office at Charing Cross. Phillpotts fell ill, and the Passion Play would not wait, so Helmore and I went alone. That was in 1890. One went to Oberammergau then in post chaise, and there was only one hotel in the village. One lodged with the peasants and shared their fare. I visited there again a few years before the war. The railway had come, and the great hotels were crowded. The bands played, and there was dancing in the evening. Of course I had written a book about it: "The Diary of a Pilgrimage": so perhaps I am hardly entitled to indulge in jeremiads.

Helmore knew Germany well. We came home through Bavaria, and down the Rhine. It was my first visit to Germany. I liked the people and their homely ways, and later some four years residence in Germany confirmed my first impressions.

Calmour was a frequent visitor of ours at Chelsea. He was secretary to W. G. Wills, who wrote blank verse plays for Henry Irving: "Charles I," "Faust," and "The Vicar of Wakefield" among others. We had a fine old row in the pit on the first night of "Charles I." I was for

Cromwell. I was training a pair of whiskers at the time, and a royalist woman behind got hold of one of them and spoilt it. Wills was a bit of an oddity. He did not keep a banking account. He would take his money always in gold, and after paying what had to be, would fling the remainder into a lumber room at the top of his house, and double lock the door. Later on when he needed cash—or when a friend did, which to Wills was much the same—he would unlock the door and on hands and knees grope about till he had collected sufficient, and then fasten up the door again. Calmour was a playwright himself: "The Amber Heart" and "Cupid's Messenger" were his best known. He wrote also songs for "Lion Comiques," as they were called: "Champagne Charlie" and "The Ghost of John Benjamin Binns" were his. He never earned much money, but had learnt to do with less. He lived in one room in Sydney Street, and wrote in bed, not getting up as a rule till the evening. Bed, he used to say, was the cheapest place he knew. The moment you got up, expense began. He had a large circle of friends, and his dinners could have cost him but little. In later years, he lived on a "system"; which he took with him each winter to Monte Carlo. The difference between his system and most others was that, in his case, it really did work. He would stay there till he had in his pocket a hundred pounds over and above his expenses; and then, with rare strength of mind, would take the next train home. He had the reputation of being the guest that lingers too long. He knew of his failing, and settled the thing with my wife on his very first visit. I had not been present at their conversation; and was shocked when, the moment our grandfather's clock had finished striking twelve, my wife got up and said quite sweetly: "You must go now, Mr. Calmour. And please be sure to shut the bottom door." Before I could recover my astonishment, he had wished us good-night and was gone. "It's all right," said my wife. "I think he's a dear."

W. S. Henley, the actor, often came. Eden Phillpotts and myself were writing him a play. Henley, like most comic actors, yearned to play serious parts. As a matter of fact he would have played them very well. He could be both grotesque and tragic; and had naturally a rich, deep voice.

"It wouldn't be any good," he once said, in answer to my suggestion. "I would like to play Caliban, but they'd only think I was trying to give a comic imitation of something from the Zoo. If I'm out at dinner and ask a man to pass the mustard, he slaps his leg and bursts out laughing. Damned silly, I call it."

Gertrude Kingston with her mother and sister lived near by, in a charming little house in Ebury Street. Pinero's "Creamy English Rose" will always remain the beloved of the British theatrical public to the exclusion of all others, or Gertrude Kingston would long before now have been London's leading actress. She used to grumble at our ninety-seven stairs, but I persuaded her they were good for her figure and, not altogether convinced, she would often climb them. Olga Brandon would arrive at the top speechless, which perhaps was just as well.

Olga Brandon lived near by. She was a beautiful young woman, serene and stately. On the stage, she played queens, martyrs and Greek goddesses as if to the manner born. Off the stage, she spoke with a Cockney accent one could have cut with a knife, as the saying is, dropped her aitches, and could swear like a trooper. She was a dear kind girl. In the end she went the way of many. I remember a first night at the Vaudeville Theatre. A young actress who was playing her first big part was standing in the wings waiting her cue. She had a glass in her hand. Old Emily Thorne had just come off the stage. She stopped dead in front of the girl, blocking her way.

"Feeling in a tremble all over, aren't you?" suggested the elder woman.

"That just describes it," laughed the girl.

"And you find a little brandy pulls you together— steadies your nerves?"

"I doubt if I'd be able to go on without it," answered the girl.

Emily covered the girl's small hand with her own, and sent the contents of the glass flying. A wandering stage carpenter got most of it.

"I've known a good many promising young actresses," she said, "and half of them have ruined their career through drink. I've followed some of them to the grave. You learn to get on without it, child."

Henry Arthur Jones' brother had the flat beneath us. He was an acting manager, and called himself Sylvanus Danncey.

Marie Corelli I came to know while living in Chelsea. I used to meet her at the house of an Italian lady, a Madame Marras, in Princes Gate. Marie was a pretty girlish little woman. We discovered we were precisely the same age. Mrs. Garrett Anderson, the first lady doctor to put up her plate in London, was sometimes of the party. We used to play games: hunt the slipper, puss in the corner and musical chairs. I can boast that more than once I sat on Marie Corelli's lap, though not for long. She was an erratic worker and contracts would often get behind time. She lived with her adopted brother, Eric Mackay, son of the poet, and occasionally when her agent would come to the house tearing his hair because of an instalment that an editor was waiting for, and that Marie did not feel like writing, they would take her up and lock her in her study; and when she had finished kicking the door, she would settle down, and do a good morning's work.

To keep friends with her continuously was difficult. You had to agree with all her opinions, which were many and varied. I always admired her pluck and her sincerity. She died while I was writing this chapter.

Arthur Machen married a dear friend of mine, a Miss Hogg. How so charming a lady came to be born with such a name is one of civilization's little ironies. She had been a first nighter, and one of the founders of the Playgoers' Club, which was in advance of its time, and admitted women members. Amy Hogg was also a pioneer. She lived by herself in diggings opposite the British Museum, frequented restaurants and Aerated Bread shops, and had many men friends: all of which was considered very shocking in those days. She had a vineyard in France, and sold the wine to the proprietor of the Florence Restaurant in Rupert Street. She had a favourite table by the window, and often she and I dined there and shared a bottle. The Florence, then, was a cosy little place where one lunched for one and three and dined for two shillings. One frequently saw Oscar Wilde there. He and his friends would come in late and take the table in the further corner. Rumours were already going about, and his company did not tend to dispel them. One pretended not to see him. Machen when he was young suggested the Highbrow. He has developed into a benevolent-looking, white-haired gentleman. He might be one of the Brothers Cheeryble stepped out of "Nicholas Nickleby." For ability to create an atmosphere of nameless terror I can think of no author living or dead who comes near him. I gave Conan Doyle his "Three Impostors" to read one evening, and Doyle did not sleep that night.

"Your pal Machen is a genius right enough," said Doyle, "but I don't take him to bed with me again."

The memory lingers with me of the last time I saw his wife. It was a Sunday afternoon. They were living in Verulam Buildings, Gray's Inn, in rooms on the ground floor. The windows looked out onto the great quiet garden, and the rooks were cawing in the elms. She was dying, and Machen, with two cats under his arm, was moving softly about, waiting on her. We did not talk much. I stayed there till the sunset filled the room with a strange purple light.

The Thames was frozen over the last year we were in Chelsea. It was the first winter the gulls came to London. One listened to the music of the sleigh bells. Down the Embankment and round Battersea Park was the favourite course.

Friends of ours lived in St. John's Wood, and possessed gardens, some even growing roses and spring onions; and their boastings made us envious. Olga Nethersole had a cottage with real ivy and a porch. Lewis Waller had a mulberry tree; and one day I met Augustus Harris carrying a gun. He told me he had bought it to shoot rabbits at his "little place" off the Avenue Road. We found an old-fashioned house behind a high wall in Alpha Place. Bret Harte was near by. He lived with great swells named Van der Velde. The old gentleman, I think, was an ambassador, and the wife, an American lady who had known Bret Harte when he was young, or something of that sort. Bret Harte remained with them as their guest till he died. He had his own suite of rooms. His hair was golden when we first knew him, but as the years went by it turned to white. He was a slight dapper gentleman, courteous and shy, with a low soft voice. It was difficult to picture him, ruffling it among the bloodstained sentimentalists of Roaring Camp and Dead Man's Gulch.

Zangwill and his family were denizens of the Wood. His brother Louis also wrote books, calling himself "Z.Z." "The World and a Man" remains the best known of them. Zangwill was accused of being a "New Humorist." He edited a comic journal called *Ariel*, and discovered the English "Shakespeare": Shakespeares were being discovered everywhere just then. J. T. Grein, the dramatic critic, had discovered a Dutch Shakespeare, and another critic, not to be outdone, had dug up one in Belgium. In the end, every country in Europe was found to possess a Shakespeare, except England. Zangwill did not see why England should be left out, and discovered one in Brixton. Judging from the extracts Zangwill published, he certainly seemed as good as any of the others. The Bacon stunt was in full swing about the same time; and again it was Zangwill who discovered that Shakespeare's plays had all been written by another gentleman of the same name. I first met Mrs. Zangwill at a dinner. She was Miss Ayrton then, daughter of the Professor, and had been assigned to me. It is not often that one vexes a woman by taking her to be younger than she really is; but I quite offended her that evening. She looked fifteen, and I did my best to adapt myself accordingly. I have a youthful side to me, and flattered myself for a time that I was doing well. Suddenly she asked me my age, and, taken aback, I told her.

"Well, if you are all that," she answered, "why talk as if you were fourteen?"

It seemed she was quite grown up. She told me her own age. She evidently thought it a lot, but anyhow it was more than I had given her credit for; and after that we found we had plenty of interests in common. I have always thought how wonderfully alike she and Lady Forbes-Robertson are to one another in appearance. I hope neither of them will be offended, but one can never tell. I was assured once, by a mutual friend, that I reminded him tremendously of Mr. Asquith; and then he added as an afterthought: "But don't ever tell him I said so."

Zangwill is, and always has been, a strong personality. You either like him immensely or want to hit him with a club. Myself I have always had a sincere affection for him. We have in common a love of Lost Causes, and Under Dogs. He confessed to me once that he had wasted half his life on Zionism. I never liked to say so to him, but it always seemed to me that the danger threatening Zionism was that it might be realized. Jerusalem was the Vision Splendid of the Jewish race— the Pillar of Fire that had guided their footsteps across the centuries of shame and persecution. So long as it remained a dream, no Jew so poor, so hunted, so despised, but hugged to his breast his hidden birthright—his great inheritance to be passed on to his children. Who in God's name wanted a third-rate provincial town on a branch of the Baghdad railway? Most certainly not the Zionists. Their Jerusalem was and must of necessity always have remained in the clouds— their Promised Land the other side of the horizon. When the British Government presented Palestine to the Jews, it shattered the last hope of Israel. All that remains to be done now, is to invite contracts for the rebuilding of the Temple.

The London Jew's progress, a Rabbi once informed me, is mapped out by three landmarks: Whitechapel, Maida Vale, and Park Lane. The business Jew is no better than his Christian competitor. The artistic Jew I have always found exceptionally simple and childlike. Of these a good many had escaped from Maida Vale, and crossing the Edgware Road had settled themselves in St. John's Wood. Solomon J. Solomon had his studio off Marlborough Road. He was, I think, the first artist to paint by electric light—a useful accomplishment in foggy London. He started to paint my portrait once, while staying with us at Pangbourne, but complained I had too many faces. At one moment I looked a murderer and the next a saint, according to him. I have the thing as he left it unfinished. It reminds me of someone, but I can't think whom. De Laszlo had the same trouble with me not long ago, but got over it by luring me to talk about myself. In his portrait of me there is a touch of the enthusiast. Cowen the composer had a big house in Hamilton Terrace and used to give delightful concerts. Sarah Bernhardt hired a house one spring. She brought a pet leopard with her: a discriminating beast, according to the local tradesmen. It dozed most of its day in front of the kitchen fire, and, so long as errand boys confined themselves to the handing in of harmless provisions, would regard them out of its half-closed eyes with a friendly, almost benevolent expression. But if anyone of them presented an envelope and showed intention of waiting for an answer, it would suddenly spring to its feet, and give vent to a blood-curdling growl that would send the boy flying down the garden.

The first time I met her was at one of Irving's first-night suppers on the stage of the Lyceum: a forlorn, somewhat insignificant little figure without a word of English. Nobody knew her. (They were informal gatherings. You just showed your card and walked on to the stage.) The only thing she would take was a glass of wine. I wanted to introduce her, but she was evidently hurt at not having been recognized and made a fuss of. She complained of a headache, and I got her a cab. There were tears in her eyes, I noticed, as I shut the door.

Joseph Hatton had a house with a big garden in the Grove End Road, and gave Sunday afternoon parties. One met a motley crowd: peers and painters, actors, and thought-readers, kings from Africa, escaped prisoners, journalists and socialists. It was there that I first heard prophecy of labour governments and votes for women.

Stepniak, the Russian Nihilist, was a frequent visitor; a vehement dark man, with an angelic smile. I met him one Sunday afternoon in an omnibus. We walked together from Uxbridge Road to Bedford Park. We were bound for the same house. The way then was through a dismal waste land, and the path crossed the North London Railway on the level. We had passed the wicket gate. Stepniak was deep in talk, and did not notice an approaching train, till I plucked him by the sleeve. He stood still staring after it for quite a time; and was silent—for him—the rest of the way. The following Sunday he was killed there by the same train. He had betrayed some secret, it was said, to the Russian Police, and had been given the choice between suicide or denunciation. The truth was never known.

We had an excellent cook named Isaacs who claimed to be related to quite important people of the same name: but whether with truth I cannot say. She encouraged us to be extravagant and give dinner-parties. W. S. Gilbert was a good talker. A strain of bitterness developed in him later, but in the nineties he was genial. I remember Miss Fortescue explaining that the Greeks had a custom of carving speeches on their seats. It seemed there was a term for these which she had forgotten. She appealed to Gilbert: "What were they called?" "*Arrière-pensée*, I expect," replied Gilbert. He and Crosse (or Blackwell, I am not sure which) had a dispute concerning shooting rights. Gilbert began his letter: "If I may presume to discuss with so well known an authority as yourself the subject of preserves."

Another evening he told us of a new dramatist just discovered by an American manager with whom he had been lunching. The manager had almost despaired of words with which to describe his prodigy. At last he had hit upon an inspiration: "I'll tell you what he is," explained the manager, "he's Mr. Barrie—" there followed an impressive pause—"with humour."

Barrie could easily be the most silent man I have ever met. Sometimes he would sit through the whole of a dinner without ever speaking. Then, when all but the last one or two guests had gone—or even later—he would put his hands behind his back and bummeling up and down the room, talk for maybe an hour straight on end. Once a beautiful but nervous young lady was handed over to his care. With the *sôle-au-gratin*, Barrie broke the silence:

"Have you ever been to Egypt?"

The young lady was too startled to answer immediately. It was necessary for her to collect herself. While waiting for the *entrée*, she turned to him.

"No," she answered.

Barrie made no comment. He went on with his dinner. At the end of the chicken *en casserôle*, curiosity overcoming her awe, she turned to him again.

"Have you?" she asked.

A far-away expression came into Barrie's great deep eyes.

"No," he answered.

After that they both lapsed into silence.

He and my wife found birds and animals a subject of never-failing wonder. I remember his explaining to her how much more intelligent lambs are than is generally supposed. He was thinking out a story, and coming to a stile had sat down and was making notes on the back of an envelope. Barrie rarely wasted an envelope, in those days. John Hare told me—to account for his having rejected "The Professor's Love Story"—that half of it was written on the inside of old envelopes. "Half" I doubt, but an eighth to a sixteenth I can well believe. Barrie was then an unknown youngster. "How could I guess the fool was a genius?" growled Hare. "Took him, of course, for a lunatic." But to return to our muttons.

In the field where Barrie sat there were lambs. One of them strayed away from its mother, turned round three times, and was lost. It was in a terrible to-do, and Barrie had to put down his story and lead it back to its mother. Hardly had he returned to his stile before another lamb did just the same. The bleating was terrific. There was nothing else to do, but for Barrie to put down his work and take it back to its mother. They kept on doing it, one after another. But the wonderful thing was that, after a time, instead of looking for their mothers themselves, they just came to Barrie and insisted on his coming with them and finding their mothers for them. It saved their time, but wasted Barrie's.

Barrie was always the most unassuming of men, but he could be touchy. On one occasion, a great lady invited him to her castle in the country. The house-party was a large one. There were peers and potentates, millionaires and magnates. Barrie found himself assigned to a small room in a turret leading to the servants' quarters. Perhaps the poor lady could not help it, and was doing her best. Barrie did not say anything, but in the morning he was gone. No one had seen him leave, and the doors were still bolted. He had packed his bag and climbed out of the window.

The Great Central Railway turned me out of Alpha Place to make way for their new line to London. A chasm yawns where it once stood; a pleasant house with a long dining-room and a big drawing-room looking out upon a quiet garden. When friends came my wife liked to receive them in the hall—she was a slip of a young thing then—standing on the bottom stair—to make herself seem taller. Wells was a shy diffident young man in those days, Rider Haggard a somewhat solemn gentleman, taking himself always very seriously. Mrs. Barry Pain was the only one of us who would venture to chaff him. George Moore was a simple kindly soul, when off his guard, but easily mistaken by those who did not know him for a poseur: he had the Balfour touch. Clement Shorter and his wife, Dora Sigerson the poetess,

George Gissing, with his nervous hands and his deep voice, Hall Caine, Conan Doyle, Hornung—but the list only grows. I had better leave them over to another chapter, lest I seem garrulous.

From St. John's Wood we went to Mayfair—to a little house, one of a row at the end of a *cul-de-sac* overlooking Hyde Park. George Alexander had told me of it. He had Number Four. It was there I first met Mark Twain. Hardly anyone knew he was in London. He was living poorly, saving money to pay off the debts of a publishing firm with which he had been connected. (Walter Scott's story over again.) Our children had met at a gymnasium. I found there were two Mark Twains: the one a humorist, the other a humanitarian reformer poet. About these two there was this that was curious: the humorist was an elderly gentleman, dull-eyed, with a slow, monotonous drawl; while the humanitarian reformer poet, was an eager young man with ever-changing eyes and a voice full of tenderness and passion.

They say a man always returns to his first love. I never cared for the West End: well-fed, well-dressed, uninteresting. The East, with its narrow silent streets, where mystery lurks; its noisome thoroughfares, teeming with fierce varied life, became again my favourite haunt. I discovered "John Ingerfield's" wharf near to Wapping Old Stairs, and hard by the dingy railed-in churchyard where he and Anne lie buried. But more often my wanderings would lead me to the little drab house off the Burdett Road, where "Paul Kelver" lived his childhood.

Of all my books I liked writing "Paul Kelver" the best. Maybe because it was all about myself, and people I had known and loved.

It changed my luck, so far as the critics were concerned. Francis Gribble, God bless him, gave me praise—the first I had ever tasted, and others followed.

I ought, of course, to have gone on. I might have become an established novelist—even a best seller. Who knows? But having "got there," so to speak, my desire was to get away. I went back to the writing of plays. It was the same at the beginning of me. My history repeats itself. Having won success as a humorist I immediately became serious. I have a kink in my brain, I suppose I can't help it.

Chapter VII

TRIALS OF A DRAMATIST

A lady, on one occasion, asked me why I did not write a play.

"I am sure, Mr. Jerome," she continued with a bright encouraging smile, "that you could write a play."

I told her I had written nine: that six of them had been produced, that three of them had been successful both in England and America, that one of them was still running at the Comedy Theatre and approaching its two hundredth night.

Her eyebrows went up in amazement.

"Dear me," she said, "you do surprise me."

George R. Sims told me that once he dined some friends at the Savoy. Over the coffee, he asked them if they would like to go to a theatre, and they said they would. He took them to a play of his own. For some reason that Sims could not explain, they did not like it. At the end of the first act, one of them, turning to him, said:

"Rather dull stuff this. Don't you find it so?"

"Well, now you come to mention it, perhaps it is, a trifle," agreed Sims.

"Let's go on to the Empire," suggested another.

The proposal was carried *nem. con.*; and leaving their programmes behind them, the troop arose and made their way out of the theatre noisily and cheerfully, followed by Sims, walking soberly.

"It used to annoy me," added Sims, "that not one theatre-goer in a hundred ever takes the trouble to read the author's name. That evening, I was glad of it."

"Barbara" was my first play. I am informed that nowadays managers read plays by unknown authors. In my young days they didn't. I read it to Rose Norreys, one evening, at her little flat in Chelsea Gardens; and good comrade that she was, she took it herself to Charles Hawtrey, and stood over him until he had finished it. He wrote me, asking me to come and see him the following Tuesday at twelve o'clock noon—he underlined "noon." He was running "The Private Secretary" at the Globe. I got there at twenty minutes to, and walked up and down Hollywell Street until I heard Big Ben strike twelve. The stage door-keeper said Mr. Hawtrey wasn't in. I said I would wait. The door-keeper—a kindly soul, I wish I could remember his name—put me a chair by the fire and gave me a thumbed copy of "The Talisman." He said that, speaking for himself, he considered it the best of all Scott's novels. Hawtrey turned up at a quarter past three.

The stage door-keeper introduced us, and explained things.

"I'm so sorry," said Hawtrey. "I thought it was Monday."

His first wife told me that, the night before their wedding, his best man had—unknown to him—put his watch on an hour and a quarter, with the result that he got there five minutes too soon; and in the Bankruptcy Court he used to be known as "the late Mr. Charles." But he was always so charming about it that one generally forgave him.

He told me that he liked my little play immensely. There was only one fault he had to find. It was too short. I record the fact as being the only known instance in the history of the stage of a manager suggesting to an author that his play was not long enough. I promised to write in an extra scene.

"My brother George will see you about terms," he concluded as we shook hands. "He will want you to sell it outright. Take my tip and don't do it. It's just the sort of thing to catch on with the amateurs."

The "producer" had not then arrived. He was an American invention. The stage manager, together with the promoter and the author, used to just worry it out. I have never been able myself to detect any difference. "Dot" Boucicault was one of the first, and for straightforward work is still among the best. If anything he is too painstaking. His method at rehearsal is to play all the parts himself, leaving the actor to copy him. On a certain occasion, he had been coaching Gertrude Kingston after this manner for about a fortnight; and then one morning, taking her aside, he asked her how she liked her part.

"What part?" asked Gertrude Kingston.

"What part?" repeated Boucicault, astonished. "Why, *your* part—the Countess."

"Oh, that," answered Miss Kingston. "I thought you were playing that."

I take it Du Maurier's dictum really sums up the matter: that a play that is worth producing, produces itself.

Cissy Grahame was my Barbara. She has not changed much, and I love her still. But she will never be quite as handsome as her mother. Their Sunday evening supper parties at Hammersmith make pleasant memories. I fancy that, when young, I must have had a face expressive of more sympathy than, perhaps, I really felt. People used to suddenly confide their troubles to me. The first time I met there Henley the actor, brother to W. E. Henley the poet, he beckoned me into a corner and poured out to me the secret history of his private life. What he wanted me to decide for him was: Should he strangle her or simply leave her? Weighing the matter as a whole, I chose for him the second alternative. He went off unexpectedly to America a short time afterwards, so I like to reflect that maybe I was of service to both parties. I have always wondered what became of him. He was a brilliant actor. He could get more passion over the footlights than any other actor I have known. McKinnel comes the nearest to him. Charles Whibley was another frequent guest there. I was a die-hard Tory at twenty-five, and Whibley was an anarchist of the reddest dye. We had some grand sets-to. John Burns was preaching revolution and the British Constitution was in danger. Whibley wanted to go a-rioting in Trafalgar Square. We had difficulty in restraining him. To make things safe, I joined the special constables and learnt to form fours and to turn my eyes right and left. Now I am a Vice-President, I believe, of the Oxford University Labour Party; while Whibley has become a pillar of the State, and writes for stodgy old *Blackwood*.

"Barbara" ran, on and off, for years, and amateurs still play it. Following Charles Hawtrey's advice, I had refused to sell it, though his brother George went up to a hundred pounds, and the temptation was sore. Another one-act play, "Fennel," I wrote for George Giddens, who had taken the Novelty, now the Kingsway—or rather adapted it from the French of François Coppée. Managers clamoured then for adaptations from the French. Sydney Grundy, one of the most successful authors on the English stage, never wrote an original play. He was quite frank about it. "Why should I cudgel my own brains," he would say, "when I can suck other men's?"

"Fennel" was chiefly remarkable for introducing Allan Aynesworth to the London stage. He played Sandro, the lover. I see that I describe him in the script as "a fine, dashing, good-looking young fellow." Aynesworth was all that right enough; but on the first night he got stage fright. I was watching from the wings. I could see him getting more and more nervous; and when he came to his big speech, his memory snapped. I had prided myself upon that speech. I had done my best to put Coppée's poetry into English blank verse. It was all about music and the sunrise, and Heaven and love: some two pages of it altogether. I could have forgiven him forgetting it, and drying up. But, to my horror, he went on. He had it fixed in his mind that until the old man returned home he had to stand in the centre of the stage and talk poetry. And he did it. Bits of it, here and there, were mine; most of it his own; a good deal of it verses and quotations that, I take it, he had learnt at his mother's knee. I shouted to Stuart Dawson, who was playing the old man, to go on and stop him. But he would finish, and threw such fervour into the last few laps, that at the end he received a fine round of applause.

"Sorry I forgot the exact lines," he said to me, as he came off. "But I was determined not to let you down."

"Woodbarrow Farm" was my first full-sized play. Gertrude Kingston produced it at a *matinée*, playing herself the adventuress. The trial *matinée* was a useful institution. I think it is a pity it has dropped out. The manager would lend the theatre in return for an option on the play; and the leading parts could generally be arranged for on a like understanding. At the cost of about a hundred pounds, a play could be put before the public and judged: in the only way a play can be judged—through the test-like tube of an audience. Three out of four, in spite of friendly stalls, were seen to be no good: the fourth won the prize. Charles Hawtrey lent us the Comedy. Frederick Harrison, now the doyen of London Managers, was in it. He played a gentlemanly villain. And Eric Lewis made the small part of a valet the chief thing in the play. John Hare bought it. He wanted a play for young Sydney Brough, son of old Lal Brough, a bright handsome lad, full of promise then. He had been a pupil of mine when I was a schoolmaster at the "South Lambeth Road Academy. For Sons of Gentlemen." I forget how it came about, but eventually Tom Thorne took it for his opening piece at the new Vaudeville. He played the valet. Bernard Partridge was the hero.

Conway had been cast for the part originally. That was another sad story. He had made his name as Romeo to Adelaide Neilson's Juliet: the best Juliet I have ever seen, though Phyllis Neilson-Terry, some years ago, ran her close. It was plain, before rehearsals were a week old, that poor Conway would have to be replaced; and the grim task of breaking it to him fell upon me. I called upon him early in the morning at the Adelphi Hotel. He was standing with his back to me when I entered the room, leaning his head against the mantelpiece.

"I know what you've come for," he said, without turning round. "It's my own fault. I thought I'd pulled myself together. I must have another try—later on."

There is no catch in being the one to put an actor out of his part. Everybody tries to shift the job on to somebody else. There was a young actress, I remember, at Terry's Theatre. She had been cast for a rattling good part on an unwise friend's recommendation, and had agreed to rehearse on approval. It was her first London engagement. She was no good; and we all of us agreed that the producer was the fit and proper person to handle the situation. The producer flatly refused; and as we still worried him, he gave us his reason.

"I had to do it once, some years ago now," he said. "She was an angelic-looking little creature. We had done the usual damn silly trick of just choosing her because of her appearance. She wasn't bad, but she hadn't the experience. The part was too big for her altogether. She took it quite nicely. I went round to see her in the evening. She had a bed-sitting-room in a street off the King's Road, Chelsea. We sat and chatted, afterwards, about the British drama in general, and she made me a cup of coffee. I flattered myself I had got out of it cheaply. She drowned herself that night—walked down the steps by Battersea bridge into the river. This child reminds me of her. Somebody else will have to tell her."

Nobody did. We let her play the part. She wasn't good.

Dan Frohman took the play for America. He wrote me that he was staying at the Hotel Victoria and would call and see me. We were living then in Alpha Place. My wife thought it would be an artful plan to lunch him well first and talk business with him afterwards. He accepted our invitation. We felt we had him in our hands. It was a gorgeous lunch. There was caviare and a stuffed bird and tricky things in French. For two days and a half my wife had lived with Mrs. Beeton. I saw to the cocktails myself, and after there was Château Lafitte and champagne. I can still see my wife's face when Frohman, in his grave emphatic way, explained that his digestion did not allow him to lunch; but might he have a few of the greens and some dry toast with a glass of apollinaris? But he smoked a cigar with me afterwards, and gave me good terms for the play.

E. H. Sothern played Bernard Gould's part in America; and fell in love with the lady who played Gertrude Kingston's part. They married during the run of the piece. I cannot claim to have been always successful as a match-maker. I introduced J. M. Barrie to Mary Ansell. That also was a by-product of "Woodbarrow Farm." I had a travelling company of my own, playing the piece in the provinces, and had engaged Mary Ansell for the *ingénue*. Barrie was producing "Walker London" with Toole at the old Folly in King William Street; and asked me if I could recommend him a leading lady. He didn't want much. She was to be young, beautiful, quite charming, a genius for preference, and able to flirt. The combination was not so common in those days. I could think of no one except Miss Ansell. It seemed unkind not to give her the chance. I cancelled the contract and sent for her; and next time it was Barrie who introduced her to me, as his wife.

It was during another play of mine, "The Prude's Progress," that a marriage was solemnized between my heroine, Lena Ashwell, and my light comedian, Arthur Playfair. The last time I saw Arthur Playfair was at Brighton. We were staying at "The Old Ship," and he was there with his then wife, and three children. She was a beautiful, healthy, jolly young woman, and boasted to my wife of never having had a day's illness in her life. She was dead three weeks afterwards; and Playfair died a few months later: of a broken heart folks would have said in a more sentimental age. He had sown his wild oats, and had grown steady and somewhat stout. Hawtrey was there at the same time. When living in Park Row, and while shaving early in the morning, I had often looked down upon Charles Hawtrey sprinting round Hyde Park, in shorts and a sweater; but it had not saved him from the common fate of middle age. And even I myself was not the figure that I once had been. Mrs. Playfair had dug up from somewhere the photo of a Playgoers' Club dinner, taken twenty years before, showing us standing side by side; three slim young gentlemen—almost, one might say, sylph-like. She had cut us out, and labelled us "The Three Graces."

The brothers Frohman, Charles and Dan, were good men to do business with. Their word was their bond. Charles used to say that no contract was ever drawn that a clever man could not get out of, if he wanted to. Towards the end, I never bothered him to sign anything. We would fix the terms over a cigar, and shake hands. He was a natural born sentimentalist: most Jews are. He spent a good deal of his time when in England at Marlow, where now stands a memorial to him. I had a house upon the hills, and Haddon Chambers used to rent a cottage at Bisham, near the Abbey. On a sunny afternoon, one often found Charles sitting on his own grave in Marlow churchyard—or rather on the spot he hoped would one day be his grave: a pleasant six foot into four of English soil, under the great willow that overhangs the river. He was still in negotiation for it the last time that I talked to him there. He went down in the "Lusitania," the year following.

Reading a play to a manager is a trying ordeal. I remember Addison Bright sending me a message at twelve o'clock one night to come at once to his flat, and bring with me a comedy of mine, "Dick Halward," that Sothern was then playing in America. Tree and Mrs. Pat Campbell were waiting for me. Tree had engaged Mrs. Pat for his "star" to open at Her Majesty's in three weeks' time; but had not found a play for her. He thought he had—some half-a-dozen of them altogether—but she had turned them all down one after the other. It was a dismal night. Tree sat watching Mrs. Pat's face, and evidently did not mind what the play was. I fell to doing the same and hardly knew what I was reading. Sometimes she laughed and sometimes she yawned, but most of the time she just sat. The dawn was breaking when I finished. She would not make up her mind, even then. Tree, on the stairs, thanked me for a pleasant night. Frederick Harrison is the most courteous manager I have ever read to. If he likes the play he shows it; and if he doesn't he makes you feel that the fault is not yours, but his. Frohman, until the end, would give no sign of what he was thinking. One hoped he was awake, but was not sure. He never pretended to know what the public wanted, and had a contempt for anyone who did.

"I'll tell you what a play is going to do, after I've seen the second Monday night's returns," he would say. "Some people will tell you before; but they're fools."

First-night receptions tell nothing. First nighters are a race apart. Like the Greeks, they hanker after a new thing. The general public, on the other hand, are faithful to their old loves. I met Arthur Shirley one afternoon. A new and original drama of his was to be produced that evening at Drury Lane.

"Feeling cheerful?" I asked him.

"Tolerably," he told me. "There are three rattling good situations in it."

"Capital," I said. "You think they will go all right?"

"Well, they ought to," he answered. "They always have."

The piece, I am glad to record, ran the whole season.

The last play I wrote for Charles Frohman was in collaboration with Haddon Chambers. He paid us a good sum down, but never produced it. We had made our chief comic character a Lord Mayor of London, and Frohman was nervous about it. He had the foreigner's fixed notion that the Lord Mayor of London is, next to the King, the most exalted personage in all England; and feared that to put him on the stage in company with ordinary mortals would be to outrage all the better feelings of the British public. I am sorry. He was a jolly old chap and, I think, original. We had given him a sense of humour.

Haddon Chambers had the reputation of being a "dangerous" character; but my wife always said she was sure it was their fault, and our two daughters loved him. The elder, who was nearly thirteen, said the great thing was to keep him to serious subjects. They taught him croquet and talked to him about horses and religion; and he used to tell them stories about Bushrangers, and Madame Melba when she was a little girl.

"New Lamps for Old," I wrote for Cissy Grahame. She produced it at Terry's Theatre. Horatio Bottomley was her backer. We all liked him. He used to take us out to lunch at the old Gaiety; and tell us stories about his early struggles, when he was a poor boy selling newspapers for his uncle, Charles Bradlaugh; and how he saved his first half-crown. Penley played the old family lawyer. He made a wonderful character of it at rehearsal. Penley was really a great actor. If he had played the part as he rehearsed it, he would have made for himself a new reputation. But he funked it at the end; and on the first night he was just Penley, as usual. Fred Kerr, Gertrude Kingston and Bernard Partridge were in the cast, in addition to Cissy herself. But the most wonderful person connected with the affair was our acting manager. I wish I could remember his name. It deserves to go down to posterity as the man who swindled Bottomley.

"He must have started faking the accounts from the very first week," commented Bottomley, more in sorrow than in anger; "and he's done it so cleverly that, although it is staring me in the face, I can't prove it. Damned scoundrel!"

Later, he got a cheque out of *The Daily Mail* for telling lies about Lloyd George. *The Daily Mail* was very indignant and charged him with fraud. The man must have had a sense of humour, when you come to think of it.

Bottomley had a wonderful tongue. I remember a shareholders' meeting, called together for the sole and express purpose of denouncing him. Half of them were in favour of lynching him. He talked to them for three-quarters of an hour; and now and then there were tears in his eyes. Before he sat down he had launched a new company on them. The majority of them subscribed to it before they left the room. He had his kindly side and was always good company. Once when I was in sore straits he lent me a thousand pounds; and never asked me for security or interest.

Augustus Daly took "New Lamps" for America; and Ada Rehan and John Drew played in it. Ada Rehan was superb in passion. Her Katharine in "The Taming of the Shrew" was a magnificent performance. It began like a tornado and ended like a summer's breeze whispering to the willows. But John Drew in Shakespeare always suggested to me "A Yankee at the Court of King Arthur." Afterwards, Daly asked me to adapt Sudermann's "Die Ehre." I had marvelled up till then at the linguistic range of the average dramatic author who at a moment's notice "adapts" you from the Russian, or the Scandinavian, or any other language that you choose. I did not then know very much German and had to confess it.

"That'll be all right," said Daly. "I'll send you the literal translation."

For translations, a shilling a folio used to be the price generally paid to the harmless necessary alien.

Somewhat against my conscience, I consented to bowdlerise Sudermann's play so as not to offend Mrs. Grundy, who then ruled the English and American stage. Poor lady! She must have done quite a lot of turning in her grave since then. Jones went further when he adapted Ibsen's "Doll's House." In the last act Helmar took the forgery upon himself, and the curtain went down on Nora flinging herself into his arms with the cry of "Husband"; and the band played "Charlie is my Darling." That was the first introduction of Ibsen to the British public. "A charming author," was the verdict first passed upon Ibsen in London.

I wrote "The MacHaggis" in collaboration with Eden Phillpotts. Penley accepted it, but fell ill, and handed the part over to Weedon Grossmith. Our heroine shocked the critics. She rode a bicycle. It was unwomanly, then, to ride a bicycle. There were so many things, in those days, that were unwomanly to do. It must have been quite difficult to be a woman, and remain so day after day. She smoked a cigarette. The Devil must have been in us. Up till then, only the adventuress had ever smoked a cigarette. In the last act, she said "damn." She said it twice. Poor Clement Scott nearly fell out of *The Daily Telegraph*. Once before, it is true, a lady (Mrs. Huntley, I think) had said "damn" upon the stage, but that was in a translation from the French. No one dreamed the day would come when Mrs. Pat Campbell would say "bloody." But it is an age of progress, we are told. One blushes at the thought of what they may say next. She cost me a friend, that heroine of ours. By chance we christened the hussy Ewretta; and it happened to be the name of an actress friend of mine, Ewretta Lawrence. She wouldn't believe we hadn't done it of *malice prepense*. She never spoke to me again. I am sorry. It is always with fear and trembling that one chooses names for one's less immaculate characters. During the run of Pinero's "Mrs. Ebbsmith," a real Mrs. Ebbsmith committed suicide. She thought that Pinero had been told her story and had used it.

Phillpotts and myself had bad luck over "The MacHaggis." It was doing well when Penley suddenly closed the theatre. His illness, it turned out, was mental.

One of the things I best remember in "The MacHaggis" was Reeves Smith's performance of a cheerful idiot. He was a delightful actor. He went to America soon after, and they never let him come back. I met him there when on a lecturing tour. He was playing with Nazimova. I went behind to see him.

"Forgive me," I said, so soon as his dresser had left the room, "but aren't you making him rather too noisy?" They were playing Ibsen—"The Master Builder," I think.

"Great heavens," he answered. "You don't think it's my idea, do you? It's the new method, over here. Everybody has to shout at the top of their voice, except the Star. 'How quiet and natural she is,' they say. 'What a contrast.' Clever idea. Gillette invented it."

Alia Nazimova was drawing all New York. I found her somewhat changed from the quiet, simple girl who with her husband (they spelt the name "Nazimof" then) had knocked at our door in London with a letter of introduction from friends of ours in Russia. They had got themselves into trouble with the political police, and had had to cut and run with barely time to pack a handbag. She spoke German, but he spoke only Russian. They looked little more than boy and girl; and he in his way was as beautiful as she was. That first evening, we taught him an English sentence. He had said it in Russian, his eyes fixed on my wife. Alla translated it into German, and then we told him the English for it, which was: "You remind me of my first love." He repeated it till he had it perfect; and subsequently quite a number of women mentioned to me casually that he only seemed to know one English sentence. We chaffed him about it. He maintained it was not humbug. All beautiful women reminded him of his first love. But his last love! There was no one like her. And kneeling, he kissed Alla Nazimof's hand. He was rather a lovable, childish person. I took them to Tree, and we fixed up a benefit performance for them at the Haymarket; and afterwards I got Frohman interested, and he fathered them into America. For some reason, the boy went back to Russia and was killed in a pogrom. The first person she asked me about, when I saw her in New York, was "Madame Needles," as she had always called a small fox-terrier of ours. They had been great friends, and had played hunt the slipper together. Madame Needles would go outside the room, while Madame Nazimof would hide one of her shoes, and then open the door. Only once Needles failed to find it, and that was when Alla had sprinkled scent upon it. Needles said, in dog language, that it wasn't fair; and wouldn't play any more that night.

Another play Phillpotts and I wrote together was "The Prude's Progress." I read it one evening to a little Jew gentleman, a friend of Fanny Brough's, at his chambers in Piccadilly. "Read it to him after dinner," she had counselled me. Dear, sentimental, fat old gentleman, how he cried over the pathetic parts! At the end, he shook me by both hands, and wrote me an agreement then and there. He left the business arrangements to me, and I took the Comedy Theatre and gathered together a company regardless of expense: among others, Fanny Brough, Teddy Righton, Cyril Maude, Lena Ashwell, glorious in her first youth and beauty. Bernard Partridge was to have played an up-to-date journalist who knew everything and was not ashamed of it: an amusing fellow, and Partridge would have played him to perfection. Alas and alack! I listened to advice. The author who listens to advice is lost. During the second rehearsal, your manager draws you aside. He has been talking the play over with his mother-in-law. It seems that she likes it, immensely. She has only one suggestion to make—or rather two. He propounds them at some length. You explain that the adoption of either would necessitate the re-writing of the piece. "Well, better do that, my dear boy," he answers, "than have a failure; I'm only advising you for your own good." The producer does not agree with the manager's mother-in-law. His advice is: "Cut the other woman out altogether. Lighten the play and save a salary." He slips his arm through yours. "If it was only a question of art," he continues in a friendly undertone, "I daresay you're right. Unfortunately, we've got to consider the great B.P. Now I've had twenty years' experience," and so on. Later on, the solicitor to the syndicate drops in and watches a rehearsal. He stumbled over the cat and reaches the stage. He has thought of an alteration that may save the play. The next afternoon, the stage door-keeper stops you on your way out. He also has been thinking the play over with the idea of helping you. They all know what the public want, and how to give it to them. It is everybody's secret, except the author's. I once overheard a producer talking to a friend concerning one of Barrie's plays.

"It was all no good," he was saying. "He wouldn't take my advice. Of course the piece was successful—in a way, I admit. But think what it might have been!"

Over the play proper, I had learnt to be firm; but I was young at producing, and I listened to George Hawtrey. He meant well. He was a dear fellow, in many respects. He always did mean well. He had discovered a genius made by the Creator on purpose to play our journalist. Partridge was my friend, he would not stand in the way of my making my fortune—of my making Phillpott's fortune—of my making everybody's fortune. To cut a sad story short, I put it to Partridge, and, of course, he agreed. But he never forgave me; and I have always felt ashamed of myself for having done it.

It was hoped, when the Dramatists' Club was formed, that it might develop into a dramatic authors' trades union on the lines of the French *Société des Auteurs Dramatiques*. It would have been a good thing. The established dramatist can, perhaps, hold his own: though even he is never sure of not being cheated, especially when it comes to dealing with the syndicates. But the young and struggling are fleeced and humbugged without mercy. Often a play out of which the management will make its tens of thousands is sold outright for a few pounds down. "Take it or leave it," is presented at the author's head; and the youngster, impatient to see his play produced, signs the receipt. Occasionally he makes good, and the future repays him. More often the play turns out to be his one and only success. We used to grumble at the actor manager. We wish now we had him back. He had his failings, but at least he was an artist. The theatrical bosses who nowadays control the English and American stage have no idea beyond that of pandering to the popular taste of the moment. They regard the author's work as raw material to be cut down, altered, added to, and generally worked up by "experts" at so much an act. They would have boiled down "Hamlet" to an hour and a half; written in some comic business for the ghost; and brought down the curtain on Hamlet cuddling Ophelia. Actors and actresses wail that not enough plays are being written. Where are the new dramatists? they bewilderedly inquire. Why don't authors write more plays? The answer is that authors with any self-respect are being practically forbidden the stage door. I asked a well-known literary man, when last in America, why he never wrote for the theatre. There could be no question of his ability.

"I haven't the courage," he answered. "I could not bear seeing my play knocked about and rendered senseless by a horde of syndicated savages. It would break my heart."

The Dramatists' Club, at one time, had the dream of starting a dramatists' theatre. That would have been a sound scheme, if only we had had faith. It may yet materialise. The plan was that ten or a dozen leading dramatists, possessing a bank balance, should form themselves into a company, lease a theatre and produce their own plays. Afterwards the doors would be thrown open to all. Cecil Raleigh and myself were appointed to report upon the scheme. I went into the City and found there would be no difficulty in obtaining, if need be, financial assistance. Your City man is a born gambler, and the theatre being a ready-money proposition, particularly appeals to him. We could have had a lease of the Savoy at eighty pounds a week, and I am still of the opinion that we missed a golden opportunity. The danger confronting a new management is that of running short of plays. We should have had a dozen to fall back upon, each one the work of an experienced dramatist. Running a theatre is the easiest business going. I ran the Comedy Theatre for six months with the "Prude's Progress." If I had had a better play I would have made a fortune. As it was I came out with a profit. All that had to be known I learnt in the first week. Bram

Stoker, Henry Irving's manager, put me up to the art of "papering." It was almost the rule then for plays to hang fire at first. The house had to be "dressed," as the saying was. Generally, this was done by handing out each morning a bundle of passes to the bill-poster for distribution. The deserving poor came in for, perhaps, more than their share. Evening dress, so far as the stalls and dress circle were concerned, was indispensable; but the term is necessarily elastic in the case of female attire, and often the appearance of the house would be irresistibly suggestive of Mrs. Jarley's wax works. Bram Stoker, in those early years when he was building up the Lyceum, took pains. With a Burke's peerage at his elbow, he would confine his complimentary admissions to Mayfair and Kensington, together with, maybe, the park end of Bayswater. It was rarely that his invitation was declined. The Lyceum floor would blaze with jewels, and the line of waiting carriages extend to Covent Garden. I followed the same plan, and kept *The Morning Post* busy recording the nobility and gentry that, the previous evening, had honoured the Comedy Theatre with their gracious presence.

Collaboration, generally speaking, is a mistake. Like on the old tandem bicycle, each man thinks he is doing all the work. The last time I tried it was with Justin McCarthy. But that was a play asking for collaboration. Its subject was re-incarnation. Our hero and heroine meet for the first time in the days of Prometheus, and he shows her how to light a fire. A million years later, they turn up in Athens. He is Socrates and she is a slave.

What they've been up to in the meanwhile we do not bother about. In the end, they come back to the Present, where the play first opened. I had submitted the idea to Phyllis Neilson-Terry in New York, and she had been tremendously keen about it. But her plans fell through. That is the heart-breaking side of play-writing: you spend a year's labour and nothing comes of it. Or it is produced only to be jeered at and promptly buried. True, what one loses on the roundabout failures one makes on the swinging successes. But, somehow, the failures seem always to be the ones that we love best.

My first collaboration was with Addison Bright. We wrote a play for Miss Eastlake. I remember Bright's reading it to Wilson Barrett in his dressing-room at Birmingham after a performance of "Claudian." Barrett had not changed his costume, and came to us with two long hat-pins sticking out of each of his calves. Miss Eastlake had stuck them into him as she had followed him up the stairs. He never noticed them until he went to cross his legs. Miss Eastlake had a great sorrow in the first act, and the curtain went down on her sobbing her heart out. During rehearsals, she came forward for the second act still weeping. Bright explained to her that six years had elapsed, and that the stage directions were: "Enters talking and laughing."

"I know," she answered, the tears still falling down her cheeks. "I can't help it, it's so absurd of me. I'll never be able to get over it in time."

There was some risk of it, especially on the first night. To avoid danger, we made the second act to take place on the anniversary of her trouble; and gave her a "pensive" entrance.

She and Annie Hughes both "came out" the same evening at the Criterion in a play, I think, of McCarthy's. They both had a wonderful success. The last time I saw poor Miss Eastlake, she was running a cheap boarding-house in Gower Street. As the result of an illness, she had lost all her beauty and had grown tremendously stout. She was still playing the heroine. She was finer than I had ever seen her: patient and cheerful. She made a jest of the whole thing. It was in a play that I wrote for Annie Hughes that the telephone first appeared on the English stage. People talked about it, and the critics said it was false realism. I wish now I hadn't done it. But maybe somebody else would have thought of it, if I hadn't.

I wrote three plays for Marie Tempest, two of which she never played in, and the third she wished she hadn't. It was her own fault. She wanted a serious play, and I gave her a serious play. She loved it when I read it to her. "Esther Castways" was the name of it. She was magnificent in it, and on the first night received an ovation. But, of course, the swells wouldn't have it. She had made a groove for herself; and her public were determined she should keep it. We ought to have known that, all of us. I didn't get on with her at rehearsals. I wore a red suit. I rather fancied it myself; but somehow it

maddened her; and I was obstinate and wouldn't change
it, though she offered to buy it off me that she might
burn it. My daughter made a successful first appearance
in the play. Marie took a liking to her. She liked young
girls, and was always very nice to women. It was men she
hadn't any use for, so far as I could gather. A pity she
ever got into that groove. She was a great actress pinned
down to frocks and frivolity. Lillah McCarthy gave me
an insight into female psychology when she told me that
the first thing she did with a new part was to dress it. She
could not imagine how the woman would think and feel
till she had visualized the clothes that she would wear.
Then she began to understand the woman, working from
the clothes inwards. I can understand: because The
Stranger in "The Third Floor Back" came to me like
that. I followed a stooping figure, passing down a foggy
street, pausing every now and then to glance up at a
door. I did not see his face. It was his clothes that
worried me. There was nothing out of the way about
them. I could not make out why it was they seemed
remarkable. I lost him at a corner, where the fog hung
thick, and found myself wondering what he would have
looked like if he had turned round and I had seen his
face. I could not get him out of my mind, wandering
about the winter streets; and gradually he grew out of
those curious clothes of his.

"Miss Hobbs" (or "The Kissing of Kate," to give the
play its original title), produced by Chas. Frohman in
America with Annie Russell as Kate and wonderful old
Mrs. Gilbert as Auntie, was my first real money-making

success: if a gentleman may mention such detail. She has been a good child to me, God bless her. The Princess Paulowa presented her in Russia and is now showing her round Italy. She was a great success in Germany. I was living in Dresden at the time; and the Kaiser sent me his congratulations, through an official of the Saxon Court, who brought it to me in a big envelope: so he couldn't have been all bad. How the coming of the Great War was kept from us common people may be instanced by the production of my play, "The Great Gamble," at the Haymarket, six weeks before the guns went off. The scene was laid in Germany. One of our chief characters was a dear old German Professor. German students, in white caps, sang German folk songs and drank Lager beer. We had incidental music, specially written, in the German style. The hero had been educated in Germany and the heroine's mother's co-respondent was an Austrian. For a solid month, we rehearsed that play without a suspicion that the Chancelleries of Europe were one and all making their secret preparations to render it a failure. Talk of organized opposition! It was a conspiracy.

"Fanny and the Servant Problem" I wrote for Marie Tempest. She was otherwise engaged when it was ready; and Frohman not wanting to wait, we gave the part to Fannie Ward. I think myself she made a quite delightful "Fanny," and Charles Cartwright's Butler was a joy. Alma Murray played the Lady's Maid. I had not seen her for nearly twenty years. She had been one of the first to put Ibsen on the London stage. But for that, she might have had her own theatre and been a leading light. But in those days the feeling against Ibsen was almost savage, and no player prominently connected with his plays was ever forgiven. For some reason or another, "Fanny" failed in London. So Fannie Ward took it to America, and there it was a big success, under the name of "Lady Bantock." The Americans love a title. Afterwards it was converted into a musical comedy and ran for four seasons. With Hamlet, I object to actors speaking more than is set down for them. But a gag by the American actor cast for the music-hall manager was quaint, I confess. He finds the Bible that her Uncle and Butler has placed open on Fanny's desk. He turns over the pages, and seems surprised. "What have you got there?" asks his companion. "I don't know," he answers. "It's all about the Sheenies."

"Fanny" has been translated and played in almost every European country, except Portugal.

"Cook" (I called it "The Celebrity," and if I had originally called it "Cook" my manager would have wanted to call it "The Celebrity") proved to me, I am sorry to say, that the power of the critics to make or mar a play is negligible. I have never written anything that has won for me such unstinted praise. I could hardly believe my eyes when I opened the papers the next morning. Generally, if your play does get through, it is the actors who have "saved" it. But in the notices for "Cook," favourable mention was made even of the author. We all thought we were in for a record run; and I ordered a new dress suit. I ought to have remembered Charles Frohman's advice and waited for the second Monday. But "Cook" also has succeeded abroad, so I comfort myself with the prophet's customary consolation.

Rehearsals are trying periods. Everybody seems to be wearing their nerves outside their skin. The question whether the actor should take three steps to the right, and pause with his left hand on the back of chair, centre, before proposing to the heroine; or whether he should do it from the hearthrug, with his left elbow on the mantelpiece, may threaten the friendship of a lifetime. The author wants him to do it from the hearthrug—is convinced that from there and there only can he convey to the heroine the depth and sincerity of his passion. The producer is positive that a true gentleman would walk round the top of the table and do it from behind a chair. The actor comes to the rescue. He "feels" he can do it only from the left-hand bottom corner of the table.

"Oh well, if you feel as strongly about it as all that, my dear boy," says the producer, "that ends it. It's you who've got to play the part."

"Do you know," says the author, "I think he's right? It does seem to come better from there."

The rehearsal proceeds. Five minutes later, the argument whether a father would naturally curse his child before or after she has taken off her hat, provides a new crisis.

In ancient times, the fashion was for movement. The hero and heroine would be seated, making love, one each side of the piano. At the end of the first minute, the stage manager, as he was then, would call out:

"Now then, come along, my dears, break it up. Put some life into it. You're not glued to those chairs, you know."

The hero and heroine would rise and change seats.

Nowadays the pendulum has swung too far the other way. I remember a rehearsal where the leading actress suddenly jumped up and began stamping about the stage.

"Whatever's the matter?" asked the producer.

"I'll be all right in a minute," she answered. "I've got pins and needles."

My own worst experience was over a musical play I wrote for Arthur Roberts, then with Lowenfeldt at the Prince of Wales'. Lowenfeldt was an Austrian who had made a fortune out of Kop's ale. It was a popular temperance beverage, twenty years ago, until the Revenue authorities discovered it contained more alcohol than the average public-house beer. His grievance against the London critics was that they didn't take cheques. "Why not?" he argued. "A good notice in a respectable paper is worth a hundred pounds to me. I give the critic ten. It pays him, and it pays me." He thought the time would come.

Arthur Roberts took me aside.

"I want you to write me a part with a touch of pathos in it," he said. "You know what I mean. Plenty of fun, but not all fun. I want them to go home saying, 'Well, I always knew Arthur could make me laugh, but damned if I thought he had got it in him to make me cry.' See what I mean?"

I retired into the country and worked hard. It seemed to me an interesting story. There were moments in it when, if properly played, a chocky feeling would, I felt sure, manifest itself throughout the audience. But it all came right in the end. I made him a licensed victualler, of the better sort. An uncle died and left him an hotel. Roberts had not attended the reading. At the first rehearsal he took me aside. He said:

"I've got an idea for this part. I'm a young farmer——" He gave me an imitation of a Somersetshire yokel. It was an excellent performance. "You know," he continued, "a Simple Simon sort of part. In the second act——"

"But you can't," I said. "You're an hotel proprietor at Maidenhead."

"Good," he answered. "All you'll have to do, is to knock out the hotel and call it a farm."

I tried reason, but he was just mad to be a farmer. He sketched out the part. It would be novel and amusing, I could see that. I sat up for a night or two, and turned him into a farmer. We struggled through one or two rehearsals; and then he had another inspiration. He wanted to be a detective, disguised as an Italian waiter.

"Where's the difficulty?" he demanded. "Somebody steals the old girl's jewels. I'm in love with the daughter. The police are no good, I take the job on for her sake."

It meant re-writing half an act. I did it. Three days later, he wanted to be a French Marquis, reduced to giving English lessons in Soho.

"Don't you see, my dear boy?" he explained. "Gives me an opportunity for pathos. I've been making them laugh, now I make them cry. Variety: that's the thing we want."

I never saw the play myself. I was told that he got them all in; and the critics spoke highly of his versatility. Adrian Ross (Arthur Ropes) took it off my hands and finished it. He was a wonderful worker. He would write a scene—quite a good scene—while Arthur Roberts walked up and down the room and acted it. The next morning, Arthur had forgotten all about it; and Ropes would write him another.

I wrote "The Passing of the Third Floor Back" for David Warfield. I worked it out first as a short story. It was John Murray, the publisher, who put the idea into my head of making it into a play; and when I saw Warfield in "The Music Master," it seemed to me he was just the actor to play it. He would not have had the dignity and compelling force of Forbes-Robertson. He would have made the character win rather through tenderness and appeal. I was on a lecturing tour in America; and I got my agent, Miss Marbury, to put me into touch with Belasco, Warfield's manager. It was in a Pullman car between Washington and New York that I sketched out the idea to him. It got hold of him. We were both doubtful as to how the public would receive it. I thought I could do it without giving offence. Belasco agreed to trust me, and on my return to England I got to work upon it. It was not an easy play to write: one had to feel it rather than think it. I was living in a lonely part of the Chiltern hills with great open spaces all around me, and that helped; and at last it was finished. I had arranged to return to America to produce "Sylvia of the Letters," a play I had written for Grace George; and I took "The Passing" with me. I read it to Warfield and Belasco late one night at Belasco's theatre in New York. We had the house to ourselves; and afterwards we adjourned to Warfield's club for supper. It was about three o'clock in the morning, and the only thing we could get was cold beef and pickles. They were both impressed by the play, and we found ourselves talking in whispers. I fancy Belasco got nervous about it, later on. We fixed things up next morning at Miss Marbury's office, and he asked me to see Percy Anderson, the artist, when I got back to England, and get him to make sketches for the characters. It was while he was drawing them, in his studio at Folkestone, that one morning Forbes-Robertson, who had a house there, dropped in upon him. Forbes was greatly interested in the sketches; and Anderson showed him the play.

Forbes-Robertson wrote me telling me this; and saying that if by any chance arrangements between myself and Belasco fell through, he would like to talk to me. His letter arrived the day after I had had one from Belasco, making it clear that he did not want, if possible, to be bound to his contract; so for answer, I called upon Forbes-Robertson in Bedford Square; and read the play to him and his wife. He also was nervous; but Gertrude Elliott swept all doubts aside and ended the matter.

We got together as perfect a cast as I think any play has ever had. Ernest Hendrie as the old Bookmaker, Ian Robertson as the Major, Edward Sass as the Jew, Agnes Thomas as Mrs. Sharpe, and Haidee Wright as the Painted Lady were all wonderful; and Gertrude Elliott played the Slavey. I was afraid, at first, that her beauty and her grace would hamper her; but she overcame these drawbacks and, even at rehearsal, invested the little slut with a spirituality that at times transfigured her. My daughter played the part in the country and afterwards in London during the war, and they two were the best Stasias I have seen. Lillah McCarthy was to have played Vivien. Granville Barker was in America, and she consulted Shaw, who read the play and told her to grab the part and hang on to it. She had an engagement she thought she could get out of; but it was not so, and we had to seek elsewhere.

"We must have someone supremely beautiful," said Forbes. "There are six women in the play; four of them have to be middle-aged, and my wife has to disguise herself. It's our only chance."

I thought of Alice Crawford. Time was pressing. We sent her a wire. She had just left for a ball at the Piccadilly Hotel.

"You must go to the ball," said Forbes.

I went as I was, in a blue serge suit, brown boots, and a collar that I had been wearing since eight o'clock in the morning. I made a sensation in the ballroom. I gathered that the people round about took me for a policeman in unnecessarily plain clothes; but I spotted Alice Crawford, and beckoned her outside. A gentleman came up and asked if he could be of any use. I take it the idea of bail was in his mind.

We produced the play at Harrowgate. The audience there mistook it for a farce. It was by the author of

"Three Men in a Boat," so they had been told. That evening the Robertsons and myself partook of a melancholy supper. It was Blackpool that saved the play. Forbes wired me—

"It's all right. Blackpool understands it and loves it."

In London, on the first night, the curtain fell to dead silence which lasted so long that everybody thought the play must be a failure, and my wife began to cry. And then suddenly the cheering came, and my wife dried her eyes.

I was not present myself. I have shirked my own first nights ever since a play of mine that Willard produced at the Garrick. I thought the applause was unanimous, but was received with a burst of booing. The argument is that if an author is willing to be applauded, he must not object to being hissed. It may be logic, but it isn't sense: as well say that because a man does not mind being patted on the back, he ought not to object to being kicked. I remember the first night of one of Jones's plays. There was a difference of opinion and Jones very properly did not appear. In the street, I overheard some critics from the gallery talking:

"Why didn't he come out," said one, "and take his punishment like a man?"

W. T. Stead used to gather interesting people round him, on Sunday afternoons, at his house in Smith

Square. Soon after the production of "The Passing of the Third Floor Back" I received an invitation from him to discuss "The Gospel according to St. Jerome." Another time, we discussed the chief motive power governing human affairs, and decided that it was hate: hatred of nation for nation, religious hatred, race hatred, political hatred. Just then the suffrage movement was in full swing, and sex hatred had been added to the list. Stead lived and died a convinced Spiritualist, in spite of the fact that his spirit friends once let him down badly. They urged him to start a daily newspaper and assured him of success. It was a grim failure, but he forgave them.

Forbes-Robertson was doubtful about taking the play to America. It was his sister-in-law, Maxine Elliott, who insisted. It was at her theatre in New York that he opened.

Matheson Lang took it East. In China, a most respectable Mandarin came round to see him afterwards and thanked him.

"Had I been intending to do this night an evil deed," he said, "I could not have done it. I should have had to put it off, until to-morrow."

Chapter VIII

I BECOME AN EDITOR

"*The Idler*. Edited by Jerome K. Jerome and Robert Barr. An illustrated monthly magazine, Price sixpence," was Barr's idea. But the title was mine. Barr had made the English edition of the Detroit Free Press quite a good property; and was keen to start something of his own. He wanted a popular name and, at first, was undecided between Kipling and myself. He chose me—as, speaking somewhat bitterly, he later on confessed to me—thinking I should be the easier to "manage." He had not liked the look of Kipling's jaw. Kipling had been about two years in London, and had just married his secretary, a beautiful girl with a haunting melancholy in her eyes that still lingers.

By writers he was recognized as a new force, though his aggressive personality naturally made enemies. The critics and the public were more squeamish then. He was accused of coarseness and irreverence. The reason, it is said, that he was never knighted was that Queen Victoria would not forgive him for having called her "The Widdy o' Windsor." He has not missed much. Lord Charles Beresford used to tell the story—and those who knew him could easily believe it—that King Edward on one occasion said to him:

"You remember L——, that fellow at Homburg. Well, I've just made him a knight."

"Dirty little bounder," said Beresford; "serve him damn well right."

The Idler was a great success, so far as circulation was concerned. Our business manager was one Robert Dunkerley. I see from "Who's Who" that he himself explains that he "took to writing as an alleviation and alternative from business, and found it much more enjoyable." He is now John Oxenham. We had pleasant offices in Arundel Street, off the Strand, and gave tea-parties every Friday. They were known as the "Idler At Homes," and became a rendezvous for literary London. Burgin, G. B., was our sub-editor. He was a glutton for work, even then; and his appetite seems to have grown. He thinks nothing of turning out three novels a year. I once wrote two thousand words in a single day; and it took me the rest of the week to recover. Wells is even yet more wonderful. He writes a new book while most people are reading his last; throws off a history of the world while the average schoolboy is learning his dates; and invents a new religion in less time than it must have taken his god-parents to teach him his prayers. He has a table by his bedside; and if the spirit moves him will get up in the middle of the night, make himself a cup of coffee, write a chapter or so, and then go to sleep again. During intervals between his more serious work, he will contest a Parliamentary election or conduct a conference for educational reform. How Wells carries all his electricity without wearing out the casing and causing a short circuit in his brain is a scientific mystery. I mentioned once in a letter to him that I was a bit run

down. He invited me to spend a day or two with him at
Folkestone: get some sea-air in my lungs and a rest. To
"rest" in the neighbourhood of Wells is like curling
yourself up and trying to go to sleep in the centre of a
cyclone. When he wasn't explaining the Universe, he was
teaching me new games—complicated things that he had
invented himself, and under stress of which my brain
would reel. There are steepish hills on the South Downs.
We went up them at four miles an hour, talking all the
time. On the Sunday evening a hurricane was raging
with a driving sleet. Wells was sure a walk would do us
good—wake us up. While Mrs. Wells was not watching,
we tucked the two little boys into their mackintoshes and
took them with us.

"We'll all have a blow," said Wells.

They were plucky little beggars, both of them, and
only laughed. But battling up the Leas against the wind,
we found the sleet was cutting their small faces. So we
made them walk one each behind us with their arms
around our waists, while we pressed forward with ducked
heads. And even then Wells talked. But one day Nature
got the better of him and silenced him. That was when
he was staying with me at Gould's Grove near
Wallingford. We climbed a lonely spur of the Chilterns,
and half-way up he gave out, and never spoke again till
we had reached the top, and had sat there for at least five
minutes, looking down upon the towers of Oxford and
the Cotswold Hills beyond. Southampton water gleamed
like a speck of silver on the horizon, and at our feet we

marked—now rutted and grass-grown—the long straight line of the old Roman way that led from Grimm's Dyke, past the camp on the Sinodun hills, and so onward to the north.

I can't remember, for certain, whether it was to Wells at Folkestone when I was staying with him, or to me at Wallingford when he was stopping with me, that there came one afternoon a company of garden city experts on the hunt for a new site. The head of the party was an American gentleman who had devoted most of his life to the building of garden cities. He had been invited over to assist with his experience. He never got further than the two words "garden city." At that point, Wells took the matter in hand, and for twenty minutes he explained to the old gentleman how garden cities should be constructed; the inherent imperfectability of all garden cities that had hitherto been built; the proper method of financing and running garden cities. The old gentleman attempted a few feeble interruptions, but Wells would have none of them.

"Your ideas are all right," said the old gentleman, when Wells at last had finished, "but they are not practical."

"If the ideas are right," said Wells, "your business is to make them practical."

Of Shaw, it is said that he is never at rest unless he is working. Shaw once told me that he only had three speeches. One about politics (including religion); one about art (together with life in general); and the other one about himself. He said he found these three—with variations—served him for all purposes.

"People think I am making new speeches," he said. "I'm repeating things that I have told them over and over again, if only they had listened. I'm tired of talking," he said. "I wouldn't have to talk one-tenth as much, if people only listened."

He used to say there were two schools of elocution: one the Lyceum Theatre (in Irving's time) and the other Hyde Park. He himself had graduated in Hyde Park, mounted on a chair without a back, opposite the Marble Arch. There is only one way of countering Shaw on a platform. It is hopeless trying to cross wits with him. The only thing is to force him to become serious. Then I have known him to flounder. His mind works like lightning. I remember the then President of the Playgoers' Club coming to him one day. It was at the beginning of the cinema boom. He was an earnest young man.

"We want you to speak for us on Sunday evening, Mr. Shaw," he said, "on the question: Is there any danger of the actor being eliminated?"

"You don't say which actor," answered Shaw, "and, anyhow, why speak of it as a danger?"

Shaw is one of the kindest of men, but has no tenderness. His chief exercise, according to his own account, is public speaking; and his favourite recreation, thinking. He admitted to me once that there have been times when he has thought too much. He was motoring in Algiers, driving himself, with his chauffeur beside him, when out of his musings came to him the idea for a play.

"What do you think of this?" he said, turning to his chauffeur; and went on then and there to tell the man all about it.

He had usually found his chauffeur a keen and helpful critic. But on this occasion, instead of friendly encouragement, he threw himself upon Shaw and, wrenching the wheel out of his hands, sat down upon him.

"Excuse me, Mr. Shaw," the man said later on; "but it's such a damn good play that I didn't want you to die before you'd written it."

Shaw had never noticed the precipice.

Conan Doyle used to be another tremendous worker. He would sit at a small desk in a corner of his own drawing-room, writing a story, while a dozen people round about him were talking and laughing. He preferred it to being alone in his study. Sometimes, without looking up from his work, he would make a remark, showing he must have been listening to our conversation; but his pen had never ceased moving. Barrie had the same gift. He was a reporter on a provincial newspaper in his early days, and while waiting for orders amid the babel and confusion of the press room, he would curl himself up on a chair and, quite undisturbed, peg away at something dreamy and poetic.

A vigorous family, the Doyles, both mentally and physically. I remember a trip to Norway with Doyle and his sister Connie: a handsome girl, she might have posed as Brunhilda. She married Hornung the novelist. Another sister married a clergyman named Angel, a dear ugly fellow. They lived near to us at Wallingford, and next door to them happened to live another clergyman named Dam. And later on Dam was moved to Goring, and found himself next door to a Roman Catholic priest whose name was Father Hell. Providence, I take it, arranges these little things for some wise purpose.

We had a rough crossing to Norway. Connie Doyle enjoyed it: she was that sort of girl: it added to her colour and gave a delightful curl to her hair. She had a sympathetic nature, and was awfully sorry for the poor women who were ill. She would burst in upon them every now and then to see if she could be of any help to them. You would have thought her mere presence would have cheered them up. As a matter of fact, it made them just mad.

"Oh, do go away, Connie," I heard one of her friends murmur, while passing the open door, "it makes me ill to look at you."

Doyle was always full of superfluous energy. He started to learn Norwegian on the boat. He got on so well that he became conceited; and one day, at a little rest house up among the mountains, he lost his head. We had come there in stoljas—a tiny carriage only just big enough for one person, drawn by a pony about the size of a Newfoundland dog, but marvellously sturdy. They will trot their fifty miles in the day and be frisky in the evening. While we were lunching, with some twenty miles still in front of us, a young officer came into the room, and said something in Norwegian. Of course we turned him on to Doyle; and Doyle rose and bowed and answered him. We all watched the conversation. The young Norwegian officer was evidently charmed with Doyle, while Doyle stood ladling out Norwegian as though it had been his mother tongue. After the officer was gone, we asked Doyle what it was all about.

"Oh, just about the weather, and the state of the roads, and how some relation of his had hurt his leg," answered Doyle carelessly. "Of course I didn't understand all of it." He turned the conversation.

When we had finished lunch, and the stoljas were brought out, Doyle's pony was missing. It appeared Doyle had "lent" it to the young officer, whose own pony had gone lame. The ostler, who was also the waiter, had overheard the conversation. Doyle had said "Certainly, with pleasure." He had said it once or twice. Also the Norwegian equivalent for: "Don't mention it."

There wasn't another pony within ten miles. One of our party, who had taken a fancy to the view, and thought he would like to spend a day or two in the neighbourhood, let Doyle have his stolja. But for the rest of that trip, Doyle talked less Norwegian.

Leprosy is still a living terror in Norway. Eating bad fish is the cause of it. Round about the fjords, preserved fish is the chief article of food during the long winter. Doyle, as a doctor, got permission to visit one of the big leper hospitals and took me with them. Not till one has seen the thing can one understand the full meaning of that awful cry: "The leper, the leper." The strange thing was the patience of the poor marred creatures, their quiet acceptance of their fate. Above the doors were texts of scripture. "His mercy endureth for ever," was one of them. The bell was ringing for service when we thanked our guide for an interesting afternoon. We left them trooping towards the little cold grey chapel.

Doyle had always a bent towards the occult. He told me once a curious story. It led him to conclusions with which he may now disagree. He and another member of the Psychical Research Society were sent down to an old manor house in Somerset to investigate a "phenomenon," as it is now termed—"ghost story," our grandmothers would have said. There lived in this house a retired Colonel and his wife with their only daughter, an unmarried woman of about five and thirty. For some time past, strange noises had been heard: a low moaning, rising to a wailing sob, and a sound as of a chain being dragged across the floor. Night after night, the noises would be heard. Then, for a while, they would cease. And then they would come again. The servants—so the old gentleman explained—were being frightened out of their lives: most of them had left; and even the dogs were becoming jumpy. Doyle and his friend were to say nothing about the Psychical Research Society. They were to come merely as guests, friends of the Colonel's, that he had run across in London. He had not told his wife and daughter. His idea was that no woman could keep a secret. The Colonel himself pooh-poohed the whole thing. He put it down to rats. But his wife's health was becoming affected. He was evidently more worried than he cared to show.

It was a lonely house. Doyle and his friend arrived there in time for dinner. In the evening, they played a rubber of whist with the Colonel and his daughter. It was before bridge was invented. The old lady looked on while knitting. They seemed a most devoted family. Doyle and his friend, pleading drowsiness, the result of country air, retired early. That night nothing happened. On the second night, Doyle, suddenly waking about two o'clock in the morning, heard the noises exactly as described: the low moaning, rising to a wailing sob, and the dragging of a chain. He was out of bed in a jiffy. The other man, whose turn it had been to keep watch, was in the gallery overlooking the hall, from where, he felt sure, the sounds had come. The old lady and gentleman joined them, almost immediately; and the daughter a few minutes later. The daughter, while comforting her mother, whose self-control seemed to be at breaking-point, declared she had heard nothing; and was sure it was all imagination, the result of "suggestion"; but admitted, after the old people had gone back into their room, that this was only pretence. She burst into a violent fit of weeping. Doyle's medical training came to his aid. The next night they laid their plans; and discovered, as Doyle had suspected, that the ghost was the daughter herself.

She was not mad. She protested her love both for her father and her mother. She could offer no explanation. The thing seemed as unaccountable to her as it did to Doyle. On the understanding that the thing ended, secrecy was promised. The noises were never heard again. The mysteries are with the living, not the dead.

From shining examples of industry and steadfastness I—being a lazy man myself—find it a comfort to turn my thoughts away to W. W. Jacobs. He has told me himself that often he will spend (the word is his own) an entire morning, constructing a single sentence. If he writes a four-thousand-word story in a month, he feels he has earned a holiday; and the reason that he does not always take it is that he is generally too tired. I once recommended him to try a secretary. I have found it so myself: the girl becomes a sort of conscience. After a time, you get ashamed of yourself, muddling about the room and trying to look as if you were thinking. She yawns, has pins and needles, begs your pardon every five minutes—was under the impression that you said something. A girl who knows her business can, without opening her mouth, bully a man into working.

"It wasn't any good," he told me later on. "I put Nance on to it" (Nance was his sister-in-law). "I felt it wasn't going to be any use; and I didn't want the disgrace of it to get outside the family. I suppose I'm too far gone, or else she was too eager. She would persist in our beginning sharp at ten, and I'm never any good before twelve."

He told me that if it hadn't been for the Night Watchman, he might have had to give up writing. He had exhausted all his own stories. For weeks he cudgelled his brain in vain. Then suddenly in desperation he seized his pen and wrote:

"Speaking of wimmen," said the Night Watchman.

And after that, it was plain sailing. He left it to the Night Watchman. The Night Watchman talked on.

I like talking to Jacobs about politics. He is so gloriously honest.

"I'm not sure that I do want the greatest happiness of the greatest number," he said to me one afternoon. We were driving across the Berkshire downs, behind a jolly little Irish cob of mine: it was before the days of motors. "So far as I can see, there's not enough of the good things of this world to go round evenly, and I want more than my share."

As a matter of fact, he doesn't. All he wants to make him happy is a pipe, two Scotch whiskies a day, and a game of bowls three afternoons a week. But he's an obstinate beggar. I asked him once why he was afraid of Socialism. I promised him—I offered to personally guarantee it—that under Socialism all his simple desires would be assured to him.

"I don't want things assured to me," he answered quite crossly. "I'd hate a lot of clever people fussing about, making me happy and doing me good. Damn their eyes."

During the Suffrage movement Mrs. Jacobs became militant. Husbands lived in fear and trembling in those days. Ladies who, up till then, had been as good as they were beautiful, filled our English prisons. Mrs. Jacobs, for breaking a post-office window, was awarded a month in Holloway. Jacobs did all that a devoted husband could do. Armed with medical certificates, he waited on the Governor: with all the eloquence fit and proper to the occasion, pointed out the impossibility of Mrs. Jacobs' surviving the rigours of prison régime. The Governor was all sympathy. He disappeared. Five minutes later he returned.

"You will be pleased to hear, Mr. Jacobs," said the Governor, "that you have no cause whatever for anxiety. Your wife, since her arrival here a week ago, has put on eight pounds four ounces."

As Jacobs said, she always was difficult.

Editorial experience taught me that the test of a manuscript lies in its first twenty lines. If the writer could say nothing in those first twenty lines to arrest my attention, it was not worth while continuing. I am speaking of the unknown author; but I would myself apply the argument all round. By adopting this method, I was able to give personal consideration to every manuscript sent in to me. The accompanying letter I took care, after a time, not to read. So often the real story was there. Everything had been tried: everything had failed: this was their last chance. The sole support of widowed mother—of small crippled brother, could I not see my way? Struggling tradesmen on the verge of bankruptcy who had heard that Rudyard Kipling received a hundred pounds for a short story—would be willing to take less. Wives of little clerks, dreaming of new curtains. Would-be bridegrooms, wishful to add to their income: photograph of proposed bride enclosed, to be returned. Humbug, many of them; but trouble enough in the world to render it probable that the majority were genuine. Running through all of them, the conviction that literature is the last refuge of the deserving poor. The idea would seem to be general. Friends would drop in to talk to me about their sons:

nice boys but, for some reason or another, hitherto unfortunate: nothing else left for them but to take to literature. Would I see them, and put them up to the ropes?

That it requires no training, I admit. A writer's first play, first book, can be as good as his last—or better. I like to remember that I discovered a goodish few new authors.

Jacobs I found one Saturday afternoon. I had stayed behind by myself on purpose to tackle a huge pile of manuscripts. I had waded through nearly half of them, finding nothing. I had grown disheartened, physically weary. The walls of the room seemed to be fading away. Suddenly I heard a laugh and, startled, I looked round. There was no one in the room but myself. I took up the manuscript lying before me, some dozen pages of fine close writing.

I read it through a second time, and wrote to "W. W. Jacobs, Esq." to come and see me. Then I bundled the remaining manuscripts into a drawer; and went home, feeling I had done a good afternoon's work.

He came on Monday, a quiet, shy young man, with dreamy eyes and a soft voice. He looked a mere boy. Even now, in the dusk with the light behind him, he could pass very well for twenty-five—anyhow with his hat on. I remember Mrs. Humphrey Ward whispering to me at a public dinner not so very long ago—

"Who is the boy on my left?"

"The boy," I told her, was W. W. Jacobs.

"Good Lord!" she said. "How does he do it?"

I made a contract with him for a series of short stories. He was diffident—afraid lest they might not all be up to sample. I had difficulty in persuading him. The story he had sent me had been round to a dozen magazines, and had been returned with the usual editorial regrets and compliments. I fancy the regrets came to be sincere.

We had an old farmhouse on the hills above Wallingford. William the Conqueror had a friend at Wallingford, who opened the gates to him. It was there he first crossed the Thames. In return, William granted to the town a boon. Curfew still rings at Wallingford, but at nine o'clock instead of eight. We would hear it clearly when the wind was in the west; and always there would fall a silence. The house was on the site of an old monastery. The ancient yews still stand. There was a corner of the garden that we called the Nook. A thick yew hedge, the haunt of birds, surrounded it, and an old nut tree gave shelter from the sun. It made a pleasant working place. An interesting tablet might be placed above its green archway, commemorating the names of those who at one time or another had written there: among others, Wells, Jacobs, Doyle, Zangwill, Phillpotts. Zangwill wrote stories of the Ghetto there; but wasted much of his time, playing with the birds, digging up worms with the end of his pen to feed the young thrushes and blackbirds.

It was a lonely house, on a western slope of the Chilterns. There were two front doors. One had to remember which way the wind was blowing. If one opened the wrong one, there was danger of being knocked down; and then the wind would rush through all the rooms and play the devil before one got him out again. I had a liking for being there alone in winter time, fending for myself and thinking. The owls also were fond of it. One could imagine all manner of sounds. Often I have gone out with a lantern, feeling sure I had heard the crying of a child. I remember reading there one night the manuscript of Wells' "Island of Doctor Moreau." It had come into the office just as I was leaving; and I had slipped it into my bag. I wished I had not begun it; but I could not put it down. The wind was howling like the seven furies; but above it I could hear the shrieking of the tortured beasts. I was glad when the dawn came.

Locke came to live at Wallingford. He had a bungalow down by the river, and lived there by himself until he married. He used to work at night. We could see his light shining across the river. His future wife lodged with an old servant of ours. He would tell my girls stories of the Munchausen family, descendants of the famous Baron. He used to stay with them in France. The family failing, judging from Locke's stories, still clung to them. An heirloom they particularly prized was the sling used by the late King David in his contest with Goliath. Locke had seen it himself: a simple enough thing, apparently home-made. We took him to Henley Regatta one year. We had the saddler's house down by the bridge. It was an awful week. We got drenched every day. I lent him some clothes. He is longer than I am. His arms were too long, and his legs were too long. Some Oxford boys with us dubbed him Dick Swiveller. He did suggest poor Dick.

Henham, or John Trevena as he called himself, was a neighbour of ours at Wallingford. He wrote some good books. "Furze the Cruel" and "Granite" are among the best. The woman to whom he was engaged died. But he always spoke of her as if she were living—would talk with her in his study and go long walks with her. He built himself a solitary house high up on Dartmoor. Lived there by himself for a time. And then quite suddenly he married his typist.

I suppose luck goes to the making of reputations, as it does to the shaping of most things human. Next to Hardy, I place Eden Phillpotts as the greatest of living English novelists: and Hardy has not his humour. But I take it he will have to wait till he is dead before full justice is done to him. He was staying with us; and one afternoon we went on a picnic. Landing at Dorchester lock, we climbed the Sinodun hills, where once was a Roman encampment, commanding the river. The ramparts still remain, and one may trace the ordered streets. And before that, in Druid times, it had been a

British fortress. A grove of trees marks the place now. "A green crown upon a lovely hill." It is a famous landmark for many miles around. We talked, as we boiled our kettle, of the danger of fire. There had been no rain for weeks and all the countryside was parched. The fear haunted us. The idea once started, we seemed unable to get away from it. There were dead trunks among the living that would have served as touchwood to ignite the whole.

After tea, we were preparing to light our pipes. Phillpotts was standing with his match-box in his hand. I was waiting to ask him for a light. It is most men's one economy, lucifer matches. Instead, he replaced the box in his pocket and, turning his back on me, walked down the hill. I called to him, but he took no notice. Later, I found him seated on the lock gates, smoking.

"Do you know what was happening to me just now?" he said. "A beastly little imp was urging me for all he was worth to set fire to that rotten tree against which we were standing. One lighted match would have done it, and burnt down the entire grove. If I hadn't come away, I believe he'd have nagged me into doing it."

Love of Nature is to Phillpotts almost a religion. I wonder if there is a Devil?

A Scotchman who signed himself Cynicus drew cartoons for *The Idler*: clever sketches, with a biting satire. He had a quaint studio in Drury Lane; and lived there with his sisters. One used to meet Ramsay MacDonald there. He was a pleasant, handsome young man—so many of us were, five and thirty years ago. He was fond of lecturing. Get him on to the subject of Carlyle and he would talk for half-an-hour. He would stand with his hat in one hand and the door-handle in the other, and by this means always secured the last word.

Gilbert Parker was another *Idler* man. He married in 1895 and became The Rt. Hon. Sir Gilbert Parker, Bart., M.P., L.L.D., D.C.L. It might have been jealousy— probably was, but there was a feeling that after his marriage he had become more impressive than was needful. I remember one evening at the Savage Club. He had kindly looked in upon us, on his way to some reception. He moved about, greeting affably one man after another. Eventually he came across Odell, an old actor; his address now is the Charterhouse, where Colonel Newcome heard the roll call. Odell was an excellent raconteur, one of the stars of the club. Sir Gilbert laid a hand upon his shoulder.

"You must come down and see me, Odell," he said. "Fix a day and write me. You know the address. B—— Court."

"Delighted," answered Odell. "What number?"

The Idler was not enough for me. I had the plan in my mind of a new weekly paper that should be a combination of magazine and journal. I put my own money into it, and got together the rest. Dudley Hardy designed us a poster. It was the first time a known artist had condescended to do poster-work. It came to be known as the "Yellow Girl." She seemed to be stepping out of the hoarding. If high up, you feared she would land on your head; and if low down, you feared for your toes. *To-day*, I suppose, is now forgotten; but though I say it who shouldn't, it was a wonderful twopennyworth. Stevenson's "Ebb-Tide" was our first serial. Myself, I never read the serial in a magazine. A month is too long: one loses touch. But a week is just right: one remembers, and looks forward. Stevenson agreed with me. I had met him some time before. He was ill, and looking forward to getting out of England. It was always a difficulty getting him to talk; but once started he would go on without a break: reminding me, in this respect, of Barrie. Maybe it is a Scotch trait. A gentle, unassuming man: he seemed to have no notion that he was anybody of importance—or if he had, he kept it hidden.

Anthony Hope wrote for both *The Idler* and *To-day*. I am sorry he came into money. He might have been writing to-day if he hadn't. Poverty is the only reliable patron of literature. He was a methodical worker. He had his "office" in a street opposite the Savoy Chapel. He would reach there as the clock struck ten, work till four, then, locking the door, go home to his flat in Bloomsbury. I met him for the first time at the house of a young couple named Baldry, who have since grown older, and become dear friends of mine. Baldry and Hall

Caine, in those days, used to be mistaken occasionally, by sinners out late at night, for Jesus Christ. Baldry now suggests Moses, and Hall Caine has come down to Shakespeare. Baldry was an artist and still is; but is best known as a critic. She was a slip of a girl then, and even more beautiful than she is now. She had been chief dancer at the Gaiety—Lily Lyndhurst on the programme. She confided to me, in the course of the evening, that she was the original "Dolly" of the famous "Dolly Dialogues." Anthony Hope had—well, not exactly told her so, but given her to understand it. He had a way with him. Since then I have met quite a dozen charming women who have confided to me precisely the same secret.

To-day was an illustrated paper. Dudley Hardy, Sauber, Fred Pegram, Lewis Baumer, Hal Hurst, Aubrey Beardsley, Ravenhill, Sime, Phil May, all drew for it. As I have said, it was a wonderful twopennyworth. It was difficult to get work out of Phil May in his later years. He would promise you—would swear by all the gods he knew; and then forget all about it. I had a useful office-boy. He had a gift for sitting still and doing nothing. He could sit for hours. It never seemed to bore him. James was one of his names.

"James," I would say, "you go round to Mr. Phil May's studio; tell him you've come for the drawing that he promised Mr. Jerome last Friday week; and wait till you get it."

If Phil May wasn't in, he would wait till Phil May did come in. If Phil May was engaged, he would wait till Phil May was disengaged. The only way of getting him out of the studio was to give him a drawing. Generally Phil May gave him anything that happened to be handy. It might be the drawing he had intended for me. More often, it would be a sketch belonging, properly speaking, to some other editor. Then there was trouble with the other editor. But Phil May was used to trouble. He was a thirsty soul. His wife used to tell the story that one night he woke her up, breaking crockery. It seemed he was looking for water. The water-bottle was empty.

"Oh, well, drink out of the jug," suggested Mrs. May; "there's plenty of water in that. I filled it myself, the last thing."

"I've finished that," said May.

He had been in the office of an art dealer in Liverpool, before he came to London. They hadn't got on together. There had been faults on both sides, one gathered. The old man also came to London and established himself in Bond Street. From him, I obtained an insight into the ways of picture dealers. He looked me up one day at my office.

"Could you put your hand on a journalist," he asked me, "who knows anything about art?"

"Sounds easy," I answered. "Most of them know everything. What is it you want?"

"He needn't know much," he went on. "I want him to write me an article about Raeburn. I'll tell him just what I want him to say. All he's got to do is to make it readable, with plenty of headlines. Then I want you to make a special feature of it in *To-day*."

"Wait a bit," I said. "From all I've heard, this man Raeburn is dead. Where does the excitement come in, from my point of view?"

"I'm not asking you to do it for nothing," he explained. "Send your advertisement man to me and he and I will fix it up."

I began to understand.

"You've been buying Raeburns?" I suggested.

"Raeburn is going to be the big thing this season," he answered. "We're just waiting for the Americans to come over."

Another view of the Press was afforded me by the late Barney Barnato. He had just arrived in London from South Africa; and *To-Day* had taken the occasion to give its readers the story of his life, putting down nothing in malice, I hope; but, on the other hand, nothing extenuating. Two days after our article had appeared, he called upon me. He was not of imposing presence; but his manner was friendly and he made himself at home.

"I've read your article," he said. He seemed to be under the impression I had written it myself. "There are one or two points about which you are mistaken."

He was looking at me out of his little eyes. There came a twinkle into them.

"I've always been friendly with the Press," he continued. "I've made a note of where you've gone wrong, here and there. What I'd like you to do is to write another little article—no immediate hurry about it—just putting things right."

He had taken from his pocket-book a sheet of note-paper. He rose, and breathing heavily, he came across and laid it on the desk before me. It was covered with small writing. I took it up to read it. Underneath it, there was a cheque for a hundred pounds, payable to bearer and uncrossed.

He was sadly out of condition, it was evident, but he had been a prize-fighter. Besides, violence is always undignified. I handed the cheque back to him; and crumpling up his sheet of paper threw it into the waste-paper-basket. He looked at me more in sorrow than in anger. A sigh of resignation escaped him. He took a fountain pen out of his bulging waistcoat and, leaning over the back of the desk, proceeded quite calmly to make alterations: then pushed the cheque across to me. He had made it for two hundred pounds and had initialled the corrections.

It was my turn to give it back to him. I wondered what he would do. He merely shrugged his shoulders.

"How much do you want?" he asked.

He was so good-tempered about it, that I could not help laughing. I explained to him it wasn't done—not in London.

There came again a twinkle into those small sly eyes.

"Sorry," he said. "No offence." He held out a grubby hand.

Barry Pain was of great help to me upon *To-day*. He wrote for me "Eliza's Husband," which myself I think the best thing he has done. "Eliza" is a delightful creation. Another series he wrote for *To-day* we called "De Omnibus." They were the musings, upon things in general, of a London omnibus conductor, with occasional intrusions from the driver. One is glad of the disappearance of the old horse 'bus, for the sake of the horses; but the rubicund-faced driver one misses with regret. His caustic humour, shouted downward from his perch, was a feature of the London streets. I remember once our driver making as usual to pull up by the kerb at the top of Sloane Street, outside Harvey & Nichols. A gorgeous "equipage"—as the newspaper reporter would describe it—drawn by a pair of high-stepping bays, and driven by a magnificent creature in livery of blue and gold, dashed in between and ousted us. Our driver bent forward and addressed him in a loud but friendly tone:

"Good-morning, gardener," he said. "Coachman ill again?"

The conductor also was a kindly soul—would recognize one as a fellow human being. One would hardly dream of trying to be familiar with the modern motor-'bus conductor.

It was to Barry Pain that the reproach "new humorist" was first applied. It began with a sketch of his in the "Granta"—a simple little thing entitled "The Love Story of a Sardine."

Le Gallienne was another of my "Young Men," as the term goes. "The Chief" they used to call me. "Is the Chief in?" they would ask of the young lady in the outer office. Just a convention, but always it gave me a little thrill of pride, when I overheard it. Le Gallienne was a great beauty in those days. He had the courage of his own ideas in the matter of dress. I remember at a *matinée*, a lady in the stall next to me looking up at him. He was sitting in the front row of the dress circle.

"Who's that beautiful woman?" she asked.

It has come to be the accepted idea that woman is more beautiful than man. It is a masculine delusion, born of sex instinct. I give woman credit for not believing it. The human species is no exception to the general law. The male is Nature's favourite. I remember at Munich a young officer going to a ball in his sister's clothes. He made a really lovely woman, but over-played the joke. It led to a duel the next morning in the Englischer Garten between two of his brother officers; and one of them was killed.

There is nothing of the celebrity about Thomas Hardy, O.M. He himself tells the story that a very young lady friend of his thought that O.M. stood for Old Man; and was very angry with King Edward. The order was created to give Watts, the painter, a distinction that he could not very well refuse. He had declined everything else. The last time I saw Thomas Hardy was at a private view of the Royal Academy. He was talking to the Baldrys. The papers the next morning gave the usual list of celebrities who had been present: all the famous chorus ladies, all the film stars, all the American millionaires. Nobody had noticed Thomas Hardy.

He lives behind a high wall in an unpretentious house that he built for himself long ago on the downs beyond Dorchester. We called upon him there, just before the war. His wife was away and it happened to be the servant's afternoon out. His secretary opened the door to us. His wife died a little later and she is now the second Mrs. Hardy. It was a warm afternoon, and we walked in the garden. At first, he appears to be a gentleman of no importance; but after a while, behind his quietness and simplicity, you catch glimpses of the real man. He shows himself in his poetry to be one of the deepest thinkers of the age. The unassuming little gentleman looking at you with pale gentle eyes does not suggest it. There was a whispering towards tea-time between Hardy and the lady. Hardy was worried. It seemed Mrs. Hardy, careful soul, not anticipating visitors, had before leaving locked up all the spare tea-things. We had some fun searching round. My wife and daughter were with me, making five of us. We got together a scratch lot; and sat down to table.

An interesting club, established in London about thirty years ago, was the Omar Khayyam club. I was never a member, but frequently a guest. In the winter, we dined at Anderton's Hotel in Fleet Street, and in the summer, wandered about to country inns. William Sharpe, the poet, was a member. So, also, was Fiona McLeod, the poetess, who wrote the "Immortal Hour." About her, there came to be a mystery. Some people must have gone about pulling other people's legs. George Meredith, in a letter to Alice Meynell, dated from Box Hill, writes: "Miss Fiona McLeod was here last week, a handsome person, who would not give me her eyes." All I know is that Sharpe himself made no secret of the fact that he and Fiona McLeod were one and the same person. It was after an Omar Khayyam dinner, at Caversham near Reading, that, walking in the garden, I mentioned to him my admiration of the lady, and my wish to obtain some of her work. He laughed. "To confess the truth," he said, "I am Fiona McLeod. I thought you knew." He told me that, when it came to writing, he really felt himself to be two separate personalities; and it seemed the better course to keep them apart.

I am writing these memoirs in a little room where, years ago, Edward Fitzgerald sat writing "The Rubaiyat of Omar Khayyam." The window looks out across the village street; and some of those who passed by then still come and go. Mrs. Scarlett, our landlady, who keeps the village shop, remembers him as a gentleman somewhat "thin on the top," with side whiskers and a high-domed forehead. He wore generally a stove-pipe hat at the back of his head (at rather a rakish angle, so I gather), an Inverness cape with a velvet collar, and a black stock round his neck. In voice and manner, Mr. Zangwill reminds her of him. He used to frighten the good fisher folk, at first, by his habit of taking midnight walks along the shore, talking to himself as he went by. A favourite working place of his was the ruined church upon the cliffs. It was still a landmark up to a few years ago, standing out bravely against the sky. But now its stones lie scattered on the beach or have been carried out to sea, and not a trace remains. There, with his back against a crumbling buttress, he would sit and write of mornings, till Mrs. Scarlett, to whom in those days steep pathways were of small account, would fetch him home to lunch. No one knew of his retreat: until one day some yachting friends dropped in at Mrs. Scarlett's shop to replenish their larder, and so discovered him.

Mrs. Scarlett's shop was, of course, the hub of the village. The gossips would gather there and talk. But Fitzgerald had a way of getting rid of them. Putting on his hat—at the back of his head, according to that rakish custom of his—he would bustle out and join them.

"Ah! Mrs. Scarlett," he would say, "you are talking about something interesting, I feel sure of it. Now tell me all about it."

The ladies would look from one to another, and assure him it was nothing of importance.

"No, no. You must not keep it from me," Fitzgerald would persist. "Do let me hear it."

It would occur to the ladies, one after another, that tasks were awaiting them at home. Excusing themselves, they would drift away. After a time, it came to be sufficient for Mrs. Scarlett to indicate by signs that Fitzgerald was in the little front room, working. He used to write, sitting by the window, in the easy chair (it isn't really very easy), with his writing-pad on his knee. The ladies would make their purchases in whispers and depart.

To-Day was killed by a libel action brought against me by a company promoter, a Mr. Samson Fox, whose activities my City Editor had somewhat severely criticised. I have the satisfaction of boasting that it was the longest case, and one of the most expensive ever heard in the court of Queen's Bench. It resolved itself into an argument as to whether domestic gas could be made out of water. At the end of thirty days, the unanimous conclusion arrived at was, that it remained to be seen; and the Judge, in a kindly speech, concluded that the best way of ending the trouble would be for us each to pay our own costs. Mine came to nine thousand pounds; and Mr. Samson Fox's to eleven. We shook hands in the corridor. He informed me that he was going back to Leeds to strangle his solicitors; and hoped I would do the same by mine. But it seemed to me too late.

A big catastrophe has, at first, a numbing effect. Realisation comes later. It was summer time, and my family were in the country. I dined by myself at a restaurant in Soho, and afterwards went to the theatre; but I recall a dull, aching sensation in the neighbourhood of my stomach, and an obstinate dryness of the throat.

Of course it meant my selling out, both from *The Idler* and *To-Day*. Barr's friends took over *The Idler*, and Bottomley bought most of my holding in *To-Day*. But it had, from the beginning, been a one-man paper, and after I went out, it gradually died.

I had always dreamed of being an editor. My mother gave me a desk on my sixth birthday, and I started a newspaper in partnership with a little old maiden aunt of mine. She wore three corkscrew curls on each side of her head. She used to take them off, before bending down over the table to write.

My mother liked our first number. "I am sure he was meant to be a preacher," she said to my father.

"It comes to the same thing," said my father. "The newspaper is going to be the new pulpit."

I still think it might be.

Chapter IX

THE AUTHOR ABROAD

It was comparatively early in my life that I found myself a foreigner. A fellow clerk and I saved up all one winter, and at Easter we took a trip to Antwerp. We went by steamer from London Bridge: return fare, including meals, twenty-six shillings; and at Antwerp, following the second mate's directions, we found an hotel in a street off the Place Verte where they boarded and lodged us for five francs a day: *café* complete at eight, *déjeuner* at twelve, and *dîner* at six-thirty, with half a bottle of wine.

I would not care to live the whole of my youth over again; but I would like to take that trip once more, with the clock just where it was then.

The following year we bestowed our patronage upon Boulogne; and ferreting about for ourselves unearthed a small hotel in the Haute-Ville, where they did us well for seven francs a day *en pension*. Étaples had just been discovered by the English artists. Dudley Hardy was one of the first to see the beauty of its low-lying dunes and pools of evening light. I became an habitué of the Continent. I discovered that with a smattering of the language, enabling one to venture off the beaten tracks, one could spend a holiday abroad much cheaper than in England. Ten shillings a day could be made to cover everything. Zangwill once told me that he travelled through Turkey in comfort on twenty sentences, carefully prepared beforehand, and a pocket dictionary. A professor of languages I met at Freiburg estimated the entire vocabulary of the Black Forest peasant at three hundred words. Of course, if you want to argue, more study is needful; but for all the essentials of a quiet life, a working knowledge of twenty verbs and a hundred nouns, together with just a handful of adjectives and pronouns, can be made to serve. I knew a man who went to Sweden on a sketching tour, knowing nothing but the numbers up to ten; and before he had been there a month, got engaged to a Swedish girl who could not speak a word of English. Much may be accomplished with economy. At Ostend, in the season, one can enjoy oneself for eleven francs a day; but to do so one should avoid the larger hotels upon the front. It was the smell of them, and of the people dining in them, that first inclined my youthful mind to Socialism.

Paris is a much over-rated city, and half the Louvre ought to be cleared out and sent to a rummage sale. On a rainy day with an east wind blowing, it isn't even gay; and its streets are much too wide and straight: well adapted, no doubt, to the shooting down of citizens, with which idea in mind they were planned, but otherwise uninteresting. All the roads in France are much too straight. I remember a walking tour in Brittany. All day long, the hot, treeless road stretched a straight white line before us. We never moved; or so it seemed. Always we were seven miles from the horizon, with nothing else to look at. There must have been villages and farmsteads scattered somewhere around, but like the events of a

Greek drama one had to imagine them. The natives were proud of this road. They boasted that an army corps could march along it thirty abreast without ever shifting a foot to right or left. But they did not use it much themselves. From morn to eve, we met less than a score of people; and half of them were mending it. A motoring friend of mine told me that touring in France was ruination. A tyre burst every day. It was the pace that did it. "But must you go so fast?" I suggested. "My dear boy," he answered, "have you seen the roads? You don't want to linger on them."

The best things about Paris are its suburbs. I am sorry they are rebuilding Montmartre. I never grew tired of the view, and one lodged there cheaply. The huge lumbering omnibus drawn by three mighty stallions served one for getting about Paris when I first knew it. And for playing the grand Seigneur there was the *petit fiacre* at one franc fifty the course; or two francs by the hour, with a *pour-boire* of twenty cents. But the drivers were cruel to their half-starved horses.

Provence is the most interesting part of France. The best way is through Blois and the region of the great châteaux. With a Dumas in one's pocket, one can dream oneself back in the days of the Grande Monarque; and when one reaches Orange, and has forgotten the railway, one hears the marching of the legions. I never succeeded in finding Tartarin's house at Tarascon, but King René still holds his court there, in the twilight. They were repairing the Palace of the Popes at Avignon when I first visited the town, some thirty-five years ago, and they were still repairing it when I was there last, the year before the war. They did not seem to me to have got much further. Maybe the British workman does not take so disproportionate a share of the cake for leisureliness as he is supposed to do. But everything goes slow, or else stands still, in sunny, sleepy Provence. I used to like it in the summer time before the tourists came. We English get accustomed to extremes. I remember, after *déjeuner* in a cool cellar, strolling through Les Beaux. The houses are hewn out of the rock on which the town stands: so much of it as still remains. From one of the massive doors a little child ran out, evidently with the idea of joining me upon my walk. And next moment came its mother, screaming. She snatched up the child and turned on me a look of terror.

"Mon Dieu!" she exclaimed. "To promenade here in the heat for pleasure! You must surely be Monsieur the Devil himself. Or else an Englishman."

Another time, at St. Petersburg on a mild winter's morning (as it seemed to me), I went out without a greatcoat; and made a sensation in the Nevski Prospect.

A curious thing once occurred to me in Russia, persuading me of the possibility of thought transference. I was staying with my friends the Jarintzoffs. General Jarintzoff had been the first governor of Port Arthur, and Madame, most fortunately for me, had constituted herself my translator; and had made my name fairly well known in Russia. A friend had dropped in, and the talk had turned on politics. Madame Jarintzoff was repeating, in Russian, a conversation I had had with her the day before on India. Suddenly she stopped and stared at me.

"I am sorry," she said. "I must have misunderstood you. But how on earth did you know what I was saying?"

Unconsciously, I had interrupted her, and corrected a statement she had made. I knew hardly a word of Russian, except a few sentences she had taught me, enabling me to go out by myself. Her voice could have conveyed nothing to me, but the thought behind it I had grasped. I may, of course, have gathered it from her expression.

The Russians are a demonstrative people. On stepping out of the train at St. Petersburg, I found a deputation waiting to receive me. The moment they spotted me, the whole gang swooped down upon me with a roar. A bearded giant snatched me up in his arms and kissed me on both cheeks; and then light-heartedly threw me to the man behind him, who caught me only just in time. They all kissed me. There seemed to be about a hundred of them: it may have been less. They would have started all over again, if Madame Jarintzoff had not rushed in among them and scattered them. Since then, my sympathies have always been with the baby. I knew it was affection; but in another moment I should have burst out crying. I never got used to it.

There used to be a special breed of fox-terrier popular in Russia, employed on bear-hunting expeditions. Being very small and very courageous, they would contrive to get behind the bear, when sheltering in his cave, and by biting at his heels drive him out. Some friends at Zarskoe Selo made me a present of one of these dogs. He was eleven weeks old at the time, but grew up to be quite the smallest and quite the fiercest animal that I have ever lived with. His name—I forget the Russian for it—signified "Seven Devils," but for short I called him Peter. He was useful on the way back from St. Petersburg to Berlin. He saw to it that we had the compartment to ourselves; and were both able to lie down and get some sleep. There were complaints, of course. But in Russia, in those days, there was a fixed tariff for officials. Railway guards and ticket-inspectors cost a rouble; station-masters two; and Divisional Superintendents, with sword, sometimes as much as five.

My wife met me at the station. Peter was lying curled up in a nest I had made him inside my fur coat. He was then nine inches long, pure white with blue eyes. He looked half asleep: that was one of his tricks. Before I could warn her, my wife stooped to kiss him. Fortunately she was quick, and saved her nose by a hair's breadth. I remember her delight, two years later, when she ran back into the bedroom to tell me that Peter had let her kiss him. I would not believe it until I had seen it myself.

Yet he was an affectionate little beggar, in his cranky way. He would sit on my desk while I worked; and would never go to sleep unless he was lying on something belonging to one or another of us. One of the girls' hats would do as well as anything. He would take it on to a chair and curl himself up inside it; and his one answer to all their storming and raving was: "What I have, I hold; what I take, I keep." Well, it taught them not to leave their things about. He would keep close enough to me in the country; but the town always confused him; and often I would lose him. He would make no attempt to find me, but would just sit down in the middle of the street where he had last noticed me, and howl. In Munich, he came to be known as: "The English dog that for his master screams." Policemen would knock at my door to inform me that he was screaming in such and such a street; and that I must come immediately and fetch him home. His chief trouble was that big dogs, as a rule, would not fight him; and for little dogs he had too much contempt. I suppose it was inherited instinct. Something about the size of a bear was his idea of a worthy antagonist. One day at Freiburg, in the Black Forest, he succeeded in persuading a great Dane to take some notice of him. So long as Peter merely leapt about in front of him and tried to reach his throat to kill him, the Dane just walked on. Peter ran after him and bit his leg. He bit it hard; and the Dane turned. Peter's every hair bristled with delight. At last, he had found a gentleman willing to oblige him. But life brings disappointments both to dogs and men. The Dane was quicker than Peter had expected. He made a sudden dive and seized Peter by the scruff of the neck. I overtook them just as the Dane, with Peter cursing and kicking, reached the middle of a bridge crossing a small stream. The Dane put his front paws on the parapet and looked over. All was clear. So he dropped Peter into the middle of the stream, waited to see Peter's head come up again, and then trotted off.

The stream flowed between walls, and Peter had to swim quite a quarter of a mile before he found a landing-place. He was still looking for that great Dane when we left Freiburg for Dresden, some six months later.

Taking summer and winter together, Dresden is perhaps the most comfortable town to live in of all Europe. Before the war, quite a large English colony resided there. We had a club; and a church of our own, with debt and organ fund just as at home. A *gemütliche* town, as the Germans say, and cheap. One went to the opera, the finest in Europe, in a tramcar. It didn't land you in the mud a quarter of a mile away, but put you down outside the door. And when you came out at ten, in time for a cosy supper and so home to bed by twelve, it was waiting there for you. For the best seats you paid six marks. You did not have to get yourself up. Nobody did, except the King's relations. (A kindly old gentleman. He sent a special messenger round to me one morning to tell how much he had enjoyed my "Three Men on the Bummel.") You just got up from the tea-table, and went. The only dress restriction was that ladies must take off their hats. You had no call to tap her on the shoulder, beg her with tears in your eyes to do so, and wonder if she would. The gentleman at the door, in a uniform suggestive of a Field-Marshal, had seen to all that. She was not bound to take off her hat. She could keep it on and go home again. It was only if she wanted to get in to hear the opera that she had to take it off, and leave it in the Garde-robe. But then the Garde-robe cost twopence, and was surrounded with looking-glasses. They think of these things, in Germany. Another Hunnish law that always shocked the English visitor at first, was one forbidding him to scatter dirty paper in the street. I once asked a Turkish celebrity I was interviewing for a newspaper what had most impressed him on his first arrival in England. We always asked them that. Generally they said it was the beauty of our women, or the greenness of our grass, or something of that sort. This ruffian was new to the business and answered without a moment's hesitation, "Dirty paper."

A kindly, simple folk, the Saxons. We spent two years in Dresden and made many friends. On Sunday evenings we had music at each other's houses. Students from the great music *schule* would drop in, armed with their favourite instrument; also full-fledged members of the orchestra. Marie Hall was a student there—a shy, diffident little girl; and Mischa Elman.

The Military were gods, and everybody feared and loved them. Gaudy officers, with clanking swords, would walk the pavements two or three abreast, sweeping men, women and children into the gutter. But indoors, they could be quite human. We had a visit from the Kaiser, during the manœuvres. He was not popular in Saxony;

and that year made himself still less so. The first-floor
window of a country villa commanded a good view of
the operations. It was five o'clock in the morning. The
Kaiser would not wait a moment. A door was forced
open and the Kaiser stamped upstairs, marched into the
bedroom, and threw open the window. The Gnädiger
Herr with his Gnädigen Frau were in bed. Both were
furiously indignant, but had to lie there till it pleased the
Kaiser to tramp out again, without so much as even an
apology. He must always have been a tactless fool.

There was good skating at Dresden in the winter.
Every night the lake in the Grosser Garten would be
swept and flooded. In the afternoon a military band
would play, and there was a comfortable restaurant in
which one took one's tea and cakes. The Crown Princess
would generally be there. She was a lovely woman. She
mingled freely with the people, and was popular with all
classes, except her own. She saw me waltzing one day,
and sent for me; and after that I often skated with her.
She was a born Bohemian, with, perhaps, the artist's love
of notoriety. The ponderous respectability of the Saxon
Court must have weighed upon her like a nightmare. But
there is no need to believe all the stories that were told
against her. A man I knew well, an Irish doctor, got
himself mixed up with the business; and was given forty-
eight hours to clear out of Dresden, taking all his
belongings, including his family, with him. He was in
good practice there, and it ruined him. It transpired
afterward that he was guiltless of all; except maybe of
having talked too much. But the court had got its dander

up, and was hitting out all round. His name was O'Brien. He was aware of his national failing. I asked him once to support me in a resolution I was putting to the club.

"Don't, my dear J.," he begged me. "Don't ask me to get on my legs. If I once start talking I go on for ever. And the Lord knows what I'll say."

We had the same sort of trouble with G. B. Shaw, another Irishman, on the dramatic committee of the Authors' Club. Shaw could be, and generally was, the most exemplary and helpful of committee men. But every now and then the old O'Adam would assert itself.

"Speaking of musical glasses," he would interrupt, "I'll tell you a thing that happened to a play of my own."

The anecdote would have all Shaw's delightful wit and inconsequence, and would invariably lead to another. Carton, our chairman, would take out his watch, and lay it ostentatiously upon the table. But hints were of no use when once Shaw had got into his stride. Carton in the end would have to use his hammer.

"I'm sorry, my dear Shaw," he would say, "I should love to hear the end of it. We all should, I am sure. But——"

With a gesture he would indicate the agenda paper.

"I'm sorry," Shaw would answer. "You're quite right. Now what were we talking about?"

Knowing Germany well, it would amuse me, if it did not so much disgust me, to hear the Germans spoken of as brutal and ferocious. As a matter of fact, they are the kindest and homeliest of people. Cruelty to animals in Germany is almost unknown. It was Barbarossa who left his war tent standing that the swallows who had built there should not be disturbed. Every public park and garden in Germany has its Fütterhaus, where, morning and evening, stern officials in grey uniform spread a table for the "singers," as they call them. They love the birds in Germany. In the Black Forest, they fix cart-wheels on the chimney tops, where the storks may build their nests. Cats are unpopular and rare for the reason that a healthy cat, in every country, slaughters on an average a hundred birds a year. How anyone who cares for birds can keep a cat, I have never been able to understand. The charge I myself should bring against the German people is that of over indulgence in patriotism. Out of it have grown most of their follies. The duelling clubs amongst the students, for example. That he may fight the better for the Fatherland, the German lad must be made indifferent to wounds and suffering: so the *mensur* with all its bloody paraphernalia was conceived. I attended one or two, while we were living at Freiburg; and to my horror found I was developing a liking for the smell of blood. The human tiger is not indigenous to any soil. He roams the whole world round. In England, we give him the run of the football field and the prize ring, where he is less harmful. A young secretary of mine that I took out with me to Freiburg, George Jenkins by name, first taught the boys there to play football. They had heard about it and were keen to learn; and when we left, they were playing it three days a week. The older professors shook their heads. Almost immediately it had had its effect upon the *mensur*. A youngster who is going to play for his corps on Saturday does not want to run the risk of having his eye put out on Friday. The women were against us, of course. The Fräulein took pride in seeing the face of her Hertzschatz half-hidden behind bandages, but shrank from him when he came back from the football field dirty and dishevelled. She agreed with Kipling in thinking him a muddied oaf; and that fighting was a much more attractive game—for the onlooker, at all events. But then women and poets (except the really big ones) are naturally bloodthirsty. Henley, and even dear Stevenson, used to warble about how fine a thing a blood bath would be for freshening up civilization. Another thing football did for them in Freiburg was to encourage them to drink less beer. The Kneiper was another thing to the debit side of German patriotism. Every true German hobbledehoy had to be capable of swilling more beer than the hobbledehoy of any other country. They would turn themselves into bulging beer-tubs for the honour of Saint Michael. Again, a boy keen on football thinks about his wind, and goes to bed sober. Perhaps we overdo sport in England. But, anyhow, it is a fault on the right side. I should like to see French boys take it up more seriously.

Not far from Freiburg, there stands, upon the banks of the Rhine, a little fortress town called Breisach. During the middle ages, the townsfolk of Alt Breisach must have been hard put to it to maintain their patriotism always at high-water mark. Every few years it changed hands. Now France would seize it, and then, of course, all the good citizens of Breisach would have to thank God that they were Frenchmen; and be willing to die for France. And hardly had the children been taught to hate the Deutscher Schwein, when, hey presto! they were Germans once again. God this time had sided with the Kaiser; and all the men and women of Alt Breisach— all of them that were left alive—praised "Unserer Gott." Until the next French victory, when they had to hurry up and praise instead "Notre Dame," and impress upon their children the glory of dying for France: and so on for three hundred years. Patriotism must have been a quick-change business to the citizens of Alt Breisach.

Tennis, also, was beginning to catch on when we were at Freiburg. There were only two tennis courts then. Last time I passed through Freiburg, I could have counted a hundred; and a little red-haired girl I had taught to play had become Germany's lady champion.

Munich is a fine town, but its climate is atrocious. I used to think that only we English were justified in grumbling at the weather. Travel soon convinced me that, taking it all round, English weather is the best in Europe. In Germany, I have known it to rain six weeks without intermission. In France, before going to bed, I have stood a pitcher of water in front of a blazing fire, dreaming of being able to wash myself in the morning. And, when I woke up, the fire was still burning, and the pitcher contained, instead of water, a block of solid ice. In Holland, there is always a cold wind blowing. In Italy, they have no winter. "In your cold England," they say, "for six months in the year you have to sit over a fire to keep yourselves warm. In Italy we have no fires. You can see for yourself." They are quite right. There isn't even a fire-place. They carry about a little iron bucket containing two ounces of burning charcoal. I have never tried sitting on it. It is the only way I can think of, for feeling any heat from it. Two good friends of mine have died of cold in Italy. In Russia—well, Englishmen who grumble at their own climate ought to be made to spend either a summer or a winter there. I don't care which. It would cure them in either case.

The chief business of Munich is dressing-up. In Munich, it is always somebody's holiday, and everybody else who has nothing better to do—and most of them have—join in. For the Christian, there are carnivals and saints' days. Munich is the paradise of saints. They swarm there, and each one has his own particular day, winding up with a dance in the evening. For the more worldly-minded, there are festivals organized by the guilds; and pageants by the students; and fancy-dress balls gotten up by the artists. Most folk walk to these glittering balls. There would not be sufficient cabs for a quarter of them. On rainy nights, one passes gods and goddesses in mackintoshes, fairies in goloshes, Socrates and Brunhilda under one umbrella. On fine nights, the dancers overflow into the streets. On one's way home to bed, one may be seized by a gang of Knight Templars and carried off to take part in a witch's sabbath.

German beer is seductive. The trouble is that it does not go to one's head: the consequence being that one never knows when one has had enough. I took a Scotchman to the Hofbrau one night.

"See that solemn old Johnny at the table opposite," he said, "looks like a professor. He's had seven of these mugs of beer—'masses,' or whatever you call them. I've counted them."

The Fräulien was just that moment passing.

"How many beers has my friend had up to now?" I asked her.

"Six," she answered.

"You're one behind him," I said. "You'd better have another."

I ordered it, and he drank it. But he stuck out to the end it was only his third: which was absurd.

But a little way outside Munich, there is a far-famed brewery, where they make it different. They brew for a year. Then they placard Munich, announcing they are ready; and all the town pours forth and climbs the hill; and in a week, the house is drunk dry and the garden is closed, till the following spring. They told me it was strong—"*heftig.*" But they did not say how *heftig.* Everybody was going. We hired a carriage, and I took my girls and their governess. My wife had left for England, the day before, to see a sick friend. Our governess, who was from Dresden, said "Be careful." She had heard about this beer. I claim that I was careful. The girls had each one mug. I explained to them that this was not the ordinary beer that they were used to; and that anyhow they were not going to have any more. It was a warm afternoon. They answered haughtily, and drank it off. Our governess, a sweet, high-minded lady—I cannot conceive of her having done anything wrong in all her life—had one and part of another. I myself, on the principle of safety first, had decided to limit myself to three. I was toying with the third, when my eldest girl, saying she wanted to go home, suddenly got up, turned round and sat down again. The younger swept a glass from the table to make room for her head, gave a sigh of contentment and went to sleep. I looked at Fräulein Lankau.

"Whatever we do," she said, "we must avoid attracting attention. You remain here, as though nothing had happened. I will lead the poor dears away, and find the carriage. A little later, you follow quietly."

I could not have thought of anything more sensible myself. She gathered her things together and rose. The following moment she sat down again: it was really one and the same movement.

"You take the two children," she said, "and find the carriage. Then come back for me. Hold them firmly, and walk straight out. Nobody is looking. Go now."

I am very intelligent, and I have formed the habit of taking notice. I had noticed a common-looking man, of powerful physique, who on three occasions had passed our table arm in arm with a different companion; each time he had come back alone. He was now returning empty-handed. I beckoned to him.

"If you, Fräulein Lankau," I said, "and you, my dear Elsie, will take this gentleman's arm—or rather arms, he will, I am sure, kindly see you into the carriage. I will rest here, and look after the child until he returns."

He put one arm round Fräulein Lankau, in quite a fatherly way; and one round Elsie. It seemed to come natural to him.

A few minutes later he reappeared. He lifted up the child without waking her. As a matter of fact, she did not wake up till much later in the day. I took his other arm and we sauntered out together. He mentioned, as he tucked a rug round me, that the price was four marks. I gave him five, and shook him by the hand.

"I am sorry," remarked Fräulein Lankau on the way home, "that dear Mrs. Jerome was called back to England to see her sick friend. And yet, perhaps, it was the hand of Providence." Having said which, she went to sleep.

Poor Fräulein! She had much faith in Providence. She died of starvation during the blockade.

Lenbach, the painter, was a prominent figure in Munich, when we were there. His daughter was a beautiful child, then about six years old. Her mother was away; and she did the honours of the studio with a grave dignity. Most of the visitors would want to kiss her. But there she drew the line, putting out her little hand with a reproving gesture. Another interesting party I met at Munich was a grand-looking, red-haired dame. She was the wife of a Baron. They were common then in Germany. She lived in a sombre, silent street, the other side of the river; and few people associated her with Clotilde von Rüdiger, who, at seventeen, had been the talk of Europe. Meredith tells her story in "The Tragic Comedians": A passionate, mad love affair. She, of the older nobility. He, Jew, rebel, demagogue, stormy leader of the people. Aristocratic family at first unbelieving, then furious, as was to be expected. All the material of an historical romance, the characters still living. Heroine devoted, ecstatic, defying her world for love. Hero, magnificent, all daring. In the last chapter, shot dead by high-born rival, the suitor approved and favoured by stern parents. So far, all in order. We prepare to shed our tears. And then the curious epilogue. Clotilde von Rüdiger gives her hand to Prince Romaris, the man who killed her lover. Meredith understands her, and is thus able to forgive. He explains her to us, but leaves us still puzzled. Talking to her—one tactfully avoids religion, politics or sex—about the opera, her stage experiences in America; answering her inquiries as to whether one takes lemon in one's tea, and so forth, it is difficult to dismiss the dismal Gastzimmer with its shabby, shop-made furniture, and think of her flaming youth, when she made havoc in the world.

One of the reasons that snobbery hardly exists upon the Continent must be that titles are so plentiful. Among others in Munich, there was an Italian Prince, of lineage dating back to Charlemagne, whom we came to know well. His wife, who was a Princess in her own right, had her "At Home" on Thursdays. They lived in a three-roomed flat not far from us. A charming little man. On Thursday mornings, one could always meet him in the neighbourhood of the Theatinerstrasse, with a basket on his arm, selecting pretty cakes and fancy biscuits against the afternoon's reception. He did most of the marketing. He was so clever at it, the Princess would explain. She, herself, took more interest in cooking. Another lady we knew, an Austrian Countess, won a carriage in a lottery. Originally, it must have been intended for a circus: a gorgeous affair, all yellow and gold, suggesting a miniature of our own dear Lord Mayor's coach. But it never occurred to her that there was anything ridiculous about it. Seated in it, very upright, behind an ancient, raw-boned steed, hired by the hour from a livery stable, and a little coachman in a chocolate coat belonging to the eighteenth century, she would solemnly, of afternoons, make the tour of the Englischer Garten. Our Dienstmädchen was related to her Dienstmädchen, and we came to know that the poor lady had put aside many a small comfort to pay for that hired horse and little coachman. But the charm of the whole turn-out was that none could pretend they had not seen and recognized it. Through the throng it would make its way, the cynosure of every eye. Hats would be raised, and fair heads bowed. The Countess, her old dull face transfigured, would shower her gracious acknowledgments.

There was a large English Colony in Brussels before the war. It is a cheap town to live in: provided you possess a knowledge of the language and are quick at mental arithmetic. At first, the new arrival, on being introduced to fellow-countrymen, is often perplexed.

"Mr. and Mrs. Blankley-Nemo," you whisper to your wife. "I seem to know the name. Where have we met them?"

"I can't be sure," your wife answers. "I know her face quite well."

Experience teaches you not to say anything much at the time, but to make discreet inquiries later on.

"Remember her face!" laughs your friend. "Well, you ought to. It was in all the newspapers every day for a fortnight. Interesting case. Three co-respondents. They called them 'The Triple Alliance.' Nemo seems to have been the leading member. Anyhow, he married her. Nice people. Give jolly little dinners."

Another, whose name sounds familiar, turns out to be an ex-company promoter, about whose previous address it is not considered etiquette to make inquiry. During our stay of two winters in Brussels I make the acquaintance of three gentlemen, all of whom, so they themselves informed me, had been known as the "Napoleon of Finance": an unfortunate family, apparently.

An added trouble besetting the newly arrived is the habit among Brussels tradesmen of calling and leaving their cards. There is nothing on the card to indicate the nature of the compliment. Just the gentleman's name and address. My wife and I made a list. None of their ladies had accompanied them, so far as we could tell; but maybe that was a custom of the country. On Sunday afternoon, we started on a round. The first people we called on lived over a grocer's shop. They were extremely affable; and yet we had a feeling that, for some reason, they had hardly been expecting us. It was so pronounced that we could not shake it off. My wife thought it might be that they were Sabbatarians; and apologized for our having come on a Sunday. But it was not that. Indeed, they were emphatic that Sunday was the most convenient day we could have chosen; and hoped, if ever we thought of calling upon them again, that it would be on a Sunday. They offered to make us tea; but we explained that we had other calls to make and at the end of the correct twenty minutes we departed.

The next people on our list lived over a boot shop. "The International Shoe Emporium." Their door was round the corner, in a side street. Monsieur was asleep, but Madame soon had him awake; and later the children came down and the eldest girl played the piano. We did not stop long, and they did not press us. Madame said it was more than kind of us to have come, and was visibly affected. The entire family came to the door with us, and the children waved their handkerchiefs till we had turned the corner.

"If you want to finish that list," I said to my wife, "you take a cab. I'm going home. I never have cared for this society business."

"We will do one more," said my wife. "At least we will see where they live."

It turned out to be a confectioner's. The name was over the door. It was the third name on our list. The shop was still open.

"We'll have some tea here," said my wife.

It seemed a good idea. They gave us very good tea with some quite delicious cream buns. We stayed there half-an-hour.

"Do we leave cards, or pay the bill?" I asked my wife.

"Well, if the former," explained my wife, "we shall have to ask them to dinner."

There is a vein of snobbery in most of us. I decided to pay the bill.

The late King Leopold was the most unpopular man in Brussels when we were there. It was the time when the Congo horrors were coming to light. One hopes, for the credit of the Belgians, this may have had something to do with it. The people would rush to the windows, when his carriage came in sight, and hastily draw down the blinds. In the streets, he was generally followed by a hooting crowd. His brother, the Vicomte de Flandres, was much liked. A quaint old gentleman. He would promenade the Avenue Louise, and talk to anyone he met: for preference anyone English. Waterloo is a pleasant bicycle ride from Brussels; through the Forêt de Soignes, where little old Thomas à Kempis once walked and thought. It was always good fun to take an Englishman there, and get a Belgian guide I knew, an old Sergeant, to come with us and explain to us the battle. We would be shown the Belgian Lion, on a pyramid, proudly overlooking the field; and would learn how on the 18th of June, 1815, the French were there defeated by the Belgian army, assisted by the Germans, and some English.

We tried to winter once in Lausanne. But Swiss town life holds few attractions. We had a villa at the top of the hill. The view was magnificent. But of an evening one yearns rather for the café and the little theatre. Oswald Crawford and his wife were staying at the Beau Rivage. It was there that he invented Auction Bridge. I used to go down and play with him. He was tired of the old game, and was working out this new idea with the help of some French officers. I took a dislike to invalids that winter. The Beau Rivage was given over to them. There were men and women who would take seven different medicines with their dinner, and then sit nipping all the evening. Young girls would lure you into a corner, and tell you all their kidney troubles; and in the middle of a game your partner would break off to give an imitation of the sort of spasms that had happened to him in the night. It was difficult at times to remember what were trumps.

It gave me a good conceit of myself, living abroad. I found I was everywhere well known and—to use the language of the early Victorian novel—esteemed and respected. I cocked my head and forgot the abuse still, at that time, being poured out upon me by the English literary journals. If it be true that the opinion of the foreigner is the verdict of posterity, said I to myself, I may come to be quite a swell dead author.

Speaking of my then contemporaries, Phillpotts I found also well read, especially in Germany and Switzerland. Zangwill was known everywhere in literary circles. Barrie, to my surprise, was almost unknown. I was speaking of him once at a party in Russia. "Do you mean Mr. Pain?" asked one of the guests. Shaw had not yet got there. Wells was popular in France, and Oscar Wilde was famous. Kipling was known, but was discussed rather as a politician than a poet. Stevenson was read and Rider Haggard. But of the really great— according to Fleet Street—one never heard.

Chapter X

THE AUTHOR AT PLAY

Advanced friends of mine, with a talent for statistics, tell me that, when the world is properly organized, nobody will work more than two hours a day. The thing worrying me is, what am I going to do with the other twenty-two. Suppose we say seven hours sleep, and another three for meals: I really don't see how, without over-eating myself, I can spin them out longer. That leaves me fourteen. To a contemplative Buddhist this would be a mere nothing. He could, so to speak, do it on his head—possibly will. To the average Christian, it is going to be a problem. It is suggested to me that I could spend most of these hours improving my mind. But not all minds are capable of this expansion. Some of us have our limits. During the process, I can see my own mind wilting. It is quite on the cards, that instead of improving myself I'd become dotty. Of course, my fears may be ungrounded. One of Shaw's ancients, in "Back to Methuselah," to whom some young persons have expressed their fear that he is not enjoying himself, retorts in quite the Mrs. Wilfer manner: "Infant, one moment of the ecstasy of life as we live it would strike you dead." After which, according to the stage directions, he "stalks out gravely." And they, the young persons, "stare after him, much damped." Just as one feels poor Mr. Wilfer would have done. It may come to that. Like the old road-mender, who sometimes sat and thought, and sometimes just sat, we may eventually acquire the habit of doing nothing for fourteen hours a day without injury to our liver. But it will have to come gradually. In the interim, we shall have to put in more play.

I have wasted a good deal of time myself on play. Gissing, in a short story, relates the history of a tramp. I have never been able to make up my mind whether Gissing intended the story to be humorous or tragic. He is quite a superior young tramp, fond of flowers and birds. He does not write poetry—is always a bit too tired for that—but thinks it. Not of much use in the world— perhaps few of us are—but, on the other hand, harmless. Unfortunately, for everybody, he awakens love in the bosom of a virtuous young woman. She reforms him: persuades him of the sin of idleness, the nobility of labour. For her sake, he borrows money and starts a grocer's shop; works up from bad to worse till he becomes a universal stores; and ends eventually a bloated capitalist. I have always told that story to my conscience whenever it has reproved me for not sticking closer to my desk. I'd only have written more books and plays: might have ended as a best seller, or become a theatrical manager.

The genius has no call to shirk his work. He likes it. Shaw never wastes his time. Hall Caine is another. You hear that Hall Caine has gone to Switzerland for the winter. You picture him dancing about on a curling rink with a broom; or flying down a toboggan slide without his hat shouting "Achtung." You find him in his study, at the end of a quiet corridor on the top floor of the hotel, doing good work. I lured him out into the snow one day. He was at St. Moritz, at the Palace Hotel, and I was at Davos with my niece. It was snowing. Sport was off. But Satan can always find some mischief for idle legs. It occurred to us to train over and disturb Hall Caine in the middle of his new novel. It happened to be "The Christian." Often a good book will exert an influence even on the author himself. He received us gladly and when, after lunch, I proposed a walk, answered with gentleness that he would be pleased.

He said he knew a short cut to Pontresina. It led us into a snowdrift up to our waists.

"I know where we are now," said Caine. "We are in a hollow. We ought to have turned to the right."

We turned to the right, then and there. A minute later, we were up to our necks.

"I've been to Pontresina," I said. "It's not particularly interesting."

"Perhaps you're right," said Caine.

It is easier to get into a snowdrift, than to get out. It was dusk before we reached Celerina. We left Caine walking up the railway track, and made ourselves for the station. It was still snowing.

"No joke," I said, to my niece in the train. "We might have been buried alive. Such things often happen."

My niece, Nellie, is a pious girl, and a great admirer of Hall Caine.

"I should have felt anxious," she said, "if we hadn't had Mr. Hall Caine with us. I felt so sure that Mr. Caine was being watched over."

St. Moritz used to be a homely little place. The Kuln was the only hotel, practically speaking. My wife and I stayed at the Palace the first winter it opened. They charged us seven francs a day, inclusive. I am told that since then prices have gone up. About a dozen of us had the place to ourselves: among us a retired Indian General who was keen on skating.

"Haven't had a pair of skates on for forty-five years," he confided to me the first morning. "Used to be rather a dab at it. Daresay it will soon come back."

A sporting old fellow! He had had pads made: two for his knees, two for his elbows, and one for the back of his head.

"My nose I can always save with my hands," he explained. "And the only other place doesn't matter. It's bones that we have to be careful of, at my age."

Jacobs contents himself with bowls. As he points out, it is a game you can play without getting hot and excited, and losing your dignity. Phillpotts and his wife used to be good tennis players, in the old days at Ealing—how many years ago there is no call to discuss. Lawn tennis had not long come in. We used to play it with any kind of racquet. Keen players designed their own. Some were the shape of a kidney, and others bent like an S, with the idea of giving the ball a twist. It was not till the time of the Renshawes that we settled down to a standard size and form. There was a period when we played it—those of us who wished to be in the fashion—in stiff shirts and stand-up collars; and women wore trains which they held up as they ran. W. S. Gilbert, always original, would persist in having his court twenty feet too long. I forget the argument. It was about as long as the court. He was an obstinate chap. I remember one man making him awfully ratty by shouting out in the middle of a game—he hadn't thought to notice the court before we started:

"I say, Gilbert, what are we supposed to be doing? Playing tennis or rehearsing a Bab Ballad?"

Tennis is the only active game that a man can play when he is old. Golf I have always regarded as a remedy rather than a game. A friend of mine was completely cured of hay fever by a six months' course of golf. For most nervous complaints it is excellent. Doctors used to recommend "a little gentle carriage exercise." Now they prescribe golf. Much more sensible. A rattling good game of tennis I have seen played by four men whose united ages totalled two hundred and forty years. I had a first-class court at "Monks Corner" on Marlow Common. It costs much labour to keep a grass court in good condition. They say that at Wimbledon, on the centre court, each blade of grass has its own pet name. I didn't go so far as that, but there was rarely a day I did not spend an hour there on my knees. Wilfred Baddeley—he held the All England Championship for three years—said it was the best private grass court he had ever played on. We used to get good players there. My neighbour Baldry, the art critic, had laid down a cement court, and a short path through the wood connected them. Both courts were well sheltered. So, except in flood time, we could always be sure of a game. Mrs. Lambert Chambers is a delightful partner to play with. She puts quietness and confidence into one. It seems quite an easy game. We had the Italian champion, one summer. He had an impossible service. He would put a backward spin on the ball. It would drop just over the net, and bounce backward. Wimbledon had to summon a meeting, and hastily make a new rule: to the effect that, in service, the ball must continue a forward course. In play, the stroke is still permissible. It is a most irritatingly difficult stroke to counter. The only chance is to volley, and even then there is the devil in it. Kathleen McKane and her sister, when they were little girls, used often to come over. The family generally put up for the summer at the lock-keeper's house at Hambledon, which was just a bicycle ride.

Doyle was an all-round sportsman; but was at his best, perhaps, as a cricketer. I was never any good at cricket myself. I had no chance of learning games as a boy, and cricket is not a thing you can pick up any time. Barrie was a great cricketer, at heart. I remember a match at Shere, in Surrey. We had a cottage there one summer. It was a little Old World village in those days. There was lonely country round it: wide-stretching heaths, where the road would dwindle to a cart track and finally disappear. One might drive for miles before meeting a living soul of whom to ask the way: and ten to one he didn't know. Barrie had got us together. He was a good captain. It was to have been Married *v.* Single. But the wife of one of the Married had run away with one of the Singles a few days before. So to keep our minds off a painful subject, we called it Literature *v.* Journalism. Burgin, who was then my sub-editor on *The Idler*, caught a ball hit by Morley Roberts, I think. But it came with such force that it bowled Burgin over. He turned a somersault, and came up again with the ball still clutched in his hands. Burgin argued that the ball had not touched the ground, and that therefore the catch ought to count. There was a distinct mark of mud on the ball. But Burgin said that was there before he caught it. He had noticed it. I forget how the argument ended.

Doyle was great on winter sports; and was one of the first to introduce ski-ing into Switzerland. Before that, it had been confined to Norway. All Davos used to turn out to watch Doyle and a few others practising. The beginner on skis is always popular. My own experience has convinced me that it is, practically speaking, impossible to break your neck, ski-ing. There may be a way of doing it: if so, it is the one way I haven't tried. I must have been forty-five when I first put on skis. I had the advantage of being a good skater, and knowing all that could be done with the old-fashioned snow-shoe. Eventually I became fairly proficient. But were I to have my time over again, I would not leave it quite so late. Back somersaults, and the splits are exercises less painfully acquired in youth.

But it was worth the cost. The last time I put on skis was at Arosa, the first year of the war. We were an oddly mixed lot. American girls and German officers skated hand in hand. French, Germans and Italians clung together on the same bob-sleigh. A kind gentleman from St. Petersburg, who claimed to be related to the Tzar, gave lessons in Russian every morning to three Austrian ladies from Vienna, who were fearful that after the war they might have to talk it. We were all on the best of terms with one another. Sport is a shameless internationalist. It was the last day of my holiday. Arosa is an excellent centre for ski-ing. I had had some fine runs and was in good form. I hired a boy from the village to come with me: and climbed the slopes of the Weibhorn. No experienced skier ever goes out alone. There are positions, quite easy to fall into, from which it is anatomically impossible to rise without assistance. The snow was just perfect that day. There had been a slight fall in the night, and the surface had not yet frozen. We climbed for two hours; and then on a narrow plateau we stripped the skins from our skis and fastened them round our waists, tightened our straps, and launched forth. Often have I envied the swallows, watching them sweep on poised wing downward through the air till they almost touch the ground. I envy them more now that I know what it feels like. I can imagine only one more wonderful sensation, and that is the "jump"—an ugly word that does not really describe it. The signal is given to go, and the skier gently moves forward, skis straight, side by side, with the knees just bent. The hard, beaten track grows steeper. The pine trees glide past him, swifter and swifter. Suddenly the trees divide: the track heads straight as an arrow to—nothing. And then that glorious leap into sheer space with arms outstretched and head thrown back. I wonder how long it seems to him until the earth comes rushing up to meet him, and he is flying through the cheering crowd towards the flagstaff. It only wants nerve.

One of the most dangerous things that can happen when ski-ing is to strike a sunk-fence. A broken ankle is generally the result of that; and once I came upon a man, sitting on the edge of a precipice, over which his skis were projecting. He dared not move. He had plunged his arms into the snow behind him and was hoping it would not give way. But having regard to all the dangers that a skier is bound to face, the marvel is that so few accidents occur: and even were they umpteen times as frequent, I should still advise the average youngster to chance it.

The thing to beware of is exhaustion. Ski-ing, like riding, requires its own particular set of new muscles. Until these have been built up, avoid long excursions. It was at Villars I first put on skis. One, Canon Savage, got up a ski-ing party and asked me to come in. I told him I was only a beginner, but he said that would be all right; they would look after me; and at eight o'clock the next morning we started. On the way home, I found it impossible to keep my legs. I would struggle up merely to go down again. Towards dusk, I fell into a drift, and lost my skis. The fastenings had become loosened. They slipped away from under me, and I watched them sliding gracefully down the valley. They seemed to be getting on better without me. I had taken an equal dislike to them and, at first, was glad to see them go. Until it occurred to me that with nothing on my feet but a pair of heavy boots, I had not much chance—in my then state of exhaustion—of extricating myself. I shouted with all the breath I had left. Maybe it wasn't much; and anyhow the Canon and his party were too far ahead to hear me. Fortunately a good Christian, named Arnold, thought of me and came back. I mentioned the incident to the Canon the next morning, but his sense of humour proved keener than mine. He found it amusing.

I never cared for the English school of skating. I have the idea it must have been invented by someone with a wooden leg. I learnt it—sufficiently, at all events, to be able to pass judgment on it. There is no joy in it. It is difficult, I admit. So, likewise, would be dancing in a strait-waistcoat. Why do a thing merely because it is against the laws of nature? Pirouetting around with arms and legs stretched out, looking like something out of a Russian ballet, may not be a dignified amusement for an elderly gentleman of middle weight. But I still enjoyed it up to fifty-eight.

Tobogganing down a carefully prepared snow run soon loses its charm. It answers too closely to the Chinaman's description of it: "Swish. Then walk a milee." Beginners can come off at a bend and perform a few more or less amusing antics before they come to a standstill. Fortunately they often do, or the spectators would have a dull time. I remember one winter, a lady at Mürren attempting to steer herself by means of a pole some twenty feet long, which she used as a rudder. She wasn't good. At every bump the pole shot up into the air; and then it was the crowd on the bank that performed the antics, and did all the swearing. The bob-sleigh is, of course, another matter. That wants both pluck and skill. Freeman of Davos, who was skipper, once broke his arm at the beginning of a race, and yet steered on to the end. It must have been grim work getting her round those hairpin bends above Klosters, with a splintered bone sticking into your flesh. The best use to make of the ordinary toboggan is to take it out for an afternoon's run down the valley. One walks a little, here and there, where the road is on the level. In the Gasthaus of the scattered village, one halts to drink a glass of beer, and to smoke. One glides through pine-woods, looking down upon the foaming torrent far below. It is good sport dodging the woodcutters' sledges.

The horses watch you out of their quiet eyes, and jingle their bells as you pass. The children, coming out of school, bar your way. You shake your fist at them and plunge on headlong. You know that, at the last moment, they will leap aside. But you must be prepared for snowballs. You overtake stout farmers' wives, seated upright with their basket of eggs between their knees; and exchange a grave "Grüss Gott." And so on till you reach the sleepy town at the gateway of the valley. There you take coffee, with perhaps a glass of schnapps. Then home in the little bustling train, crowded with chatty peasant folk; and maybe, if your seat is near the stove, you fall asleep.

Climbing, so far as Switzerland is concerned, will soon be a thing of the past. Every peak will have its railway. The fine thing was to talk about it afterwards, round the great pitcher of wine in the Gastzimmer of the village inn, listening to the wisdom of the guides, comparing notes with your fellow climbers, recounting your dangers and hairbreadth escapes. Who cares to do that now, when a sportsman in spats and a jazz jumper may, at any moment, burst in upon your tale of peril and exhaustion with a cheery: "Oh, yes, we bumped up there this morning by the nine forty-five. Not a bad view, but a rotten lunch"?

Only on one occasion have I been mixed up with a mishap. We were crossing a glacier, and my friend Frank Mathew fell into a crevass. We were roped together, and he did it so carelessly that he nearly pulled me in after him. The guide, of course, stood firm; but it took some time to get him out. I was all for going on; but Mathew took a more serious view of it; and we helped him to limp home.

Frank Mathew was a nephew of Father Mathew, the great temperance preacher. Frank wrote delightful Irish stories for *The Idler*. I am convinced he would have made a name for himself in literature if he had stuck to it. Alas! he came into money and married happily.

A snow slope is the most dangerous thing to negotiate. One day, Mathew and I walked up the Scheidegg. The hotel was not then built. It was only a hut in those days. We were looking forward to getting something to eat, but found the old landlord too scared to attend to us, crying, and hardly able to stand. He had been watching through his telescope, and had just seen three men follow one another down a snow slope and over one of the precipices of the Jungfrau. Their bodies were recovered a few days later. They were three young Italians who had ventured without a guide.

The amateur photographer is the curse of Switzerland. One would not mind if they took one at one's best. There was a charming photograph in *The Sphere* one winter of my daughter and myself, waltzing on the ice at Grindelwald. It made a pretty picture. But, as a rule, beauty does not appeal to the snap-shotter. I noticed, in my early ski-ing days, that whenever I did anything graceful the Kodak crowd was always looking the other way. When I was lying on my back with my feet in the air, the first thing I always saw when I recovered my senses, was a complete circle of Kodaks pointing straight at me. Poor Rudyard Kipling never got a chance of learning. I was at Engelberg with him one winter. He was in the elementary stage as regards both skating and ski-ing; and wherever he went the Kodak fiends followed him in their hundreds. He must have felt like a comet trying to lose its own tail.

I took him one morning to a ski-ing ground I had discovered some mile or more away: an ideal spot for the beginner. We started early and thought we had escaped them. But some fool had seen us, and had given the hulloa; and before we had got on our skis, half Engelberg was pouring down the road.

Kipling is not the meekest of men and I marvelled at his patience.

"They might give me a start," he sighed; "I would like to have had them on, just once."

Engelberg is too low to be a good sports centre. We had some muggy weather, and to kill time I got up some private theatricals. Kipling's boy and girl were there. They were jolly children. Young Kipling was a suffragette and little Miss Kipling played a costermonger's Donah. Kipling himself combined the parts of scene-shifter and call boy. It was the first time I had met Mrs. Kipling since her marriage. She was still a beautiful woman, but her hair was white. There had always been sadness in her eyes, even when a girl. The Hornungs were there also, with their only child, Oscar. Mrs. Hornung, *née* Connie Doyle, was as cheery and vigorous as ever, but a shade stouter. Both boys were killed in the war.

It was election time in England, and the hotel crowd used to encourage Kipling and myself to political argument in the great hall. I suppose I was the only man in the hotel who was not a Die-hard conservative. Kipling himself was always courteous, but not all the peppery old colonels from Cheltenham and fierce old ladies from Bath were. Notwithstanding, on wet afternoons, when one couldn't go out, it wasn't bad sport. Conan Doyle in his memoirs writes me down as one "hot-headed and intolerant in political matters." When I read the passage I was most astonished. It is precisely what I should have said myself concerning Doyle. I suppose the fact is that tolerance is another name for indifference. A man convinced that his views, if universally adopted, would be of ineffable service to humanity, is bound to attribute opposition to stupidity or else to original sin. Socrates himself—if Plato is to be trusted—was quite an intolerant person. I am not sure that, arguing with Socrates, I would not rather he called me a fool and have done with it, than proceed to prove it to me, step by step, according to that irritating method of his. Thrasymachus, I am prepared to wager, thought Socrates one of the most intolerant men he had ever met. If Doyle can get into touch with Thrasymachus, he might put it to him if I am not right. Not until we have come to see that man's goal lies within him, not without—that what we call the "progress of the Race" is never towards the truth, but always round it, do we become tolerant—on most matters of opinion.

The road has disappeared. The motor track has taken its place. But the wheel is a poor substitute for the ribbons. I speak as an old coachman. It was good sport, going for a drive with jolly horses that you loved; who knew they were part of the game, and took care that it never got dull. I have a city friend who, in the old days, whenever he would take his mind off business worries, would have out his dog-cart, and drive tandem through Piccadilly and the Broadway, and so home by Richmond Hill and Brentford. Now, he takes out his motor, and all he has to do is to watch the policeman. It is no help to him whatever. Driving a coach and four was interesting but, compared with tandem driving, it was restful. In a team your leaders were coupled together and, unless they had talked it over beforehand and arranged upon a signal, could not suddenly turn round and look at you. Your tandem leader could, and sometimes would; and then you had to be quick with the flick of your whip: and maybe an oath or two, thrown in. Of course, the perfectly trained tandem was easy to take anywhere; but such was only for the rich: and, after all, there was more fun when your horses were not mere machines, and you had to watch their twitching ears and try to guess what they were thinking. I had a little Irish horse. He was a born leader. I did not have to drive him, beyond just giving him a general idea of where I wanted to get. He would pick his own way through an agricultural town on market day, leaving me to concentrate myself upon the wheeler. But that was when he was feeling good. And when he wasn't, he was just a little devil. I had some Oxford boys staying with me one summer. The horses hadn't been out all day, and the boys suggested a tandem drive by moonlight. We didn't take my old coachman, and he didn't clamour to come.

"I should keep my eye on the Little 'un, if I were you, sir," he advised me, as he handed me the reins. "I don't like the way he has been picking up his feet."

We started all right. "Pat" let his collar hang and seemed sleepy, but I knew his head was full of mischief: I could feel it through the eighteen feet of rein. In the hope of discouraging him, I turned up a narrow road with a high bank on either side. He still seemed drowsy, but I wasn't trusting him. It was a winding road. Suddenly, at a bend, he flung up his head and laid back his ears. "Hold on," I shouted. The next moment we were charging up the bank. There was nothing else to be done but to let the wheeler follow: a dear quiet girl, when left to herself; but Pat always gave her a bit of his devil. The two men behind were shot out, but hung on, and managed somehow to scramble back. I wish they hadn't. I could have got on better without them. We cleared the top, and then they started cheering. We went through that cornfield at twenty miles an hour. I saw an open gate and made for that. We crossed a lane and through the hedge to the other side: by good luck it was chiefly bramble. The two fools at the back, I gathered, were unhurt. They were singing "Annie Laurie." We took the Ewelme golf links still at the gallop. They seemed to me to be all bunkers. At the Icknield corner, I managed to get the horses on to the road. It rises four hundred feet in a mile and a half; and at Swyncombe, Pat agreed to my suggestion that we should pull up and have a look at the view. We returned home, via Nettlebed, at a gentle trot. Beyond having lost our hats, and the temporary use of my left eye, we were not much damaged. My Oxford friends crowded round Pat and congratulated him. The youngest of them, who had an indulgent mother, offered me my own price for him, then and there. He had been bitten with the idea of starting a tandem of his own.

Poor Pat! I had to shoot him when the motors came. He had never let anything pass him on the road, before, and one day, at the Henley Fair Mile, he ran his last race. He was only a few days short of twenty then: though you wouldn't have thought it. He had had a good time.

Tandem driving is asking for trouble, sooner or later. I had driven tandem, summer and winter, for over ten years, in and out among the Chilterns, which isn't an easy country; and my escapes had put it into my head, I suppose, that nothing ever could happen to me. And then, one afternoon, driving quietly round a corner at eight miles an hour, I tilted over a heap of stones that had been shot out there that morning for road-mending and broke poor Norma Lorimer's leg. She and Douglas Sladen were staying with us at the time. Sladen had remained behind to write a book-review in answer to a telegram: which shows how wise it is always to put duty before pleasure. Fortunately, we were near home, and some labourers quickly came to our assistance. I got on my bicycle and rode down to Wallingford, and wired for a bone setter; and when I started to return, I discovered I had broken an ankle. I had not known it till then, when my excitement had begun to cool down. I remember we boys had a way of getting into the Alexandra Palace by climbing a tree and dropping down inside the fence. One day, I slipped and fell upon the spikes. I felt nothing at the time, except the desire to put distance between myself and a young policeman who seemed to have suddenly sprung out of the earth. It was my mother who noticed that my arm was in ribbons. Nature, red though she be in tooth and claw, provides an anæsthetic. It was man who invented cold-blooded cruelty. Miss Lorimer stayed with us for a month, and forgave me. She talked as if all I had done had been to provide her with a good excuse for a pleasant holiday. But I was glad of that broken ankle. I'd have felt mean merely saying "I'm sorry." We used to play croquet on crutches.

Killing has never attracted me. I give myself no airs. As Gilbert points out, there is no difference, morally speaking, between the Judge who condemns a man to be hanged and the industrious mechanic who carries out the sentence. If I like eating a pheasant (which I do) I ought, logically, to take a pleasure in shooting it. Possibly, if we all had to be our own butchers, vegetarianism would be less unpopular. But there would still remain a goodly number to whom the cutting of a pig's throat would afford enjoyment; and such, alone, are entitled to their bacon. There was an old farmer I knew in Oxfordshire, a simple soul. He owned the shooting over one solitary field, in the centre of which was a three-acre copse of beech wood. All round him, for miles, were rich men who spent quite fabulous sums on rearing pheasants.

"No," he said to me one day during a big shoot. We were leaning over the gate of his one small field. "No, I don't myself go in for breeding. I just take what the Lord sends me."

I didn't count them but, speaking roughly, I should say about a hundred birds had gained the shelter of that three-acre copse while we had been talking.

"They've got more sense than people think," he added musingly. "They know they'll find a little corn there; and will be safe, poor things—till after Christmas."

Riding to hounds would be good sport, if it were not for the fox. So long as the gallant little fellow is running for his life, excitement, one may hope, deadens his fear and pain. But the digging him out is cold-blooded cruelty. He ought to have his chance. How men and women, calling themselves sportsmen, can defend the custom passes my understanding. It is not clean.

As for the argument about the dogs, that is sheer twaddle. Is anybody going to tell me that my terrier will decline to chase rabbits on Tuesday, because the rabbit he ran after on Monday had the good luck to get away from him! I only wish it were so. Many a half-crown I'd have been saved, in my time.

I learnt riding with the Life Guards at Knightsbridge barracks. It was a rough school, but thorough. You were not considered finished until you could ride all your paces bareback, with the reins loose; and when the Sergeant-Major got hold of a horse with new tricks, he would put it aside for his favourite pupil.

"I've got a daisy for you, sir, this afternoon," he would whisper to you, his honest face illumined with a kindly grin. "As full of play as a litter of kittens. Look at her—she's laughing."

You looked. She would be standing with her head stretched out straight, and all her teeth showing. And you would wonder if the Sergeant-Major had noticed that, while he was patting her neck, you had slipped off your spurs and put them in your pocket.

There used to be a belt of well-kept grass along most country roads; and riding was a pleasant mode of taking a short journey. While for the joy of a stretch gallop on the turf, there were the commons. There was a fine straight course from the top of Nuffield Hill to Heath Bottom, across what are now the Huntercombe golf links. All the commons have been appropriated by the golfers; and the grass-way by the roadside is a tangle of briar and weed: and one comes across the old brown saddle in a corner of the loft, covered with cobwebs, and dreams of days gone by: as old men will.

The river must have been the mother of sport. Little brown-skinned picaninnies of the Stone Age must have played upon its banks; pushed each other in: splashed and shouted; learnt to swim and dive. Hairy, low-browed Palæolithic gentry must have crouched there with their fishing spears; launched their bark canoes. One day, some blue-eyed, lithe young cave man must have shouted that first challenge to a friendly race. Most of my life, I have dwelt in the neighbourhood of the river. I thank old Father Thames for many happy days. We spent our honeymoon, my wife and I, in a little boat. I knew the river well, its deep pools, and hidden ways, its quiet backwaters, its sleepy towns and ancient villages. It is pleasant to feel tired when evening comes and the lamp is lighted in the low-ceilinged parlour of the inn. We stayed a day at Henley for the Regatta.

It was King Edward who spoilt Henley Regatta. His coming turned it into a society function, and brought down the swell mob. Before that, it had been a happy, gay affair, simple and quiet. People came in craft of all sorts, and took an interest in the racing. One could count the people on the tow-path: old blues, the townsfolk, with the farmers and their families from round about. The line of house-boats, decked with flowers, stretched from Phyllis Court to the Island, and we all came to know one another. My nephew, Harry Shorland, brought his houseboat up from Staines by easy stages, one year. A pair of swallows had started building on it, and came with him all the way. They finished the nest just in time to take a day off, and watch the finals.

Goring Regatta was always good fun when Frank Benson, the actor, stage-managed it. He lived at Goring, and was an all-round sportsman. One year, his ambition ran away with him. He planned an aquatic drama. I am a little confused, regarding the details. I was at the time, I remember. The main idea was that a bevy of beauteous damsels—some half a dozen of them—had to be rescued from an island in mid-stream; and that time was the essence of the contract, as we say in the law. The mistake Benson made, in my opinion (and I was not the only one), was in arranging for the rescue to be made in a canoe. Myself, I should have given the young man a fishing punt, or one of those old-fashioned dinghies that ferrymen used to ply. The journey might have taken him longer, but time would have been saved in getting the lady on board and comfortably seated. The first young man dashed off at a terrific pace. His particular damsel was on the bank of the island, waiting for him, holding up her skirts. (They wore them, in those days.) Not a moment was to be lost. The husband—I think he was the husband: of the whole six, if I remember rightly—was already in sight. The gentleman, with one foot in the canoe and one foot on the island, held out his arms; and the lady sprang. Having said this much, I need hardly add that they both sat down in the water. Fortunately, the gentleman's right leg was still in the canoe. With great presence of mind, he dragged the lady on board and, stepping lightly over her, regained the opposite bank: where there was much cheering. The second lady may have been rendered nervous by seeing what had happened to the first. The general opinion was that, if she had kept her head, it might have been avoided; and that after all there are worse things than being soused in the river on a pleasant July afternoon. The remaining four ladies elected to be rescued by the umpire's launch.

Croquet is an irritating game; but a boon to cripples. I took it up when I was suffering from a broken ankle. The more you try, the worse you play. I know a man who never touches a mallet except once a year, when he enters for the county tournament, and carries off half the prizes. Children, before they are old enough to have known trouble, make good players. What the game seems to require is a thoughtless temperament. My eldest girl, at the age of about twelve, was a demon. She'd just whack round and hit everything. It used to make me mad. I remember being Lady Beresford's partner against Lord Charles and Miss Beresford. Three times that child croquetted her mother to the other end of the lawn, and then Lady Beresford—very properly, as it seemed to me—put an end to the atrocity.

"You do that again, my girl, and you go straight to bed," she told the child. Eventually, Lady Beresford and myself won that game.

Zangwill used to be keen on croquet, but never had the makings of a great player. Wells wasn't bad. Of course, he wanted to alter all the laws and make a new game of his own. I had to abandon my lawn, in the end. I had laid it out in the middle of a paddock where the farmer kept his young bulls. They couldn't resist the sight of the fresh green grass. I had fenced it round with barbed wire, but they made light of that. They would gather into a little group and confabulate, and then suddenly would lower their heads and charge. Sometimes they got through and sometimes they didn't: but it used to distract us. I remember a nightingale that would perch on one of the sticks and sing—often while we were playing. Nightingales love an audience. There was another that had his nest in a garden of ours by Marlow Common. Like the swallows, they return each year to the same loved spot. If one went to the gate and whistled, he would soon appear and, perching on the branch of an old thorn, sing for so long as one remained there, listening.

Chapter XI

AMERICA [1]

"How do you like America?"

"Oh," I said, "are we there?"

"Soon will be," he answered. "How do you pronounce your name?"

I told him. He repeated it louder, for the benefit of the others—some dozen of them, grouped around him. They made a note of it.

"What would you say was the difference between English and American humour?"

A chill north wind was blowing, and I hadn't had my breakfast. I did my best.

"These things," I said, "are a natural growth, springing from the soil. In England, to go no further back than Chaucer——" Nobody was listening. They were all busy writing. I wondered where they had come from. Out of the sea, apparently. I had been pacing the deck, scanning the horizon for my first sight of New York, and suddenly had found myself in the midst of them. Their spokesman was a thick-set, red-haired gentleman. He had a military manner. The rest were a mixed collection. Some of them looked to me to be mere boys.

"Say, can you tell us a story?" he questioned me.

I stared at him. "A story?" I repeated. "You want me to tell you a story?"

"Why, sure," he answered.

What on earth did they mean! Did they want me to start off and spin them a yarn, at a quarter to eight in the morning? And if so, was it to be adventure or romance, or just a simple love episode? I had a vision of being, perhaps, expected to sit down in the centre of them, taking the youngest of them on my knee.

He saw I was bewildered. "Anything happened to you on the voyage," he suggested, "anything interesting or amusing?"

I had the feeling of a condemned prisoner, reprieved at the last moment. In gratitude, I tried to think of something interesting and amusing that really might have happened to me. Given time, I could have done it. But they stood there waiting with their pencils poised, and I had to fall back upon the truth. I told them the only thing that had happened—that, three days out, we had sighted an iceberg. It was a silly little iceberg. I had mistaken it, myself, for a portion of a wreck; and a man who had been looking at it through a telescope had pronounced it to be a polar bear. If it had not been for the bartender, none of us would have known it was an iceberg. I made the most of it, describing how we had "run before it," and speaking highly of the Captain. It appeared in the evening papers under the heading, "The Ice Queen shows her Teeth."

We got on better after that. They saw that, at all events, I was trying. I told them how the American woman struck me—or rather how I felt sure she was going to strike me when I saw her; and gave them (by request) my opinion of Christopher Columbus, the American drama, the future of California, President Roosevelt and Elizabeth B. Parker. Who Elizabeth B. Parker was I have never discovered to this day; but that, I take it, is my fault. I gathered her to be one of America's then leading idols (they don't last long); and said that one of my objects in coming to America was to meet her. This seemed to give general satisfaction, and we parted friends.

I make no charge against the American interviewer. One takes the rough with the smooth. I have been described, within the same period of seven months, as a bald-headed elderly gentleman, with a wistful smile; a curly-haired athletic Englishman, remarkable for his youthful appearance; a rickety cigarette-smoking neurotic; and a typical John Bull. Some of them objected to my Oxford drawl; while others catalogued me as a cockney, and invariably quoted me as dropping my aitches. All of them noticed with unfeigned surprise that

I spoke English with an English accent. In the city of Prague, I once encountered a Bohemian ruffian who claimed to be a guide—a Czecho-Slovakian, I suppose he would be called to-day. He had learnt English in New York from a Scotchman. Myself, I could not understand him; but the New York interviewer would, I feel sure, have found in him his ideal Englishman. To anyone visiting America for a rest cure, I can see the American interviewer proving a thorn in the flesh. In pursuit of duty, he makes no bones about awakening you at two o'clock in the morning to ascertain your opinion of the local baseball team; and on arriving at your hotel, after a thirty-six hours' journey, you may find him waiting for you in your bedroom, accompanied by a flashlight photographer. But not many people, I take it, go to America for their health. At Pittsburgh, my wife woke with a sick headache, and I had to leave her behind me for a day or two. In the evening, better but still shaky, she dressed herself and slipped down into the lounge. Little black things were running about the floor. She thought they were kittens and tried to make friends with them, but they none of them would come to her. The place was poorly lighted, but there seemed to be about a score of them; sometimes more and sometimes less. The chambermaid looked in. She was an Irish girl. My wife drew her attention to these black kittens, as she thought them, commenting upon their shyness.

"Oh, they're not kittens," explained the chambermaid, "they're rats."

It seemed they came up from the kitchen, making use of the air shaft. If you did not interfere with them or tease them, they did you no harm.

It was a slack time and the girl, at my wife's earnestly expressed wish, brought in her sewing. The girl was full of stories about rats, but doubted their being as intelligent as it was said. Otherwise, so the girl argued, you would hardly find them in Pittsburgh.

"But you yourself are in Pittsburgh," said my wife, "and you told me yesterday you had been here six years."

The girl explained the seeming riddle. She hoped in another three years to have saved enough to be able to return to Ireland and settle down. She had pigs and a small holding in her mind, not unconnected with one named Dennis. Thousands of Irish girls, she assured my wife, came to America with similar intention. Not all of them, of course, succeeded, but it was long before they lost hope. It is the dream of every "Dago" to return to his native village and open a shop with dollars brought back from America. Nor is it only the hyphenated alien who looks forward to spending abroad money got out of the United States. In travelling about, I have discovered that all the best parts of Europe are inhabited by hundred-per-cent Americans. Sooner or later, it occurs to the English literary man that there is money to be made out of lecturing in America. But without the American interviewer to boom us in advance, and work up the local excitement for us when we arrive, we would return with empty pockets. For what I have received in the way of lecturing fees out of America the Lord make me truly thankful to the American interviewer: and may his sins be forgot.

The most impressive thing in America is New York. Niagara disappointed me. I had some trouble in finding it. The tram conductor promised to let me know when we came to the proper turning, but forgot; and I had to walk back three blocks. I came across it eventually at the bottom of a tea garden, belonging to a big hotel. My tour did not permit me to visit the Yellowstone Park. But I saw the Garden of the Gods in Colorado, and it struck me as neglected. The Rockies are imposing, but lack human interest. The Prairies are depressing. One has the feeling of being a disembodied spirit, travelling through space, and growing doubtful as to one's destination. To the European, what America suffers from is there being too much of it. In Switzerland, one winter, I met a man from Indianapolis. We were looking out of the window on our way to Grindelwald.

"This would be quite an extensive country," he said, "if it were rolled out flat."

In America everything seems to have been sacrificed to making an extensive country. In Arizona, they point out to you the mirage; but to the stranger it still looks like salt. The American lakes are seas surrounded by railways. In New Orleans, there are old-world nooks and corners, but these are disappearing. The first thing they do with you in New Orleans is to take you a drive through the cemeteries. There are miles and miles of them. You go in a char-à-banc, and the gentleman with the megaphone draws your attention to the most important tombs. "Seeing New Orleans" they call it.

California is beautiful (one can forget the "movies"). I was in San Francisco the week before the earthquake. My wife and I were the guests of Bancroft, the historian. I shall never forget the kindness of himself and his sweet wife. He took us drives into the country behind two grand grey horses. He was a splendid whip. One afternoon, he proposed an excursion down into the town: "But we will leave your dear little lady to rest herself," he said. And, later, I understood and was grateful to him. It was a curious experience. During the war, round Verdun, I came across roads that reminded me of that drive. Every few yards we went down into a hole and often it took the horses all their strength to pull us out. I asked if there had been an earthquake; but my host said no. For years the roads had never been repaired, the mayor and corporation ("Grafters" they are termed in America) having found another use for the money.

In Florida, one seems to have dropped back into antediluvian times, or, to be more exact, the third day of the Creation, before God had quite finished separating the dry land from the waters, and creeping things sat about, wondering which they were.

Virginia has an atmosphere and speaks English; but the new towns in the Middle states, with their painted canvas "Broadways," suggest a Wild West exhibition at Earl's Court. One looks instinctively for the sign-board, pointing to the switchback. Here and there, New England reminds one of the old country. I forget who it was said he would like to come back and see America when it was finished. One has the fancy that, returning in a thousand years or so, one might find there little cottages standing in gay gardens; pleasant rambling houses amid soft lawns and kindly trees. But there will never rise the clustering chimneys with the blue smoke curling upward. America will still be central-heated. I missed the friendly chimneys. Elsewhere in America, there is no country. There are summer resorts, and garden cities, and health centres; and just outside the great towns long avenues of "homes," each on its parallelogram of land. The larger ones have verandahs and towers and gables; and the smaller ones are painted red. They told me that the reason why all the houses in America are painted red was that the Trust made red paint only. You can paint your house red or leave it alone, according to your taste and fancy. In America, a man who wants to paint his house any other colour than red is called a radical. America never walks. I am told that now every fifth American owns an automobile and the other four crowd in. In my time, you took a surface car. I used to dream of going for a walk, and when I asked my way, they would direct me to go straight on till I came to nine hundred and ninety-ninth street—or some such number—and there I would find the car.

"But I want to walk," I would explain.

"Well, I'm telling you," they would reply, "you walk to the end of the block. The car starts from round the corner."

"But I don't want the car," I would persist. "I want to walk—all the way."

Then they would dive into their pocket and press a twenty-five cent piece into my hand and hurry off to catch their own car.

But New York reminds you of nothing, suggests no comparison. New York is America epitomized: fierce, tireless, blatant if you will, but great. Nature stands abashed before it. The sea crawls round it, dwarfed, insignificant. Trees, like waving grasses, spring from its crevices. The clouds are rent upon its pinnacles.

It strikes a new note. Behind the mere bigness is a new idea: something that you feel is tremendously important. You worry for a time, wondering. And then suddenly it springs upon you. In London, Paris, Rome— go where you will in the old world it is the great cathedral, the spires of a hundred churches, the minarets, towers, domes, the theatres and palaces that pierce the sky-line: that rise serene above the market place, the byways of the money-changers. In New York it is Business Triumphant that towers to heaven, dominating, unchallenged. The skyscraper alone is visible. Religion, art: they have their hiding-places, round its feet.

In a town of the middle west, a kind man put me up. He was rich and had one child, a daughter Margaret, who was the apple of his eye. She was twelve years old at the time. She had her own banking account, and drew her own cheques. I remember a conversation between them one evening. He had just returned home from his office; and she had fetched him his house shoes and was sitting on his knee.

"I brought off a good stroke of business to-day, Maggie," he said to her, while stroking her hair. "So I paid five thousand dollars into your account. How do you propose to invest it?"

The child sat for a while with puckered brows, one arm about his neck.

"Well," she answered at length, "if, as the papers say, there is going to be a famine in Russia this winter, hadn't I better put it into wheat?"

He kissed her.

"That's right," he answered. "I'll fix it up for you in the morning."

I have made three American tours. It was offered to me to make a fourth just after the war. My agent assured me there would be no difficulty about drinks; but there were other reasons also, and I shirked it. The first must be twenty years ago by now. That it was not as profitable to me as it might have been was my own fault. Never in my life have I felt so lost and lonesome as during my first days in New York. Everything was so strange, so appallingly "foreign." I had never been outside Europe before. Never, so it seemed to me, would I be able to adapt myself to the ways and customs of the country. And then there was the language problem. In Vevey, on Lake Leman, there sits cross-legged—or used to sit—a smiling small Italian shoeblack: behind him on the wall a placard with this wording, "English spoken—American understood." I thought of him, as I wandered bewildered through the New York streets, and wondered how long it had taken him.

At the end of a fortnight, I cabled what would now be called an S.O.S. to my wife, and she, gallant little lady, came to my help.

And she it was who persuaded me to further extravagance, as is the way of women. Major Pond, or rather his good widow, had booked me a stupendous tour. It took in every state in the Union, together with Canada and British Columbia. Five readings a week, the average worked out; each to last an hour and twenty minutes. I showed my wife the list. She said nothing at the time, but went about behind my back, and got round my agents. Among them, they decided that, to avoid a funeral, I had best have help; and found one Charles

Battell Loomis. He was, I think, the ugliest man I have met. But that was only the outside of him. All the rest of him was beautiful; and sad I am to have to speak of him in the past tense. Through him, I came to know the other America—the America of the dreamers, the thinkers, the idealists. He took me to see them in their shabby clubs; to dine with them in their fifty-cent restaurants; to spend fine Sundays with them in their wooden shanties, far away where the tram-lines end. He was a wonderful actor, but had never been able to afford a press agent. His writings, as scattered through the magazines, were mildly amusing, but that was all. Until he stood up before an audience and read them: when at once they became the most humorous stories in American literature. He made no gestures; his face, but for the eyes, might have been carved out of wood; his genius was in his marvellous voice. His least whisper could be heard across the largest hall. He had to be careful when using the telephone. Once, when I was with him, a Hello girl irritated even him after a time and, forgetting himself, he shouted "No, I didn't." There was no answer. After a while the bell boy knocked at the door to suggest that if we wanted to go on talking we had better come downstairs. For some reason or another, our telephone had suddenly gone out of order.

I envied him. The lecturer through America has to cultivate adaptability. For one night a rich man would hire us to read to his guests in a drawing-room. He was always very kind, and would make us feel part of the party. The next evening we would find ourselves booked to perform in a hall the size of Solomon's Temple, taking Mr. H. G. Wells' figures as correct. There was a "Coliseum," I think they called it, down South. I forget the name of the town. But I am sure it was down South, because of the cotton that floated on the wind, and turned our hair grey. Even Loomis had found the place difficult. The first few dozen rows must have heard him. Anyhow they laughed. But beyond and above brooded the silence of the grave. By rare chance, we had a few hours to spare the next morning; and coming across the place I stepped in, wondering how it looked in daylight. Men were busy hauling scenery about. It served for all purposes—mass meetings, theatrical performances, religious revivals, prize fights. On one wet fourth of July, a display of fireworks had been given there with great success. A small lady in black was standing just inside the door, likewise inspecting. It was Sarah Bernhardt. She was billed to play there that evening. She was finishing a tour with a few one-night stands, and had been travelling all night. She recognized me, though we had met only once before, at a Lyceum supper in Irving's time.

"My God!" she said, throwing up her arms. "Why, it's as deep as hell. How do they expect me to reach them?"

"They don't," I told her. "They want to see you, that's all. They are a curious people, these Americans. They paid last night to see me. They must have known they would not hear me."

"But they will not see her," she answered. "They will see only a little old woman. I am not Sarah Bernhardt until I act. It would be a swindle."

"Well, isn't that their affair?" I suggested.

She drew herself up. She was quite tall when she had finished—or looked it.

"No, my friend," she answered, "it is mine. Sarah Bernhardt is a great artist. And I am her faithful servant. They shall not make a show of her."

She held out her hand. "Please do not tell anyone that you have seen me," she said. She drew down her veil and slipped out.

What actually happened I do not know. They were posting notices up when we left, announcing with regret Madame Sarah Bernhardt's sudden indisposition.

I have always found American audiences most kind. Their chief fault is that they see the point before you get there, which is disconcerting. One morning I woke up speechless with a sudden cold. I could not even use the 'phone. I telegraphed to my chairman, explaining, and asking him to call the reading off. In half-an-hour the answer came back: "Sorry you won't be able to read but do come or it will be a real disappointment to us we want to see you and thank you for the pleasure your books have given us as for fee that has been posted to your agent and is too unimportant a matter to be talked about among friends."

I went and had a delightful evening. They put me in the middle of the room and entertained me. We had music and songs and stories. I whispered a few to my chairman, and he translated them. They turned the whole thing into a joke. At the end, one of them, a doctor, gave me a draught to take in bed. I wish I had asked him what it was. My cold was gone the next morning.

At Salt Lake City, we ought to have arrived with an hour to spare, instead of which our train was three hours late. A deputation met us on the platform with hot coffee and sandwiches. They put us into cabs and took us straight to the platform. An audience of three thousand people had been waiting patiently for two hours. Our chairman, in his opening, apologized to us for the train service; and asked everybody to agree that, as we must be tired, we should be asked to read for only half-an-hour, unless we felt ourselves equal to more. Both Loomis and myself felt bucked up, and gave them the full programme. Not one of them left before the end, which must have been about twelve o'clock; and if they didn't like it they were good actors.

A leading Elder put us up in Salt Lake City. He introduced us to his wife. He noticed I was looking expectant.

"There are no more," he explained. He put his arm round her. "The modern American woman," he continued, "has convinced us that one wife is sufficient for any man."

I was told that domestic establishments on a more generous basis still existed; but they were rare; and later on the law put an end to them.

It is difficult to know what your audience really thinks of you. Even if bored, I feel convinced they would pretend to be enjoying themselves. There are times when hypocrisy can he a virtue. But hidden behind a newspaper in a smoking car, I once overheard praise of myself.

"Were you at the lecture last night?" asked one man of another.

"Yes," came the answer in a soft, low, drawling voice. "The wife thought she'd like to go. I'd never heard of him myself."

"What was he like?"

"Well"—there was a pause. I guessed he was fixing a plug of tobacco—"for an Englishman—good."

Once only—at Chattanooga—did I meet with disagreement: and then I was asking for it. Two negroes had been lynched a few days before my arrival on the usual charge of having assaulted a white woman: proved afterwards (as is generally the case) to have been a trumped-up lie. All through the South, this lynching horror had been following me; and after my reading I asked for permission to speak on a matter about which my conscience was troubling me. I didn't wait to get it, but went straight on. At home, on political platforms, I have often experienced the sensation of stirring up opposition. But this was something different. I do not suggest it was anything more than fancy, but it seemed to me that I could actually visualize the anger of my audience. It looked like a dull, copper-coloured cloud, hovering just above their heads, and growing in size. I sat down amid silence. It was quite a time before anybody moved. And then they all got up at the same moment, and turned towards the door. On my way out, in the lobby, a few people came up to me and thanked me, in a hurried furtive manner. My wife was deadly pale. I had not told her of my intention. But nothing happened, and I cannot help thinking that if the tens of thousands of decent American men and women to whom this thing must be their country's shame, would take their courage in both hands and speak their mind, America might be cleansed from this foul sin.

American hospitality is proverbial. If I had taken the trouble to arrange matters beforehand, I could have travelled all over America without once putting up at an hotel. Had I known what they were like, I would have made the effort. In the larger cities they are generally of palatial appearance. If their cooking and attendance were on a par with their architecture and appointments, there would be no fault to find with them. But often I have thought how gladly I would exchange all the Parian marble in my bathroom, all the silver fittings in my dressing-room, for a steak I could cut with a knife. It appears from the statistics of the Immigration Bureau that there arrive every year in the United States well over four thousand professional cooks. What happens to them is a mystery. They can't all become film stars.

On the great routes, European customs prevail; but in the smaller towns, hotels are still run on what is termed the "American plan." A few days after landing in New York, I went to Albany to give a reading. I was due on the platform at eight. I did not have any lunch. I thought I would dine early and afterwards sit quiet. I put out my clothes and came downstairs. The dining-room was empty. There didn't seem to be any bell. I found the gentleman who had sent me up to my room. He was sitting in a rocking-chair, reading a newspaper.

"I beg your pardon," I said. "But are you the hotel clerk?"

"Yup," he grunted and went on reading.

"I am sorry to disturb you," I continued, "but I want the head waiter."

"What do you want him for?" he said. "Friend of yours?"

"No," I answered, "I want to order dinner."

He was still reading his newspaper. "You haven't got to order it," he said. "It will be ready at half-past six."

"But I want it now," I said. The time was a little after four.

He put down his paper and looked at me.

"Say, where do you come from?" he asked me.

"I have come from New York," I answered him.

"You ain't been even there long," he commented. "Englishman, aren't you?"

I admitted it.

He rose and laid a kindly hand on my shoulder.

"You run along and take a look round the town," he said. "Interesting city. Anyhow, there's nothing else for you to do, till half-past six."

I followed his advice. It wasn't really an interesting city. Or maybe I was not in the mood. At six o'clock I came back and dressed. I was feeling hungry. When I saw the "menu" I felt hungrier still. It would have made Lucullus sit up and smile. It covered two closely written pages, and contained, so far as I could judge, every delicacy in and out of season.

I order caviare and clam soup, to open with. I was doubtful about the clam soup, being new to it. But if too rich, I could just toy with it. The waiter, a youthful gentleman who apparently had mislaid his coat, remained standing.

"I'll think of the next thing to follow," I said, "while you are getting that."

"Better think of it now," he said. "We haven't got the time to spare over here that you have in the old country."

I did not want to antagonize him. I took up the menu again. I ordered whitebait to follow the soup. I told him I liked them crisp. A slice of broiled ham with truffles. Peas in butter. Lamb cutlet with tomatoes. Asparagus. Chicken (I mentioned I preferred the wing). A caramel ice cream. Dessert, assorted. Coffee, of course, to finish up with.

I was sorry to miss all the rest; but I had to think of my lecture. Even as it was I feared I had overdone it.

"That all?" asked the coatless young gentleman.

I thought he meant to be sarcastic, and put a touch of asperity into my tone.

"That is the order," I said.

He was gone longer than I had expected. When he reappeared he was carrying a sort of butler's tray. He put it down in front of me, straightened out the four sides and left me.

There was everything on it—everything I had ordered, beginning with the caviare and ending with the coffee. All the things (except the soup and the coffee) were on little white saucers, all the same size. The whole thing suggested a doll's tea party. The soup was in a little white pot with a handle. That also might have been part of the furnishing of a doll's house. One drank it out of the pot—about a tablespoonful altogether. There were six whitebait and one shrimp. Thirteen peas. Three ends of asparagus. Five grapes and four nuts (assorted). Two square inches of ham, but no truffle: the thing I took for the truffle turned out to be a dead fly. The lamb cutlet I could not place. I fancy they must have given me the wrong end. The tomato I lost trying to cut it. It rolled off the table and I hadn't the heart to follow it up. For some reason or another they had fried the chicken. I did my best, but had to put it back. It didn't look any different. I wondered afterwards what happened to it.

I suppose it was not having had any lunch. If I had been by myself, I'd have put my head down on the tray and have cried. But three or four other men were feeding near me and I pulled myself together. I started with the coffee. It was still lukewarm. It seemed a pity to let it get quite cold. The caviare did not appeal to me. It may have been the smell. After the coffee, I tackled the ice cream, which by that time was already half melted. I stole a glance at my companions. None of them were bothering about a knife. They were just picking up things with a fork, first from one saucer and then from another. Somehow they suggested the idea of mechanical chickens. But it seemed the simplest plan and I followed their example.

I never got used to it. Natives, to whom occasionally I talked upon the subject, admitted that, considered as an art, the "European plan" of dining might be preferable; but would hasten to explain that America was "too busy"—the spry American citizen had not the time for all these social monkey tricks. I would leave them, settling themselves into their rocking-chairs, ranged round the hotel lounge, preparing to light their cigars and shape their plugs of tobacco. On my return some two or three hours later, they would still be there, smoking and spitting.

America can be proud of her railways. An American train with its majestic engine and its thousand feet of steel cars, is a fine sight. Always, we were glad to get into them, away from the comfortless hotels where one is harassed by the bell boy, bullied by the waiter, and patronized by the clerk. The darky porter welcomes one with a smile, and is not above being courteous. It is only in the dining-car that one can hope for a decently cooked meal. In the sleeping-car there is no telephone over one's bed, no patent improved radiator to go wrong, and keep one awake all night. There are stretches where for miles one can look out of the window without being pestered with advertisements. But one knows one is nearing a town by the hoardings each side of the track. The magnificent approach to San Francisco is spoilt by twenty miles of boards, advertising somebody's stores. "Carter's Little Liver Pills" does the same thing in England, to a lesser degree. I used to find them helpful, but have given up taking them, myself. At a Rotary dinner in London Mr. Carter (not to be personal) made quite a good speech on the subject of how one could best serve God. Anthony Hope suggested that one way might be not to mar God's landscapes with advertisement signs. In New York, I was arrested by a notice in a shop window. It ran: "Come unto me, all ye that labour and are heavy laden, and I will give you rest." It was an advertisement for somebody's spring mattress. Except on a few main routes, punctuality is rare. There is excuse. The distances are enormous. The permanent ways are still in the making. Nature plays her tricks upon them. One does not bother about time-tables—the "schedule" as they call it. One waits until the message is sent round the town from the depôt that the train is signalled. One day, to my amazement, my train came in on time. It was at a junction. I had just got out of the branch train and was wondering what I would do with myself. The station-master was passing by.

"Any notion when she is likely to turn up," I asked him—"the 11.33 for Sioux Falls?" It was then a minute past the half hour.

"Hurry up," he said, "she's coming in now."

She glided in as he was speaking, and drew up with a soft low sigh as of self-satisfied content. He was a big, genial man. He looked at my face and laughed.

"It's all right," he said. "To be quite candid, this is yesterday's train."

Sioux Falls, by the way, is—or was then—the centre of the American divorce trade. The hotels were filled with gorgeous ladies waiting their turn: many of them accompanied by "brothers." It was a merry crowd. Three ladies, a mother and her two daughters, the younger just seventeen, sat at the table next to us and were friendly. The mother had been divorced before, but the two girls were new to it. They expected to be through by the end of the week.

Roosevelt was President at the time of my first tour; and was kind enough to express a wish to see me. By a curious coincidence, he had received that morning a letter from his son, then at school, talking about my books. He had the letter in his hand when we were shown in. Somewhat the same thing happened the first time I met Lloyd George. A relation had written him, a day or two before, urging him to read my last book. He was then in the middle of it. I couldn't get him to talk about anything else. There was a delightful boyishness about Roosevelt. You were bound to like him if he wanted you to. My wife has still the gloves in which she shook hands with him. They lie in her treasure box, tied with a ribbon and labelled.

Joel Chandler Harris ("Uncle Remus") lives in my memory. A sweet Christian gentleman; even if he did spit. We spent an afternoon with him at Atlanta. Frank Stanton dropped in, and brought with him a volume of his songs which he had dedicated to me. James Whitcomb Riley was kind and hospitable, but made me envious, talking about the millions his books had brought him in.

I was in America when Maxim Gorky came to lecture upon Russia. He was accompanied by a helpmeet to whom he had not been legally married. America is strict on this point. So was Henry VIII. At a Press lunch in Chicago, I sat next to a man who that morning had published a leader, fiercely demanding the immediate shipping back to Europe of Maxim Gorky and his "concubine." America must not be contaminated and so forth. A few evenings before he had introduced Loomis and myself to his mistress, a pretty Swedish girl with flaxen hair. His wife was living abroad, the air of Chicago not agreeing with her. I admit the sign-post argument. I have found it useful myself. But in America there would appear to be almost more sign-posts than travellers. I have been about a good deal in America. My business has necessitated my spending much time in smoking-cars and hotel lounges. My curiosity has always prompted me to find out all I could about my fellow human beings wherever I have happened to be. I maintain that the

American man, taking him class for class and individual for individual, is no worse than any of the rest of us. I will ask his permission to leave it at that.

The last time I visited America was during the first year of the war. America then was all for keeping out of it. I had friends in big business, and was introduced to others. Their opinion was that America could best serve Humanity in the bulk by reserving herself to act as peace-maker. In the end, she would be the only nation capable of considering the future without passion and without fear. The general feeling was, if anything, pro-German, tempered in the East by traditional sentiment for France. I failed to unearth any enthusiasm for England, in spite of my having been commissioned to discover it. I have sometimes wondered if England and America really do love one another as much as our journalists and politicians say they do. I had an interesting talk with President Wilson, chiefly about literature and the drama. But I did get him, before I left, to say a little about the war; and then he dropped the schoolmaster and became animated.

"We have in America," he said, "twenty million people of German descent. Almost as many Irish. In New York State alone there are more Italians than in Rome. We have more Scandinavians than there are in Sweden. Here, side by side, dwell Czechs, Roumanians, Slavs, Poles and Dutchmen. We also have some Jews. We have solved the problem of living together without wanting to cut one another's throats. You will have to learn to do the same in Europe. We shall have to teach you."

Undoubtedly at that time Wilson was intending to remain neutral. Whether his later change of mind brought about good or evil is an arguable point. But for America the war would have ended in stalemate. All Europe would have been convinced of the futility of war. "Peace without Victory"—the only peace containing any possibility of permanence would have resulted.

To the democrat, America is the Great Disappointment. Material progress I rule out. Beyond a certain point, it tends to enslave mankind. For spiritual progress, America seems to have no use. Mr. Ford has pointed out that every purchaser of a Ford car can have it delivered to him, painted any colour he likes, so long as it's black. Mr. Ford expresses in a nutshell the mental attitude of modern America. Every man in America is free to do as he darn well pleases so long as, for twenty-four hours a day, he does what everybody else is doing. Every man in America is free to speak his mind so long as he shouts with the crowd. He has not even Mr. Pickwick's choice of choosing his crowd. In America there is but one crowd. Every man in America has the right to think for himself so long as he thinks what he is told. If not—like the heretics of the middle ages—let him see to it that his chamber door is locked, that his tongue does not betray him. The Ku Klux Klan, with its travelling torture chamber, is but the outward and visible sign of the spirit of modern America. Thought in

America is standardized. America is not taking new wine, lest the old bottles be broken.

I ask my American friends—and I have many, I know—to forgive me. Who am I to lecture the American nation?—I feel, myself, the absurdity of it—the impertinence. My plea is that I am growing old. And it comes to me that before long I may be called upon to stand before the Judge of all the earth, and to make answer, concerning the things that I have done and—perhaps of even more importance—the things that I have left undone. The thought I am about to set down keeps ringing in my brain. It will not go away. I am afraid any longer to keep silence. There are many of power and authority who could have spoken it better. I would it had not been left to me. If it make men angry, I am sorry.

The treatment of the negro in America calls to Heaven for redress. I have sat with men who, amid vile jokes and laughter, told of "Buck Niggers" being slowly roasted alive; told how they screamed and writhed and prayed; how their eyes rolled inward as the flames crept up till nothing could be seen but two white balls. They burn mere boys alive and sometimes women. These things are organized by the town's "leading citizens." Well-dressed women crowd to the show, children are lifted up upon their fathers' shoulders. The Law, represented by grinning policemen, stands idly by. Preachers from their pulpits glorify these things, and tell their congregation that God approves. The Southern press roars its encouragement. Hangings, shootings would be terrible enough. These burnings; these slow grillings of living men, chained down to iron bedsteads; these tearings of live, quivering flesh with red-hot pinchers can be done only to glut some hideous lust of cruelty. The excuse generally given is an insult to human intelligence. Even if true, it would be no excuse. In the majority of cases, it is not even pretended. The history of the Spanish Inquisition unrolls no greater shame upon the human race. The Auto-da-fé at least, was not planned for the purpose of amusing a mob. In the face of this gigantic horror, the lesser sufferings of the negro race in America may look insignificant. But there must be tens of thousands of educated, cultured men and women cursed with the touch of the tar-brush to whom life must be one long tragedy. Shunned, hated, despised, they have not the rights of a dog. From no white man dare they even defend the honour of their women. I have seen them waiting at the ticket offices, the gibe and butt of the crowd, not venturing to approach till the last white man was served. I have known a woman in the pains of childbirth made to travel in the cattle wagon. For no injury at the hands of any white man is there any redress. American justice is not colour blind. Will the wrong never end?

Chapter XII

THE WAR

One of my earliest recollections is of myself seated on a shiny chair from which I had difficulty in not slipping, listening to my father and mother and a large, smiling gentleman talking about Peace. There were to be no more wars. It had all been settled at a place called Paree. The large gentleman said Paris. But my mother explained to me, afterwards, that it meant the same. My father and my mother, so I gathered, had seen a gentleman named Napoleon, and had fixed it up. The large gentleman said, with a smile, that it didn't look much like it, just at present. But my father waved his hand. Nothing could be done all at once. One prepared the ground, so to speak.

"The young men, now coming forward," said my mother, "they will see to it."

I remember feeling a little sad at the thought that there would be no more war—that, coming too late into the world, I had missed it. My mother sought to comfort me by talking about the heavenly warfare which was still to be had for the asking. But, in my secret heart, it seemed to me a poor substitute.

With the coming of the Alabama claim things looked brighter. My father, then President of the Poplar branch of the International Peace Association, shook his head over America's preposterous demands. There were limits even to England's love of Peace.

Later on, we did have a sort of war. Nothing very satisfying: one had to make the best of it: against a King Theodore, I think, a sort of a nigger. I know he made an excellent Guy Fawkes. Also he did atrocities, I remember.

At this period France was "The Enemy." We boys always shouted "Froggy" whenever we saw anyone who looked like a foreigner. Crécy and Poitiers were our favourite battles. The "King of Prussia," in a three-cornered hat and a bob-tailed wig, swung and creaked in front of many a public-house.

I was at school when France declared war against Prussia in 1870. Our poor old French Master had a bad time of it. England, with the exception of a few cranks, was pro-German. But when it was all over: France laid low, and the fear of her removed: our English instinct to sympathize always with the underdog—not a bad trait in us—asserted itself; and a new Enemy had to be found.

We fixed on Russia.

Russia had designs on India. The Afghan War was her doing. I was an actor at the time. We put on a piece called "The Khyber Pass"—at Ashley's, if I remember rightly. I played a mule. It was before the Griffith Brothers introduced their famous donkey. I believe, if I had been given a free hand, I could have made the little beast amusing. But our stage-manager said he didn't want any of my damned clowning. It had to be a real mule, the pet of the regiment. At the end, I stood on my hind legs, and waved the British flag. Lord Roberts patted my head, and the audience took the roof off, nearly.

I was down on my luck when the Russo-Turkish War broke out. There were hopes at first that we might be drawn into it. I came near to taking the Queen's shilling. I had slept at a doss-house the night before, and had had no breakfast. A sergeant of Lancers stopped me in Trafalgar Square. He put his hands on my shoulders and punched my chest.

"You're not the first of your family that's been a soldier," he said. "You'll like it."

It was a taking uniform: blue and silver with high Hession boots. The advantages of making soldiers look like mud had not then been discovered.

"I'm meeting a man at the Bodega," I said. "If he isn't there I'll come straight back."

He was there; though I hadn't expected him. He took me with him to a Coroner's inquest, and found a place for me at the reporter's table. So, instead, I became a journalist.

The music-hall was the barometer of public opinion in those days. Politicians and even Cabinet Ministers would often slip in for an hour. MacDermott was our leading Lion Comique. One night he sang a new song: "We don't want to fight, but by Jingo if we do." Whatever happened, the Russians should not have Con-stan-ti-no-ple, the "no" indefinitely prolonged. It made a furore. By the end of the week, half London was singing it. Also it added the word Jingo to the English language.

Peace meetings in Hyde Park were broken up, the more fortunate speakers getting off with a ducking in the Serpentine. The Peacemonger would seem to be always with us. In peace-time we shower palm leaves upon him. In war-time we hand him over to the mob. I remember seeing Charles Bradlaugh, covered with blood and followed by a yelling crowd. He escaped into Oxford Street and his friends got him away in a cart. Gladstone had his windows broken.

And, after all, we never got so much as a look in. "Peace with Honour," announced Disraeli; and immediately rang down the curtain. We had expected a better play from Disraeli.

To console us, there came trouble in Egypt. Lord Charles Beresford was the popular hero. We called him Charlie. The Life Guards were sent out. I remember their return. It was the first time London had seen them without their helmets and breastplates. Lean, worn-looking men on skeleton horses. The crowd was disappointed. But made up for it in the evening.

And after that there was poor General Gordon and Majuba Hill. It may have been the other way round. Some of us blamed Gladstone and the Nonconformist conscience. Others thought we were paying too much attention to cricket and football, and that God was angry with us. Greece declared war on Turkey. Poetical friends of mine went out to fight for Greece; but spent most of their time looking for the Greek army, and when they found it didn't know it, and came home again. There were fresh massacres of Armenians. I was editing a paper called *To-day*, and expressed surprise that no healthy young Armenian had tried to remove "Abdul the damned," as William Watson afterwards called him. My paragraph reached him, by some means or another, and had the effect of frightening the old horror. I had not expected such luck. The Turkish Constitution used to be described as: "Despotism tempered by assassination." Under the old régime, the assassin, in Turkey, took the place of our Leader of the Opposition. Every Turkish Sultan lived in nightly dread of him. I was hauled up to the Foreign Office. A nice old gentleman interviewed me.

"Do you know," he said, "that you have rendered yourself liable to prosecution?"

"Well, prosecute me," I suggested. Quite a number of us were feeling mad about this thing.

He was getting irritable.

"All very well, for you to talk like that," he snapped. "Just the very way to get it home into every corner of Europe. They can't be wanting that."

The "they" I gathered to be the Turkish Embassy people.

"I am sorry," I said. "I don't seem able to help you."

He read to me the Act of Parliament, and we shook hands and parted. I heard no more of the matter.

It was about this time that America made war upon Spain. We, ourselves, had just had a shindy with America over some God-forsaken place called Venezuela, and popular opinion was if anything pro-Spanish. The American papers were filled with pictures of Spanish atrocities, in the time of Philip II. It seemed the Spaniards had the habit of burning people alive at the stake. Could such a nation be allowed to continue in possession of Cuba?

The Fashoda incident was hardly unexpected. For some time past, France had been steadily regaining her old position of "The Enemy." Over the Dreyfus case it occurred to us to tell her what we thought of her, generally. In return, she mentioned one or two things she didn't like about us. There was great talk of an Entente with Germany. Joe Chamberlain started the idea. The popular Press, seized with a sudden enthusiasm for the study of history, discovered we were of Teutonic origin. Also it unearthed a saying of Nelson's to the effect that every Englishman should hate a Frenchman like the Devil. A society was formed for the promotion of amicable relationship between the English and the German-speaking people. "Friends of Germany" I think it was called. I remember receiving an invitation to join it, from Conan Doyle. An elderly Major, in Cairo, who had dined too well, tore down the French flag, and performed upon it a new dance of his own invention. This was, I believe, the origin of the Fox-trot. One of the Northcliffe papers published a *feuilleton*, picturing the next war: England—her Navy defeated by French submarines—was saved, just in the nick of time, by the arrival of the German Fleet.

The Boer War was not popular at first. The gold mines were so obviously at the bottom of it. Still, it was a war, even if only a sort of a war, as the late Lord Halsbury termed it. A gentleman named Perks resigned from the Presidency of the Peace Society, in order to devote himself to war work. Other members followed his example. There were Boer atrocities. But they were badly done and, for a while, fell flat.

It was the Kaiser's telegram that turned the wind. I was in Germany at the time, and feeling was high against the English. We had a party one evening, at which some Dutch ladies were present—relations of De Wet, we learnt afterwards. I remember in the middle of the party, our Dienstmädchen suddenly appearing and shouting "Hoch die Buren," and immediately bursting into tears. She explained to my wife, afterwards, that she couldn't help it—that God had prompted her. I have noticed that trouble invariably follows when God appears to be interesting Himself in foreign politics.

In France it was no better. Indeed, worse. In Paris, the English were hooted in the street, and hunted out of the cafés. I got through by talking with a strong American accent that I had picked up during a lecturing tour through the States. Queen Victoria was insulted in the French Press. *The Daily Mail* came out with a leader headed "Ne touchez pas la Reine," suggesting that if France did not mend her manners we should "roll her in the mud," take away her Colonies, and give them to Germany. The Kaiser had explained away his famous telegram. It seemed he didn't really mean it. In a speech at the Vagabonds' Club, I suggested that God, for some unrevealed purpose of His own, had fashioned even Boers, and was denounced the next morning in the Press for blasphemy.

At the time, there was much discussion throughout Europe as to when the twentieth century really began. The general idea was that it was going to bring us luck. France was decidedly reforming. On the other hand, Germany was "dumping" things upon us. She was dumping her goods not only in England, but in other countries, where hitherto we had been in the habit of dumping ours, undisturbed. After a time we got angry.

There was talk of an Entente with France, who wasn't dumping anything—who hadn't much to dump. The comic papers took it up. France was represented to us as a Lady, young and decidedly attractive. Germany as a fat elderly gentleman, with pimples and his hair cropped close. How could a gentlemanly John Bull hesitate for a moment between them!

Russia also, it appeared, had been misunderstood. Russia wasn't half as bad as we had thought her: anyhow, she didn't dump.

And then, out of sheer cussedness as it seemed, Germany, in feverish haste, went on building ships.

Even the mildest among us agreed that Britannia could tolerate no rival on the waves. It came out that Germany was building four new cruisers. At once we demanded eight. We made a song about it.

"We want eight, And we won't wait."

It was sung at all the by-elections. The Peace parties won moral victories.

Sir Edward Grey has been accused of having "jockeyed" us into the war—of having so committed us to France and Russia that no honourable escape was possible for us. Had the Good Samaritan himself been our Foreign Secretary, the war would still have happened. Germany is popularly supposed to have brought us into it by going through Belgium. Had she gone round by the Cape of Good Hope, the result would have been the same. The Herd instinct had taken possession of us all. It was sweeping through Europe. I was at a country tennis tournament the day we declared war on Germany. Young men and maidens, grey-moustached veterans, pale-faced curates, dear old ladies: one and all expressed relief and thankfulness. "I was so afraid Grey would climb down at the last moment"—"It was Asquith I was doubtful of. I didn't think the old man had the grit"—"Thank God, we shan't read 'Made in Germany' for a little time to come." Such was the talk over the tea-cups.

It was the same whichever way you looked. Railway porters, cabmen, workmen riding home upon their bicycles, farm labourers eating their bread and cheese beside the hedge: they had the faces of men to whom good tidings had come.

For years it had been growing, this instinct that Germany was "The Enemy." In the beginning we were grieved. It was the first time in history she had been called upon to play the part. But that was her fault. Why couldn't she leave us alone—cease interfering with our trade, threatening our command of the sea? Quite nice people went about saying: "We're bound to have a scrap with her. Hope it comes in my time"—"Must put her in her place. We'll get on all the better with her afterwards." That was the idea everywhere: that war would clear the air, make things pleasanter all round, afterwards. A party, headed by Lord Roberts, clamoured for conscription.

Another party, headed by Lord Fisher, proposed that we should seize the German Fleet and drown it. Books and plays came out one on top of another warning us of the German menace. Kipling wrote, openly proclaiming Germany, The Foe, first and foremost.

In Germany, I gather from German friends, similar thinking prevailed. It was England that, now secretly, now openly, was everywhere opposing a blank wall to German expansion, refusing her a place in the sun, forbidding her the seas, plotting to hem her in.

The pastures were getting used up. The herds were becoming restive.

The only contribution of any value a private citizen can make towards the elucidation of a National upheaval is to record his own sensations.

I heard of our declaration of war against Germany with cheerful satisfaction. The animal in me rejoiced. It was going to be the biggest war in history. I thanked whatever gods there be that they had given it in my time. If I had been anywhere near the age limit I should have enlisted. I can say this with confidence because later, and long after my enthusiasm had worn off, I did manage to get work in quite a dangerous part of the front line. Men all around me were throwing up their jobs, sacrificing their careers. I felt ashamed of myself, sitting in safety at my desk, writing articles encouraging them, at so much a thousand words. Of course, not a soul dreamt the war was going to last more than a few months. Had we known, it might have been another story. But the experts had assured us on that point. Mr. Wells was most emphatic. It was Mr. Wells who proclaimed it a Holy War. I have just been reading again those early letters of his. A Miss Cooper Willis has, a little unkindly, reprinted them. I am glad she did not do the same with contributions of my own. The newspapers had roped in most of us literary gents to write them special articles upon the war. The appalling nonsense we poured out, during those hysterical first weeks, must have made the angels weep, and all the little devils hold their sides with laughter. In justice to myself, I like to remember that I did gently ridicule the "War to end war" stuff and nonsense. I had heard that talk in my babyhood: since when I had lived through one of the bloodiest half centuries in history. War will go down before the gradual growth of reason. The movement has not yet begun.

But I did hate German militarism. I had seen German "offizieren" swaggering three and four abreast along the pavements, sweeping men, women and children into the gutter. (I had seen the same thing in St. Petersburg. But we were not bothering about Russia, just then.) I had seen them, insolent, conceited, over-bearing, in café, theatre and railway car, civilians compelled everywhere to cringe before them, and had longed to slap their faces. In Freiburg, I had seen the agony upon the faces of the young recruits, returning from forced marches under a blazing sun, their bleeding feet protruding from their boots. I had sat upon the blood-splashed bench and watched the Mensur—helpful, no doubt, in making the youngsters fit for "the greatest game of all," as Kipling calls it. I hated the stupidity, the cruelty of the thing. I thought we were going to free the German people from this Juggernaut of their own creation. And then make friends with them.

At first, there was no hate of the German people. King George himself set the example. He went about the hospitals, shook hands with wounded Hans and Fritz. The Captain of the *Emden* we applauded, for his gallant exploits against our own ships. Kitchener's despatches admitted the bravery of the enemy. Jokes and courtesies were exchanged between the front trenches. Our civilians, caught by the war in Germany, were well treated. The good feeling was acknowledged, and returned.

Had the war ended with the falling of the leaves—as had been foretold by both the Kaiser and our own Bottomley—we might—who knows?—have realized that dream of a kinder and better world. But the gods, for some purpose of their own, not yet perhaps completed, ordained otherwise. It became necessary to stimulate the common people to prolonged effort. What surer drug than Hate?

The Atrocity stunt was let loose.

A member of the Cabinet had suggested to me that I might go out to America to assist in English propaganda.

On the ship, I fell in with an American Deputation returning from Belgium. They had been sent there by the United States Government to report upon the truth—or otherwise—of these stories of German frightfulness. The opinion of the Deputation was that, apart from the abominations common to all warfare, nineteen-twentieths of them would have to be described as "otherwise."

It was these stories of German atrocities, turned out day by day from Fleet Street, that first caused me to doubt whether this really was a "Holy War." Against them I had raised my voice, for whatever it might be worth. If I knew and hated the German military machine, so likewise I knew, and could not bring myself to hate, the German people. I had lived among them for years. I knew them to be a homely, kind, good-humoured folk. Cruelty to animals in Germany is almost unknown. Cruelty to woman or child is rarer still. German criminal statistics compare favourably with our own. This attempt to make them out a nation of fiends seemed to me as silly as it was wicked. It was not clean fighting. Of course, I got myself into trouble with the Press; while a select number of ladies and gentlemen did me the honour to send me threatening letters.

The Deputation published their report in America. But it was never allowed to reach England.

America, so far as I could judge, appeared to be mildly pro-French and equally anti-English. Our blockade was causing indignation. In every speech I made in America, the only thing sure of sympathetic response was my reference to the "just and lasting" peace that was to follow. I had been told to make a point of that. A popular cartoon, exhibited in Broadway, pictured the nations of Europe as a yelling mob of mud-bespattered urchins engaged in a meaningless scrimmage; while America, a placid motherly soul, was getting ready a hot bath and bandages. President Wilson, in an interview I had with him, conveyed to me the same idea: that America was saving herself to come in at the end as peace-maker. At a dinner to which I was invited, I met an important group of German business men and bankers. They assured me that Germany had already grasped the fact that she had bitten off more than she could chew, to use their own expression, and would welcome a peace conference, say at Washington. I took their message back with me, but the mere word "conference" seemed to strike terror into every British heart.

It was in the autumn of 1916 that I "got out," as the saying was. I had been trying to get there for some time. Of course my age, fifty-five, shut all the usual doors against me. I could have joined a company of "veterans" for home defence, and have guarded the Crystal Palace, or helped to man the Thames Embankment; but I wanted to see the real thing. I had offered myself as an entertainer to the Y.M.C.A. I was a capable raconteur and had manufactured, or appropriated, a number of good stories. The Y.M.C.A. had tried me on home

hospitals and camps and had approved me. But the War
Office would not give its permission. The military
gentleman I saw was brief. So far as his information
went, half the British Army were making notes for future
books. If I merely wanted to be useful, he undertook to
find me a job in the Army Clothing Department, close
by in Pimlico. I suppose my motives for wanting to go
out were of the usual mixed order. I honestly thought I
would be doing sound work, helping the Tommies to
forget their troubles; and I was not thinking of writing a
book. But I confess that curiosity was also driving me. It
is human nature to jump out of bed and run a mile
merely to see a house on fire. Here was the biggest thing
in history taking place within earshot. At Greenwich,
when the wind was in the right direction, one could hear
the guns. Likewise masculine craving for adventure.
Quite conceivably, one might get oneself mixed up with
excursions and alarms: come back a hero. Anyhow, it
would be a relief to get away, if only for a time, from the
hinterland heroes with their shrieking and their cursing.
The soldiers would be gentlemen.

I had all but abandoned hope, when one day, outside
a photographer's shop in Bond Street,—I met an old
friend of mine, dressed up in the uniform of a Major-
General, as I took it to be at first sight.

You could have knocked me down with a feather. I
knew him to be over fifty, if a day. The last time I had
seen him, about three weeks before, had been in his
office. He was a solicitor. I had gone to him about some

tea-leaves my wife had been saving up. She was afraid of getting into trouble for hoarding.

He shook hands haughtily. "Sorry I can't stop," he said. "Am sailing from Southampton to-night. Must look in at the French Legation."

"One moment," I persisted. "Can't you take me out with you, as your Aide-de-camp? I don't mind what I do. I'm good at cleaning buttons——"

He waved me aside. "Impossible," he said. "Joffre would——"

And then, looking at my crestfallen face, the soldier in him melted. The kindly stout solicitor emerged. Taking out a note-book, he wrote upon a page. Then tore it out and gave it me.

"You can tell them I sent you," he said. "Ta-ta." He dived into a waiting taxi. The crowd had respectfully made way for him.

It was an address in Knightsbridge that he had given me. I saw a courteous gentleman named Illingworth, who explained things to me. The idea had originated with a French lady, La Comtesse de la Panousse, wife of the military attaché to the French Embassy in London. The French Army was less encumbered than our own with hide-bound regulations. Age, so long as it was not accompanied by decrepitude, was no drawback to the driving of a motor ambulance. I passed the necessary tests for driving and repairs, and signed on. Thus I became a French soldier: at two and a half sous a day (paid monthly; my wife still has the money). The French Legation obtained for me my passport. At the British War Office I could snap my fingers. Passing it, on my last day in London, I did so: and was spoken to severely by the constable on duty.

Upon our uniform, I must congratulate La Comtesse de la Panousse. It was, I understand, her own creation: a russet khaki relieved by dark blue facings, with a swordbelt and ornamental buttons. It came expensive. Of course, we paid for it ourselves. But I am sure that none of us begrudged the money. The French army did not quite know what to make of us. Young recruits assumed us, in the dusk, to be Field-Marshals. One day, in company with poor Hutchinson, the dramatist, who died a few months after he got back to England, I walked through the gateway of the Citadelle at Verdun, saluted in awed silence by both sentries.

I sailed from Southampton in company with Spring-Rice, brother to our Ambassador at Washington, and our Chef de Section, D. L. Oliver, who was returning from leave in England. We took out with us three new cars, given by the British Farmers' Association. The ship was full of soldiers. As we stepped on deck, we were handed life collars, with instructions to blow them out and tie them round our necks. It gave us an Elizabethan touch. One man with a pointed beard, an officer of Engineers, we called Shakespeare. Except for his legs, he looked like Shakespeare. But lying down in them was impossible. Under cover of darkness, we most of us disobeyed orders, and hid them under our greatcoats. Passing down the Channel was like walking down Regent Street on a Jubilee night. The place was blazing with lights. Our transport was accompanied by a couple of torpedo destroyers. They raced along beside us like a pair of porpoises. Every now and then they disappeared, the waves sweeping over them. About twelve o'clock the alarm was given that a German submarine had succeeded in getting through. We returned full speed to Southampton dock, and remained there for the next twenty-four hours. On the following night, we were ordered forward again; and reached Havre early in the morning. The cross-country roads in France are designed upon the principle of the Maze at Hampton Court. Every now and then you come back to the same village. To find your way through them, the best plan is to disregard the sign-posts and trust to prayer. Oliver had been there before but, even with that, we lost our way a dozen times. The first night we reached Caudebec, a delightful mediæval town hardly changed by so much as a stone from the days of Joan of Arc, when Warwick held it for the English. If it hadn't been for the war, I would have stopped there for a day or two. As it was, Spring-Rice and myself were eager to get to the front. Oliver, who had had about a year of it, was in less of a hurry. At Vitry, some hundred miles the other side of Paris, we entered "the zone of the Grand Armies," and saw the first signs of war. Soon we were running through villages that were little more than rubbish heaps. The Quakers were already there. But for the Quakers, I doubt if Christianity would have survived this particular war. All the other denominations threw it up. Where the church had been destroyed the "Friends" had cleared out a barn, roofed it, and found benches and a home-made altar— generally, a few boards on trestles, with a white cloth and some bunches of flowers. Against the shattered walls they had improvised shelters and rebuilt the hearth-stone. Old men and women, sitting in the sun, smiled at us. The children ran after us cheering. The dogs barked. Towards evening I got lost. I was the last of the three. Over the winding country roads—or rather cart tracks—it was difficult to keep in touch. I knew we had to get to Bar-le-Duc. But it was dark when I struck a little town called Revigny. I decided to stop there for the night. Half of it was in ruins. It was crowded with troops, and trains kept coming in discharging thousands more. The *poilus* were lying in the streets, wrapped in their blankets, with their knapsacks for a pillow. The one miserable hotel was reserved for officers. My uniform obtained me admission. The *salle-à-manger* was crammed to suffocation: so the landlady put me a chair in the kitchen. The cockroaches were having a bad time. They fell into the soups and stews, and no one took the trouble to rescue them. I secured some cold ham and a bottle of wine; and slept in my own ambulance on one of the stretchers. I pushed on at dawn; and just outside Bar-le-Duc met Oliver, who had been telephoning everywhere, enquiring for a lost Englishman. I might have been court-martialled, but the good fellow let me off with a reprimand; and later on I learnt the trick of never losing sight of the car in front of you. It is not as easy as it sounds. At Bar-le-Duc we learnt our destination. Our unit, Convoi 10, had been moved to Rarécourt, a village near Clermont in the Argonne, twenty miles from Verdun. We reached there that same evening.

We were a company of about twenty Britishers, including Colonials. Amongst us were youngsters who had failed to pass their medical examination, and one or two officers who had been invalided out of the army. But the majority were, like myself, men above military age. Other English sections, similar to our own, were scattered up and down the line. The Americans, at that time, had an Ambulance Service of their own: some of them were with the Germans. A French officer was technically in command; but the chief of each section was an Englishman, chosen for his knowledge of French. It was a difficult position. He was responsible for orders being carried out and, at the same time, was expected to make things as easy as possible for elderly gentlemen unused to discipline: a few of whom did not always remember the difference between modern warfare and a Piccadilly club. Oliver was a marvel of tact and patience. We drew the ordinary army rations. Meat and vegetables were good and plentiful. For the rest, we had a mess fund, and foraged for ourselves. Marketing was good fun. It meant excursions to Ste. Menehould or Bar-le-Duc, where one could get a bath, and eat off a clean tablecloth. For mess-room, we had a long tent in the middle of a field. In fine weather it was cool and airy. At other times, the wind swept through it, and the rain leaked in, churning the floor into mud. We sat down to *la soupe*, as our dinner was called, in our greatcoats with the collars turned up. For sleeping, we were billeted about the village. With three others I shared a granary. We spread our sleeping sacks upon stretchers supported on trestles, and built ourselves washing-stands and dressing-tables out of packing-cases that we purchased from the proprietress of the *épicerie* at a franc a piece. Later, I found a more luxurious lodging in the house of an old peasant and his wife. They never took their clothes off. The old man would kick off his shoes, hang up his coat, and disappear with a grunt into a hole in the wall. His wife would undo hidden laces and buttons and give herself a shake, put her shoes by the stove, blow out the lamp, and roll into another hole opposite. There was a house near the church with a bench outside, underneath a vine. It commanded a pretty view, and of an evening, when off duty, I would sit there and smoke. The old lady was talkative. She boasted to me, one evening, that three officers, a Colonel and two Majors, had often sat upon that very bench the year before and been quite friendly. That was when the Germans had occupied the village. I gathered the villagers had made the best of them. "They had much money," added Madame.

Fuel was our difficulty. It's an ill wind that blows nobody good. The news that a shelled village had been finally abandoned by its inhabitants flew like wildfire. It was a question of who could get there first, and drag out the timbers from the shattered houses. Green wood was no good: though, up in the dug-outs, it was the only thing to be had. They say there is no smoke without fire. It is not true. You can have a dug-out so full of smoke that you have to light a match to find the fire. If it's only French matches you have, it may take a boxfull. It was our primus stoves that saved us. Each man's primus was his vestal fire. We kept them burning day and night: cooked by them, dried our clothes, and thawed our feet before going to bed. Mud was our curse. The rain never ceased. We lived in mud. Our section worked the Argonne forest. Our *point de secours*, where we waited, was some hundred yards or so behind the front trenches. The wounded, after having passed through the Field Dressing Station, were brought to us on stretchers; or came limping to us, twisting their faces as they walked. So long as we were within call we could wander at our will, creep to where the barbed-wire ended, and look out upon the mud beyond. Black, silent, still, like some petrified river piercing the forest: floating on it, here and there, white bones, a man's boot (the sole uppermost), a horse's head (the eyes missing). Among the trees the other side, the stone shelters where the German sentries watched.

The second night I was on duty, I heard a curious whistling just above my head. I thought it some night bird, and looked up. It came again, and I moved a few steps to get a better view. Suddenly something butted me in the stomach and knocked me down; and the next moment I heard a loud noise, and a little horse, tethered to a tree some few yards off, leapt up into the air and dropped down dead. It was Monsieur Le Médecin, a chemist from Peronne, who had bowled me over, and was dragging me down the steps into his dug-out. I didn't hang about another time, when I heard that whistling in the trees.

There must have been some means of communication between the men themselves on either side. During the two hours, every afternoon, when the little tramway was kept busy, hauling up food, both French and German batteries were silent. When the last barrel of flour, the last sack of potatoes, had been rolled in safety down the steps of the field kitchen, the firing would break out again. When a German mine exploded, the Frenchmen who ought to have been killed, were invariably a quarter of a mile away sawing wood. One takes it that the German peasant lads possessed like gift of intuition, telling them when it would be good for their health's sake to take walking exercise.

A pity the common soldiers could not have been left to make the peace. There might have been no need for Leagues of Nations. I remember one midday coming upon two soldiers, sitting on a log. One was a French *poilu* and the other his German prisoner. They were sharing the Frenchman's lunch. The conqueror's gun lay on the ground, between them.

It was the night call that we dreaded. We had to drive without lights: through the dense forest, up and down steep, narrow ways with sudden turns and hairpin bends—one had to trust to memory: and down below, in the valley, were the white mists into which one strained one's eyes till it felt as if they were dropping out of their sockets. We had to hasten all we dared, the lives of men behind us depending upon time. Besides, we might be wanted for another journey. We often were. There ought at times to have been a moon, according to the almanac: but to that land of ceaseless rain she rarely came. It was nerve-racking work. The only thing to do was not to think about it till the moment came. It is the advice that is given, I understand, to men waiting to be hanged. One takes off one's boots, and tunic, blows out the candle and turns in. A rat drops from somewhere on to the table, becomes immovable. By the light of the smouldering logs, we look at one another. One tries to remember whether one really did put everything eatable back into the tin. Even then they work the covers off, somehow— clever little devils. Well, if he does, he does. Perhaps he will be satisfied with the candle. Ambulance Driver Nine turns his head to the wall. Suddenly he is up again. A footstep is stumbling along the wooden gangway. It is coming nearer. He holds his breath. The gods be praised, it passes. With a sigh of relief he lies down again, and closes his eyes.

The next moment—or so it seems to him—a light is flashing in his eyes. A bearded, blue-coated figure is standing over him. Ambulance to start immediately!

("*Ambulance faut partir.*") The bearded figure, under its blue iron helmet, kindly lights the candle (rat having providentially found something more tasty) and departs. Ambulance Driver Nine struggles half unconsciously into his clothes and follows up the steps. Pierre, the *aide*, is already grinding away at the starting handle, and becoming exhausted. One brushes him aside and takes one's turn, and with the twentieth swing—or thereabouts—the car answers with a sudden roar, as of some great drowsy animal awakened from its slumbers; and Pierre, who has been cursing her with all the oaths of Gascony, pats her on the bonnet and is almost amorous. A shadowy group emerges apparently from the ground. Two stretchers and three assis is the tale. The stretchers are hoisted up and fitted swiftly into their hangings. The three assis mount slowly and shuffle painfully into their places. Rifles and knapsacks are piled up beside them, and the doors are clanged to. Another "case" is to be picked up on the way—at Champ Cambon. You take the first road on the left, after passing the ruins of the Ferme de Forêt, and the camp is just beyond the level crossing. It seems you cannot miss it. And Ambulance Driver Nine climbs into his seat.

Through the forest, he keeps his eyes upon the strip of sky above his head. Always he must be in the exact centre of that narrow strip of sky. And it will wobble. Pierre sits on the foot-board, his eyes glued to the road. "*Gauche, gauche,*" he cries suddenly. Driver Number Nine pulls the wheel to the left. "*A droit,*" shrieks Pierre. Which the devil does he mean? And what has become of

the sky? Where's the damned thing gone to? The deep
ditch that he knows to be on either side of the road
seems to be calling to him like some muddy Lorelei.
Suddenly the sky reappears. It seems to have come from
behind him. He breathes once more.

"*Arretez*," cries Pierre, a little later. He has detected a
vague, shapeless mass that might be the ruins of a farm.
He descends. One hears his footsteps squelching through
the mud. He returns triumphant. It is a farm. Things
seem to be shaping well. Now, all they have to do is to
look out for a road on the left. They find a road on the
left—or hope they have. The descent appears to be steep.
The car begins to jump and jolt. "*Doucement,
camarade—doucement!*" comes an agonized cry from
within. Pierre opens the little window and explains that
it cannot be helped. It is a *mauvaise* route: and there is
silence. The route becomes more and more *mauvaise*. Is
it a road, or are they lost? Every minute the car seems as
if it were about to stand on its head. Ambulance Driver
Nine recalls grim stories of the mess-room: of nights
spent beside a mud-locked car, listening to groans and
whispered prayers: of cars overturned, their load of dying
men mingled in a ghastly heap of writhing limbs, from
which the bandages have come undone. In spite of the
damp chill night, a cold sweat breaks out all over him.
Heedless of Pierre's remonstrances, he switches on his
electric torch and flashes it downwards. Yes, it is a road
of sorts, chiefly of shell-holes, apparently. The car crashes
in and out of them. If the axles do not break, they may
get down. The axles do not break, by some miracle.

Pierre gives a whoop of joy as the car straightens herself out. They have reached the level, and the next moment they bump over the crossing, and hear the welcome voice of a sentry.

The *blessé* is brought out. He has been unconscious for two hours. Driver Nine had best make speed. The mist that fills the valley grows whiter and whiter. It is like a damp sheet, wrapped round his head. Shadows move toward him, and vanish; but whether they were men or trees or houses he cannot tell. Suddenly he jams on his brakes and starts up. It is clear enough this time—a huge munition wagon, drawn by a team of giant horses. They are rearing and plunging all round him.

But no sound comes from them! Pierre has sprung to the ground and is shouting. Where is their driver?

The whole thing has vanished. They listen. All is silence. Pierre climbs up again and they break into a loud laugh.

But why did Pierre see it, too!

They crawl along on bottom gear. There comes a low crashing sound. Even the torch is useless, a yard in front of them. They find by feeling that they are up against a door. Fortunately the back wheels are still on the road, so that they can right themselves. But it seems useless going on. Suddenly, Pierre dives beneath the car and emerges, puffing a cigarette. He dances with delight at his own cleverness. He holds the lighted cigarette behind his back and walks jauntily forward, feeling the road with his feet. Ambulance Driver Nine drives on, following the tiny spark. Every now and then, the invisible Pierre puffs the cigarette, covered by his hand, and it reappears with a brighter glow. After a time the mist rises; and Pierre bursts into song and remounts. A mile or so farther on they reach the barrier, beyond which lamps are permitted, but decide not to light up. Their eyes are in training now, and had better not be indulged; it will spoil them for the journey back. They are both singing different tunes when they arrive at the Base Hospital, twenty kilometres behind the lines.

"Have any trouble?" asks a fellow driver from another section, who has just discharged his load and is drawing on his gloves.

"The mist was a bit trying," answers Driver Nine. "We had to come round by Champ Cambon."

"Nasty bit of road, that, down the hill," agrees the other. "So long!"

From Rarécourt we were moved to Verdun. It was in ruins then. From some of the houses merely the front wall had fallen, leaving the rooms intact, just as one sees them in an open dolls' house: two chairs drawn close together near the hearth, the crucifix upon the wall, a child's toy upon the floor. In a shop, were two canaries in their cage, starved to death, a little heap of feathers that fell to pieces when I touched them. In a restaurant, the soup still stood upon the table, the wine half finished in the glasses. The Citadelle was still occupied: an underground city of galleries and tunnels, streets of dormitories, mess-rooms, a concert hall, stores, hospitals and kitchens. Here and there, one came across groups of German prisoners removing the débris, tidying up generally. There must have been great shortage of wool in Germany, at that time. It was a bitter winter, yet the most of them had no underclothing but a thin cotton shirt. One could see their naked bodies through the holes. A company of French Engineers was quartered in the Cathedral. The altar served them for a kitchen table. The town was strangely peaceful, though all around the fighting still continued. Our Unit, Section 10, had been there the winter before, during the battle, and had had a strenuous time. During the actual fighting, Hague Conventions and Geneva regulations get themselves mislaid. The guns were eating up ammunition faster than the little tramways could supply them, and the ambulances did not always go up empty. Doubtless the German Red Cross drivers had likewise their blind eye. It is not the soldiers who shout about these things. I was on the "Lusitania," the last voyage she made from New York to Liverpool, before she was torpedoed. We were loaded to the Plimsol line with war material. The Germans were accused of dropping shells on to the hospital. So they did. How could they help it? The ammunition park was one side of the railway head and the hospital the other. It was the most convenient place for both. Those who talk about war being a game ought to be made to go out and play it. They'd find their little book of rules of not much use. Once we were ordered to take a company of staff officers on a tour of inspection. That did seem going a bit too far. Spring-Rice bluntly refused: but not all of us had his courage.

From rain the weather had turned to frost. Often the thermometer would register forty degrees below zero. The Frenchmen said it was "*pas chaud.*" A Frenchman is always so polite. It might hurt the Weather's feelings, telling it bluntly that it was damn cold. He hints to it that it isn't exactly warm, and leaves the rest to its conscience. Starting the cars was horse's work. We wrapped our engines up in rugs at night and kept a lamp burning under the bonnet. One man made a habit of using a blow-pipe to warm his cylinders, and the rest of us gave him a wide berth. The birds lost the use of their wings. They lay huddled up wherever there was shelter from the wind. Some of the soldiers took them scraps of food, but others caught and cooked them. It wasn't worth the trouble: there was nothing on them.

One day, in a wood, I chanced upon a hospital for animals. It was a curious sight. The convalescents were lying about in the sun, many of them still wearing bandages. One very little donkey was wearing the Croix de Guerre. His driver had been killed and he had gone on by himself, with a broken leg, and had brought his load of letters and parcels safely up to the trenches. The transport drivers were kind to their beasts; and many of the soldiers had their little dog that marched with them and shared their rations. But they used to pour petrol over the rats, when they caught them, and set fire to them. "He ate my sausage," a bright-eyed little *poilu* once answered me. He regarded it as an act of plain justice. Some of the officers had made gardens in front of their dug-outs; and the little cemeteries, dotted here and there about the forest, were still bright with flowers when I first saw them. A major I used to visit had furnished his dug-out with pieces of genuine Louis Quatorze: they had been lying about the fields when he had got there. We used to drink coffee out of eggshell china cups. In the villages further back, life went on much as usual. Except when a bombardment was actually in progress, the peasants still worked in the fields, the women gossiped and the children played about the fountain. Bombardment or no bombardment, Mass was celebrated daily in the church—or what was left of it. A few soldiers made the congregation, with here and there a woman in black. But on Sundays came the farmers with their wives and daughters in fine clothes and the soldiers—on week days not always spick-and-span—had brushed their uniforms and polished up their buttons.

But within the barrier, which ran some ten kilometres behind the front, one never saw a woman or a child. Female nurses came no nearer than the hospitals at the base. It was a dull existence, after the first excitement had worn off. We worried chiefly about our food. The parcel from home was the great event of the week. Often, it had been opened. We had to thank God for what was left. Out of every three boxes of cigarettes that my wife sent me, I reckon I got one. The French cigarettes, that one bought at the canteens, were ten per cent poison and the rest dirt. The pain would go out of a wounded soldier's face when you showed him an English cigarette. Rum was our only tipple, and the amount that each man could purchase was limited. It was kind to us, and warmed our feet. The Paris papers arrived in the evening—when they did arrive. They told us how gay and confident we were. For news, we preferred reading the daily bulletin, posted up each morning outside headquarters: it told the truth, whether pleasant or unpleasant. We got used to the booming of the guns. At the distance of a few miles the sound was not unmusical. Up in the dug-outs, we were close to our own batteries. They were cleverly hidden. I remember once sitting down upon a log to read. It was a pretty spot, underneath a bank that sheltered one from the wind. Suddenly something happened. I thought, at first, my head had come off. I was lying on the ground, and became aware of a pair of eyes looking at me through a hole in the bank. I had been sitting outside a battery of seventy-fives. The boyish young officer invited me inside. He thought I'd be more comfortable. Round Verdun, they barked incessantly, and got upon one's nerves. Sometimes the order would be given for "all out" on both sides, and then the effect was distinctly terrifying. But one had to creep out and look. The entire horizon would be ablaze with flash-lights, stars and rockets, signalling orders to the batteries. Towards dawn the tumult would die down; and one could go to bed. One had no brain for any but the very lightest literature.

Small books printed on soft paper, the leaves of which could be torn out easily, were the most popular. We played a sort of bridge and counted the days to our leave. The general opinion among the French was, that the English had started the war to capture German trade, and had dragged France into it. There was no persuading them of their mistake.

It had been a trying winter, and my age had been against me. At the end of it, I was not much more good for the work. I came back cured of any sneaking regard I may have ever had for war. The illustrations in the newspapers, depicting all the fun of the trenches, had lost for me their interest. Compared with modern soldiering, a street scavenger's job is an exhilarating occupation, a rat-catcher's work more in keeping with the instincts of a gentleman. I joined a little company who, in defiance of the Press and of the Mob, were making an appeal for a reasonable peace. We made speeches in Essex Hall and in the provinces. Among others on our platform, I recall Lord Parmoor, Buckmaster, the Earl of Beauchamp, Ramsay MacDonald, Dean Inge, Zangwill, the Snowdens, Drinkwater, and E. D. Morel the great-hearted. We had one supporter in the Press, *Common Sense*, edited by F. W. Hirst, who right through the war kept his flag flying with tact and good-humour. Later, Lord Lansdowne came to our aid. Lord Northcliffe, who died not long afterwards of a lingering brain disease, suggested he must be suffering from senile decay. Whether we did any good, beyond satisfying our own consciences, I cannot say.

The war ended in 1918. From 1919 to 1924 there was every prospect of France's regaining her old position as The Enemy. Reading the French papers, one gathered that nothing would please France better. At the present moment (1925) a growing party would seem to be in favour of substituting Russia. It may be that the gods have other plans. The white are not the only herds. The one thing certain is that mankind remains a race of low intelligence and evil instincts.

Chapter XIII

LOOKING FORWARD

We were chapel folk. My mother came of Welsh Nonconformist stock; and my father, until he was forty-five, had been an Independent minister—Congregationalists they call them now—and had preached from his own pulpit. I remember talk of pamphlets he had written. One had been in answer to a writer named Thomas Paine, who, according to a great-aunt of mine, credited with knowing the whole of the New Testament by heart, was really Antichrist, and had been prophesied. I was brought up to believe in a personal God who loved you if you were good; but, if you were wicked, sent you, after you were dead, to a place called Hell, where you were burnt alive for ever and ever. My mother had the idea that it was not really for ever and ever; because God was so full of loving-kindness that He would not want to hurt any creature more than He could help; and that, when they had been punished sufficiently and had repented, He would forgive them. But that was only her fancy; and perhaps it was wrong of her to think so. I had had a little brother who had died when I was a baby. My mother would never tire of telling me about him, repeating all the wonderful things that he had said. She would always end by explaining that he was now in Heaven with Jesus, and far happier than he ever could have been on earth: adding, as she would wipe the tears from her cheeks, that it was wicked and selfish of her not to be able to help crying when she thought of

323

him. I remember the look of happiness that came into her eyes, years later, a few days before she died. She had been lying very quiet, with her eyes wide open. Suddenly she clasped her hands. "I shall see him soon now," she said, "and he will be so beautiful." It was a queer place, this Heaven of my people. It rather frightened me. Gold entered a good deal into the composition of it. You wore a golden crown, and you played upon a golden harp, and God sat in the centre of it—I pictured it a bare, endless plain—high up upon a golden throne; and everybody praised Him: there was nothing else to do. My mother explained that it was symbolism. All it meant was that we should be for ever with the Lord, and that He would take away all pain. But it was the ever-and-everness of it that kept me awake of nights. A thousand years—ten thousand—a million! I would try to count them. And still one would be no nearer to the end. And God would always be there with His eyes upon one. There would never be any getting away by oneself, to think.

Until I was fourteen, I used to kneel and say my prayers each night and morning. I was told that whatever I prayed for, really believing that I should obtain it, would be granted me. If it were not, that proved I had not had sufficient faith. They were a mixed collection, those childish prayers of mine. If they ever did reach Heaven, I cannot help thinking they must have caused amusement, even up there: that God would wake me early in the morning; that He would forgive me for having wished that the boy at the coalshed was dead—he used to run after me and kick me; that God would put it into somebody's heart to give me a white rabbit; that He would make me like fat—preferring it, if anything, to lean—because it was good for me. There were others: some of them quite reasonable. Once, I prayed that I might find a half-sovereign I had lost. My father had sent me out with it to buy a post-office order. It was in my trousers pocket when I started. Both my mother and I had felt it there. But, when I went to pay for the order, it was gone. I had run up and down the crowded streets for hours, though knowing it was useless. My father had said nothing; but my mother's face had gone white; and I had cried myself to sleep. I went straight to the post office the next morning, getting there before the doors opened. It was lying in the dust, underneath the counter, just where I had been standing. And that time, I had not believed, or attempted to believe: it had seemed too impossible. While other times, when I really had believed, God had taken no notice.

My mother thought the explanation was that God granted us only those things that were good for us: and that always He knew best.

"Papa and I," she confided to me, "so often kneel and pray that business may improve, and that He will bless papa's enterprises, so that our burthen may be lighter. But things don't seem to get any better."

God tried us in the furnace. But whatever happened we must always believe in Him. "Though He slay me, yet will I trust in Him."

But why then all this fuss about faith, if He did not really mean it? And why did He think things were not good for us that were good for other people? It was not till long after, when I came across an old diary of my mother's, that I learnt how hard had been the struggle for bare existence during those last years of my father's life. But I knew that we were poor. I remember how tired my mother would get, walking, and yet would never take the omnibus. She promised she would always do so when our ship came home. Sometimes, I could not help feeling angry with God for showering favours upon others while being so stingy, as it were, to us. There was a white-whiskered old gentleman, who occasionally asked us to tea, a Mr. Wood, with fat fingers and a great gold chain, of whom God must have been particularly fond. He rode in a carriage and pair, and had servants to wait upon him. He told me once it was God who had given him everything. God had "prospered" him. He had lately built God a chapel, and as a result was richer than ever. My father had built a chapel, mostly out of his own money, when he was a young man. True, it was only a little one, compared with Mr. Wood's great red-brick edifice off the Bow Road; and God had apparently forgotten it, altogether.

For in those days, among religious folk, there was no doubt that God gave all things literally: the good things of this world as well as of the next. I remember a hymn I learnt at Sunday school:

"Whene'er I take my walks abroad, How many poor I see. How grateful should I be to God For all His gifts to me."

I was to praise God that I was well fed and warmly clad, while others wore but filthy rags, and begged from door to door. God ordered all things, and was satisfied with them, presumably.

"The rich man in his castle, The poor man at his gate, God made them, high or lowly, And ordered their estate."

I remember the cold sweat that broke out over me one grey chill evening in the street, when suddenly I heard my own voice saying out aloud: "It isn't right of Him. It isn't just."

After my mother's death, my prayers were few and far between—occasional cries for help such as a shipwrecked swimmer might fling out into the darkness without any real hope of response. I did not pray that she might live. I had prayed so hard that my father might live, spending whole nights upon my knees. Of what use? If it depended upon children's prayers, what loved father or mother would ever die? The thing was absurd. I was beginning to doubt the whole story. The more I thought about it, the more unbelievable it seemed to me.

As it had been presented to me—as to this day it is still taught to Youth—it was this. God the omniscient, the omnipotent creator of all things had made man in His own image, and had placed him in a garden, in the centre of which grew the tree of the knowledge of good and evil. The fruit of this particular tree man was forbidden to eat. Even as a child, I had never been able to understand what the tree was doing there. God had planted this garden Himself, had meant it for man's dwelling-place. It seemed to me it could have been put there for no other purpose than to be a perpetual temptation to poor Adam, to say nothing of Eve. To add to their difficulties, a serpent—which likewise God had made and placed in the garden—was allowed to come and talk to Eve and to persuade her. God must have known of this serpent and that it was very subtle. It seemed to me that God might, at least, have warned them. Man, evidently a simple soul, easily beguiled, listened to the cunning words of the serpent and ate of the forbidden fruit. God's astonishment on discovering that he had done so, I was never able to entirely credit.

For this one act of disobedience, Adam—and not only Adam but all his descendants, myself included— had been condemned by God to everlasting perdition. When I was older, Bishop Butler and other worthy writers, sought to point out to me how just and reasonable had been God's behaviour in this matter. But I was never able to see it. To me it seemed that Adam, and with him the entire human race, had been treated with undue severity, to say the very least of it. Indeed, God Himself, later on, must have felt that He had been too harsh. To put matters right, He sent His only-begotten Son into the world to die for our sins. By this means Adam and Eve's original transgression had been wiped out and mankind given another chance. Why God, who was all-powerful and could do anything, had not chosen some simpler and more human method was never explained to me; and the question I felt was too awful to be uttered aloud. Even as it was, not all mankind were to be saved, but only those who "believed." If you didn't believe the story you were still to be damned.

As a child, my difficulty was that I was never quite sure whether I believed it or not. That I made every effort in my power to believe it, goes without saying. My not believing would break my mother's heart: that I knew. Added to which, it meant going to Hell. From many a fiery pulpit, I had heard vivid and detailed descriptions of Hell. The haunting horror of it was ever present to my mind. Face downwards on my pillow, I would repeat "I do believe," over and over again: ending by screaming it out aloud, sometimes, in case God had not heard my smothered whisperings. For periods, I would be confident that I had conquered—that I really did believe: there could be no doubt about it. And then the fear would come to me that, after all, I was only pretending to believe; and that God saw through me and knew I didn't. I dared not open my mouth. To ask questions would be to confess my disbelief. I tried not to think about it. But the thoughts would come. It was the Devil tempting me, I told myself. But neither prayers nor fasting drove him away. And as the years passed by he became more persistent.

I could not understand God going about His work in this hole-and-corner way. All men were surely His children. Why had He revealed Himself only to the Jews, an insignificant tribe of wandering shepherds, leaving it to them to disseminate His message or not as they thought fit? As a matter of fact, they had made no attempt to do so. Regarding Him as their own property, they had done their best to keep Him to themselves. Even among the early Christians, it was fiercely debated whether Christ should be shared with the Gentiles or confined to the circumcised. The vast majority of mankind are to this day in ignorance of the Gospel upon which their salvation depends. Why had God made a secret of Himself? Why had He not spoken His commands in trumpet tones that all the world might hear?

Why did He not speak to me? If it really was the Devil that was whispering to me my doubts, why did not God speak also, and with a word dispel them? Why had reason been given me, if blind faith—the instinct of an animal—was all that was required of me? Why would not God speak? Or couldn't He?

Was there a God? This God of Abraham, Isaac and Jacob, what had I to do with Him? This God who made blunders and "repented" them: who "grieved" at the result of His own work—would destroy what He had made. This God of punishments and curses. This "jealous" God, so clamorous for His meed of praise and worship, His sacrifices and burnt offerings, His blood of lambs and goats. This God with a pretty taste in upholstery. This Designer of curtains and of candlesticks, so insistent on His shittim wood and gold. This God of battles. This God of vengeances and massacres. This God who kept a Hell for His own children. This God of blood and cruelty! This was not God. This was a creature man had made in his own image.

There were three subjects about which, when I was a young man, respectable folk were not supposed to talk: politics, sex, and religion. I remember how fervently my early editors would seek to impress upon me this convention. Round about me, must have been many, sharing my doubts and difficulties. We might have been of help to one another. But religion, especially—even in Bohemian circles—was strictly taboo. To be interested in it stamped a youngster as not only priggish but unEnglish. Books dealing with the subject from the free thinker's point of view I knew existed: but for such I had no use. The usual standard works in support of orthodox opinion I did read. I do not think it altogether my fault that, instead of removing, they had the effect of increasing my perplexities.

I passed through a period of much mental suffering. The beliefs of childhood cling close. One tears them loose at cost of pain. Gradually, I arrived at what Carlyle terms the centre of indifference. What did we know—

what could we know? What were all the creeds but the jargon of a High Court affidavit, to be sworn before the nearest solicitor at a fee of eighteenpence? "I have been informed, and I believe."

And, after all, what did it matter? Beliefs did not alter facts. There must be a God. The watch proclaims the watchmaker. The starry firmament above me proved that. Some time—somewhere, the Truth would be revealed to us. Meanwhile, what needed man other than the moral law within him? That was the only true religion. The voice of God Himself, speaking to us direct, requiring no interpreter. That, one could believe.

I remember a conversation I once had with Zangwill. We were sitting in a wood upon a fallen tree. My little dog was with us. A cute little fellow. He sat between us, looking intently from one to the other as we talked. Zangwill thought that, as a dog is able to conceive of certain attributes of man, so man is able to grasp and understand a little part of God. A portion of man's nature is shared by the dog. So far, my dog, looking up into my eyes, knows me—can translate my wishes and commands. But for the rest, I remain a mystery to him. His earnest eyes look up at me, wondering, troubled. Till a rabbit crosses his path, and he scampers off.

A part of God's nature man shares. To that extent, he apprehends God—can be the friend, the helper of God. But God Himself, man's finite mind cannot

conceive. For knowledge of God, we must be content to
wait. But, meanwhile, our business is to seek Him, lest
we lose touch with Him. The creeds will pass away. But
the altar to the Unknown God will still remain.

For man's desire will ever be towards God. He
cannot help himself. It is the part of God within him,
seeking to return to its source. If there be any meaning in
this life, beyond the mere animal existence we share with
the dumb beasts, it is that we may prepare ourselves to
meet God.

That man is immortal seems to me self-evident. Not
even a cabbage is lost. It is but resolved into its
component parts, to be used again. There is no road by
which man's soul can escape out of the Universe. The
only question is whether it be absorbed back into the
fountain of all life from which it came, or retain its
separate existence. But, if the former, why should it have
been given a separate existence only on this earth: where
it is so soon to be done for: where its opportunities for
development are so limited? The chief argument against
the immortality of man is that of his kinship with the
lower animals. Man's intellect he shares with all sentient
creation. The difference between instinct and reason is
merely of degree. At their extremes, they overlap. In the
unfolding of man's brain, instinct has been the chief
educator. That many animals exhibit powers of reasoning
is capable of proof. Man's superior intelligence entitles
him to the lordship of the world, but cannot be held to
guarantee him a future beyond its boundaries.

Nor in his moral nature does man stand apart from the transient life around him. The creeping myriads of the dust labour and sacrifice themselves unceasingly for the good of their community, for love of their offspring. The law of the tribe—of the nation is but the law of the herd, amplified, extended. Man shares his virtues, with the inhabitants of the jungle. Courage, devotion, faithfulness even unto death are theirs too. God speaks to them also. The moral law within them guides them likewise through the darkness.

Any claim of man to immortality, based upon his intellectual or moral perception, would have to apply equally to the entire animal creation. The argument may be granted. Yubisthira's dying prayer to Brahma that his dog might be suffered to accompany him does not strike one as altogether without reason. It may be that all life is struggling upward by many ways, through many stages. King Yubisthira and his dog may yet meet, and remember.

But man, in his journey, has already made the tremendous leap from blind existence to self-consciousness. Still trembling, wondering, amazed, he stands upon the other side of the immeasurable gulf separating him from all other living creatures.

When did it happen, this new birth of man, through which he acquired kinship with God, also? At what turning-point of man's story first came the thought to him: "What am I? Whence came I? Whither goeth?"

How long had man been wandering upon earth before he discovered the unseen land around him, and made himself a grave to mark the road?

The desire—the intuitive belief in a future state must have grounds for its growth, or it would not have taken root in us. If our souls, like our bodies, were to be dissipated, we should not possess this instinct: it would be useless to us—a hindrance. The stoics were prepared to face the possibility; but that was that they might be free from all fear. They acknowledged that God moved in them. Their ideal was absorption back into the Godhead—the Nirvana of the Buddhists. It may be so. Eternity is a long lane. It may lead to rest.

But surely labour will come first. Kant put the moral law within him and the starry firmament above him as parts of the same whole. Man's soul must have been given to him that he should become the helper—the fellow-labourer with God. The building of the Universe is not completed. God is still creating.

That a man shall so spend his life that, when he leaves it, he shall be better fitted for the service of God, that surely is the explanation of our birth and death.

The battle of life is a battle not for, but against self. One has not to subscribe literally to the book of Genesis to accept the doctrine of original sin. How sin came into the world, we shall know when we have learnt the secrets of Eternity. Meanwhile, our business is to fight it. By wrestling with it, we strengthen our souls. Of all who have been given power to help man in his struggle for spiritual existence, one must place Christ Jesus as the highest. As a child, I had been taught that Christ was really God. There was some mystery about a Trinity, which I did not understand—which no one ever has understood, which the early Church wisely forbade its votaries from even trying to understand. Christ, himself I could have loved. I doubt if any human being has ever read or heard his story without coming to love him—certainly no child. It was thinking of him as God that caused me to turn away from him. If all the time he was God then there had been no reality in it. It had all been mere play-acting. If Christ was God, what help to me the example of his life?

But Christ my fellow-man—however far above me—was still my brother, sharer of my bonds and burthens. From his sufferings, I could learn courage. From his victory, I could gather hope. What he demanded of me, that I could give. Where he led, I too might follow.

The Christ spirit is in all men. It is the part of man that is akin to God. By listening to it, by making it our guide, we can grow more like to God—fit ourselves to become His comrade, His fellow-labourer. By neglecting it, by allowing it to be overgrown with worldliness, stifled under the evil that is also within us, we can destroy it. That the wages of sin is death is literally true. Sin drives out the desire for God. If we do not seek Him, we shall not find Him. Christ was the great Exemplar. By his teaching, by his life and death, he showed us how a man may become truly the Son of God. All the rest makes only for confusion. The idea that Christ was sent into the world to be the scapegoat for our sins is not helpful. If God has no further use for us—if all that awaits us is an eternal idleness, to be passed in either bliss or pain, the doctrine might conceivably be comforting. But if it is for labour that God is seeking to prepare us, then it is but a stumbling-block.

It is not our sins that will drag us down, but our want of will to fight against them. It is from the struggle, not the victory, that we gain strength. "Not what I am, but what I strove to be, that comforts me." It was not that we might escape punishment, win happiness, that we were given an immortal soul. What sense would there have been in that? Work is the only explanation of existence. Happiness is not our goal, either in this world or the next. The joy of labour, the joy of living, are the wages of God. Those realms of endless bliss in which, according to popular theology, we are to do nothing for ever and ever, one trusts are but a myth—at least, that they will still recede as we advance. Perfect rest, perfect content, can only be the final end, when all things shall have been accomplished, and even thought has ceased. Until that far-off twilight of creation, we trust that, somewhere among His many mansions, God will find work for us, according to our strength.

To prepare ourselves for the service of God: for that purpose came we into the world. How have we quitted ourselves? How have we prospered? Who among us dare hope to meet The Master, face to face, with head erect, saying, "Lord, I have done my best"?

But if we have truly sought Him, let us not lack courage. It may be, in some contest by ourselves forgot, that we won further than we knew. Where we have succeeded, He will remember. And where we have failed, we trust He, understanding, will forgive.

FOOTNOTES:

[1] The Author made three visits to America, separated by a number of years, the first at a time when both he and America were younger than they are now. The incidents and the observations made on all of these visits are recorded together in this chapter. It is natural in such a brief account that the date, or even the visit, on which a given incident occurred could not be recorded. The reader will readily see that, in many cases, the Author is recounting to-day the American scene of a day that is long since past.—The Publishers.